THE USES AND ABUSES OF ECONOMICS
and other essays

by the same author

A HISTORY OF ECONOMIC THOUGHT

THE USES AND ABUSES OF ECONOMICS

and other essays

by ERIC ROLL

FABER AND FABER · London and Boston

First published in 1978
by Faber and Faber Limited
3 Queen Square London WC1N 3AU
Printed in Great Britain by
Latimer Trend & Company Ltd Plymouth
All rights reserved

British Library Cataloguing in Publication Data

Roll, *Sir* Eric
   The uses and abuses of economics
    1. Economic policy
    I. Title
    330.9   HD82
    ISBN 0–571–11228–5

CONTENTS

ACKNOWLEDGEMENTS   *page* 9

PREFACE   11

I. ECONOMICS AND ECONOMIC POLICY   13
   The uses and abuses of Economics (1968)   15
   Economics and economic policy since Keynes (1971)   30
   The Wealth of Nations 1776–1976 (1976)   46
   Marx's *Capital*—an assessment (1967)   58

II. MONEY, BANKING AND INTERNATIONAL FINANCE   67
    The impact of economic policy on the financial system of
        the United Kingdom (1970)   69
    International capital movements past, present, future
        (1971)   90

III. THE BRITISH ECONOMY   131
     Our present discontents (1968)   133
     Is Britain prepared to pay the price of growth? (1968)   138
     Britain and world trade (1969)   143

IV. EUROPE   153
    Ten years of European co-operation (1958)   155
    Britain and the Common Agricultural Policy (1961)   168
    Commonwealth and Common Market (1961)   171
    Agriculture and international trade (1962)   187
    Europe—the only way (1968)   203
    International monetary developments and the European
        Common Market (1972)   207
    Britain in the Community (1973)   222
    Towards economic and monetary union (1973)   228

V. GOVERNMENT   235
   British experience and a point of view (1964)   237
   The Department of Economic Affairs (1966)   249
   The economist in the market-place (1972)   262
   Economics, government and business (1976)   269

INDEX   291

ACKNOWLEDGEMENTS

The author makes grateful acknowledgement to the following for permission to republish the essays and lectures contained in this volume:

The Editor of *Oxford Economic Papers* (the Sidney Ball Lecture, 'The uses and abuses of Economics')

The Central Bank of Ireland ('Economics and economic policy since Keynes')

The Editor of *Lloyds Bank Review* ('*The Wealth of Nations* 1776–1976' and 'Ten years of European co-operation')

The Editor of *The Listener* ('Marx's *Capital*—an assessment')

The University of Reading (the Mercantile Credit Lecture, 'The impact of economic policy on the financial system of the United Kingdom')

The Per Jacobsson Foundation (the Per Jacobsson Lecture, 'International capital movements past, present, future')

The Editor of *The Accountant* ('Our present discontents')

The Editor of *The Times* ('Is Britain prepared to pay the price of growth?' and 'Europe—the only way')

The Editor of *The Round Table* ('Commonwealth and Common Market')

The University of Nottingham (the Heath Memorial Lecture, 'Agriculture and international trade')

The Editor of *The Banker* ('Britain in the Community')

The Editor of *The Financial Times* ('Towards economic and monetary union')

The Committee for Economic Development ('British experience and a point of view')

The Editor of *The Journal of the Royal Institute of Public Administration* ('The Department of Economic Affairs')

The Editor of *The Times Literary Supplement* ('The economist in the market-place')

The Athlone Press of the University of London (the Stamp Memorial Lecture, 'Economics, government and business')

PREFACE

This selection has been made from articles, speeches, and lectures produced during the last two decades. They are all, in one way or another, concerned with economic and financial aspects of public policy. Partly through preference (I have always believed that in the social sciences, too, Bacon's belief that philosophy has the purpose 'to endow the condition and life of man with new power or works' is valid), partly through force of circumstance, both in my theoretical and in my practical occupations, public policy has loomed large.

I have completely excluded anything produced before the late fifties: much of it has now mainly historical interest, though it may still provide some raw material for any future reflections on my activities that I may be able to write down. I have made a rigorous selection of my more recent work so as to include only material which continues to have a bearing on current preoccupations and debates. However, much of what I committed to paper between 1941 and 1966 is in official files and remains, therefore, unavailable. Nevertheless, what I have been able to include here that falls within that period is indicative of many matters with which I was officially concerned.

E. R.

I.

ECONOMICS AND ECONOMIC POLICY

THE USES AND ABUSES OF ECONOMICS

The Sidney Ball Lecture 1968. Published in Oxford Economic Papers, *Vol. 20 No. 3, November 1968.*

When, fourteen years ago, Sir Robert Hall chose as his title for the Sidney Ball Lecture 'The place of the economist in government', both the subject and its practitioners were already launched on what was to prove an unprecedented boom. By whatever standards one likes to measure it: the literary output on the subject, the number of people studying it, the space devoted to it in the popular press, and, above all, the status and remuneration of economists, Economics has certainly proved to be a growth industry. Not even the upward movement of the American economy that followed on the Kennedy tax cut can compare with it in duration and rate of advance. This boom is by no means at an end, but I see some signs of concern here and there: that slight erosion of confidence which is so often the harbinger of a down-turn. It seems to me useful, therefore, to pause at this moment, to take stock of the situation and to see whether the prestige which Economics has enjoyed for so long is solidly founded, to examine also whether the insight it offers is properly applied and how far those who possess it are effectively employed in our society. Finally, to ask whether they deserve the acclaim—or the blame—which they have been getting.

The reflections which I want to put before you stem on the one hand from an interest over some forty years in the development of economic thinking, and on the other from a practical concern over nearly a generation with problems of government, largely in the economic sphere.

I shall speak of the uses and abuses both of the subject and of its practitioners. Let me first take the subject—and, to begin with, a word about the function of Economics and the frame of reference within which I wish to distinguish between uses and abuses. I want to say at once that I always have been, and continue to be, of the view that the words of Boyle, one of the founders of the 'invisible college' that had its origin in this University and that later became the Royal Society, apply with special force to Economics, namely that knowledge should only be valued 'as it hath a tendency to use'. Thus, I consider Economics to be an essentially practical subject. I do not propose to dwell at any length on its purely cognitive use, that is as an instrument for the enlargement of the human understanding. What I have to say on this point is only in relation to my main theme, namely the application of the understanding which economic analysis can provide towards the better ordering of human affairs. This is not to deny the achievements of Economics as a purely philosophical discipline. He who lacks its basic propositions lacks something important in his intellectual make-up. I have known, for example, the opportunity-cost principle, perhaps the quintessence of elementary economic reasoning, come, like M. Jourdain's prose, as a revelation to those to whom it is pointed out for the first time.

But there is something to be said on the other side. When some thirty years ago I first set down my ideas on this subject, there was a strong school of thought in this country which followed Weber in refusing to be concerned about the mundane purposes of Economics. I felt unhappy then about the view of Economics as a purely taxonomic science and I still do. I refer to it now because this tendency was at that time closely bound up with a vigorous rejection of economic planning; and controversy on this point still rears its head from time to time, though it has become largely free of the methodological trappings of the thirties. It is showing some signs of revival at this moment and, without entering into a debate which I find weary, stale, flat, and unprofitable, I feel it right to repeat the warning against closed philosophical systems erected on the basis of certain simple, supposedly immutable, principles of human behaviour. Like other closed systems, its chief danger lies in the fact that it provides deceptively simple ready-made answers: in this instance not far removed from Bastiat's notorious *Economic Harmonies*. There are some in every generation who fall in love with them; like all love affairs, this can be particularly virulent in the case of those who succumb at a mature age, after a blameless life spent not in the study of Economics but, say, in that of Herodotus or Nietzsche.

Since I shall have a good deal to say about the limits to which I think the sophistications of modern economic management are subject and to warn you against excessive reliance on the instruments now at our disposal, I think it only right to emphasize at this point that I would warn you even more strongly not to accept a simple faith in a pair of orthodox supply and demand curves as better than a sophisticated national accounts analysis.

When, fifteen years ago, I came to re-examine the progress of Economics, the situation had changed dramatically. We had been through the Keynesian revolution and the New Economics was firmly installed. There were all the signs then of a remarkable synthesis of different strands of thinking, of a union of new statistical techniques with the new analysis of the aggregates of the economy as a whole which Keynes had made possible. There was, moreover, fairly widespread agreement on the practical advantages that could be gained for public policy from the use of these new developments. The new concepts and the new techniques had been tried out during the war, whose pressures quickly eroded the traditional bureaucratic framework and made an experimental attitude more readily acceptable. The immediate post-war transition, too, was, thanks to the New Economics, accomplished with strikingly greater ease than that after the First World War. And the institutions set up to build a better economic world order were inspired—though alas as it has turned out insufficiently so—by the new view of Economics.

If at about the time that I am speaking of I felt some uneasiness despite these welcome developments it was because they seemed subject to the risk that they would once again be regarded as offering easy answers to all the most perplexing questions of human society.

For most of the period since then this sort of apprehension may have appeared unfounded. The New Economics seemed to go from success to success until one of its most eminent operators could say a year or so ago: 'Although we have made no startling conceptual breakthroughs in economics in recent years we have more effectively than ever before, harnessed the existing economics—the economics that has been taught in the nation's college classrooms for some twenty years—to the purposes of prosperity, stability, and growth.'

Let me recall briefly what this new form of economic management —macro-economic management—consists of. The first thing to note is that it is based on an explicit acceptance of a positive role for the State. The State is no longer a 'night-watchman' confining itself to the three basic tasks which Adam Smith thought legitimate. The Authority is now charged, and it accepts this charge, with a duty to promote the highest level of economic activity consistent with the avoidance of inflationary pressure and the fastest rate of economic growth consistent with continued membership, in good standing, of the international economic community, that is to say with a high degree of equilibrium in international payments. These new desiderata of economic policy are distinguished from more traditional ones (which they have not, of course, superseded), such as the pursuit of economic justice, that is the diminution of inequality, or that of economic security, that is a tempering of the hazards of employment, sickness, and old age, by being much less controversial politically. In Britain and in the United States they are enshrined in policy statements, or even in legislation, which no political party would nowadays question, let alone repudiate.

The second thing that is new about them is that while it is generally accepted that these aims are by no means easy to achieve—simultaneously that is—it is believed that Economics now enables us both to measure and to accelerate our progress towards them. The main instruments to these ends are national accounts analysis and fiscal and monetary policy.

The novelty, I think you will agree, lies primarily in the means now at our disposal for determining the current position of the economy and for forecasting its course in the immediate future. The means for influencing that course, on the other hand, are basically traditional. I do not propose here to go into the details either of the problem of forecasting or of the pros and cons of the application of different doses of fiscal and monetary policies or of their timing in relation to particular positions of the economy. What I am more concerned about is whether reliance on this new form of short-term economic management has significantly improved the chance of policy turning out right.

I would like to say straight away that I hold the achievements in this respect of the New Economics in considerable regard and if I now want to emphasize some of its shortcomings, I certainly do not want to be identified with those who decry its use, particularly as far as forecasting is concerned. After all, as Walter Heller so rightly said, 'to refuse to act on one forecast is to act on another. To refuse to act on any explicit forecast is to act on an implicit one.' So, I would stress that the detractors render a great disservice to the progress of our science, certainly a greater one than those who have been making exaggerated claims for our ability to, as it is sometimes put, 'keep the economy on an even keel'.

I repeat, there are many solid achievements. I have already referred to the comparative ease of the post-war transition, much of the credit for which must go to the New Economics. In international co-operation, too, the spread of the concepts and the techniques of short-term economic management and the elaborate machinery now in existence for a mutual comparison and discussion of them has had a very beneficial effect, which has been instrumental, at any rate until relatively recently, in deepening the understanding of each other's problems on the part of different countries. As a result, it has helped to maintain a high degree of co-operation by making a country more ready to adjust its policies in the light of their effects on its neighbours. It is also true to say (or at least it was until quite recently) that the New Economics has banished some of the spectres of the pre-war era. We may even be reasonably confident that we shall not again witness the march of the hungry and the workless on London and Washington—or the hyper-inflations that ravaged so much of Europe in the early twenties.

Nevertheless, it is not possible to be wholly satisfied. If we look at the two instruments of economic policy, progress appears to have been rather slower than is sometimes thought. Monetary policy continues to be very closely tied in with the traditional features of the classical payments mechanism and shows little evidence of the influence of the new theories of full employment equilibrium that was so strongly felt in the field of fiscal policy. Of course, once the problem of short-term economic management is posed in terms of the highest level of economic activity that can be sustained without inflationary pressures, the relatively subordinate role of monetary policy becomes clear. Nevertheless, it still has to play an important, and sometimes vital, part in sustaining the purposes of fiscal policy and in preventing them from being frustrated by a series of short-term deviations which end up by taking the economy along a quite different path from that originally mapped out. I feel that much more needs to be done to bring monetary policy up to date.

However, it is fiscal policy that will continue to have to bear the brunt. In this regard it is undoubtedly a great achievement that for so many years now it has been universally accepted that the national budget is no longer to be thought of in terms of the public household as such but as an estimate of the total economic prospects ahead, as a judgement of the extent to which the level of demand is likely to be above or below that which can sustain the general balance of the system and which will correspond to a desired rate of growth or to a specific desired result as far as the balance of payments is concerned. In short, it is accepted that it is the task of the budget to provide a measure of the total which by fiscal means would need to be injected into, or taken out of, the economy to maintain short-term balance—the fiscal means being either changes in government expenditure (which, of course, are difficult to achieve in the short run), or of changes in taxation.

Experience has shown that the new methods can be efficacious up to a certain point. In this country, where they have now been practised with remarkable consistency and continuity for the greater part of the post-war period, they have proved to be capable, if, and only if, the necessary measures are applied quickly and with sufficient force, of producing a particular result with a high degree of certainty.

The experience is, however, far from reassuring; and this has led, particularly recently, to considerable questioning. The main doubt that has been expressed can be put in this way. While it may prove relatively easy to create a sharp down-turn in economic activity, or, at other times, a considerable, though not quite so sharp, up-turn, exclusive reliance on short-term economic management runs the risk of itself producing great fluctuations, that is of having a de-stabilizing effect. Moreover, the record does not show that short-term management is able to make a contribution towards the more important long-term goals such as the creation of a healthy balance of payments or the maintenance of steady economic growth. I shall revert shortly to the wider question posed by this new scepticism about the proper function of short-term economic management. But, as we are all aware, it has led to attempts, particularly in this country, and more particularly in the last three or four years, to supplement macro-economic management by the use of other instruments designed to influence the economic process more directly and in quite specific respects. Even if the inadequacies of macro-economic measures had not become so apparent, another factor would have led to increasing interest in specific policies, namely the growth and complexity of the government's own expenditure. When this reaches, as it has done in many countries, one-third or more of the national product, it must be clear that changes in it, even when they do not affect the general balance of expenditure and revenue, can produce very marked effects through the detailed changes which they bring about in the pattern of specific resource-allocation. Cutting back the defence programme, for example, in order to increase school construction, highway improvement, or subsidy for home-owners, can have as important a bearing on the economy as a decision to increase total expenditure, raise more revenue, raise the debt ceiling, or increase the proportion of direct as against indirect taxation.

Every major government programme involves constant decisions which change not only the proportion devoted to different types of expenditure but also as between public consumption and public investment. Between them, these changes have most important consequences for different sectors of the private economy: as important, but far too little studied, as the changes that affect the general level of demand. Moreover, these decisions which the government is inexorably obliged to take will have effects on the economy which may only become apparent many years later and which may then be seen to conflict with the broad objectives sought in the short-term through fiscal and monetary policy decisions. The trouble, therefore, seems to me to be that economic policy cannot be constricted within the scope of a search for short-term balance. The basic desiderata of economic policy—stable and high employment levels, rising living standards, balance in international payments—are not spontaneously consistent with each other, and it follows therefore that the fiscal and monetary decisions of short-term management nearly always involve consciously giving one desideratum of policy priority over another.

The failure in the post-war period, despite the apparent successes of the New Economics, to achieve in this country these longer-term objectives, has naturally led to concentration on so-called structural defects of the economy and therefore to a search for policies appropriate to curing them. Regional policy, industrial policy, and, above all, incomes policy are three such fields in which successive governments have now been active for some years. But it is certainly too soon yet to say whether, between them, these new areas of policy will make a decisive difference.

Do they order these things better in the United States, where the New Economics has found so congenial a foster-home? In some respects the answer must clearly be yes. In the first place, economies of scale have operated in analytical work itself: its volume and quality in the American universities and research institutions are unsurpassed. To take only one example, the work done at Brookings in fiscal policy, in the analysis of international growth comparisons, in the study of factors accounting for technological disparities, or of the economic behaviour of the 'affluent' have no adequate counterpart elsewhere. It is not without significance that a soon-to-be-published American assessment of the British economy[1] is likely to prove the most penetrating yet made.

[1] *Britain's Economic Prospects*, a Brookings Institute study, a review of which is included in this volume, see pp. 138–42.

Even more important is the strikingly high level of professionalism applied to statistical and analytical material produced by governmental agencies and available to American policy-makers. We certainly have nothing to equal what is produced by the Federal Reserve Board and Banks on changes in the monetary system or in regard to the indicators of economic activity as regularly turned out by the Department of Commerce.

Of course, we must recognize that the whole climate is more propitious in the United States. Business itself uses the new techniques much more readily than is common in this country; and the general predisposition towards occupational and geographical mobility helps greatly. Superiority of performance in reaching the elusive goals of growth with stability of payments balance and full employment without inflation, is, however, more difficult to demonstrate.

The movement from a sluggish economy to an uninterrupted growth for five or six years as a result of a mixture of fiscal and monetary policy (though with heavy reliance on the former) appeared to be the final vindication of the New Economics and led many to expect even greater triumphs to come as a result of the introduction of what is so deceptively called 'fine tuning'. Unhappily, the reverse movement, a moderation of threatening inflationary pressures and particularly an adjustment of the domestic economy to improve the balance of payments has turned out to be much more difficult. Both the achievement and the lack of it have, however, interesting lessons for us. In particular, they seem to me to point to the need for caution in the use of the new short-term economic management techniques.

I have, myself, often wondered whether the rapid acceptance of the new concept and practice of short-term management in this country does not really prove the opposite of what is sometimes alleged, namely an exceptionally close alliance between officialdom and the economists. It is not difficult to see why this should be so. There is something almost automatic about the technique as it has been developed which fits in admirably with the demands of an official machine with its regularity of time-table, its elaborate system of clearance through departmental and inter-departmental committees, and its production of papers for Ministers in standardized form. Thus the use of the new technique was bound to be congenial to the official mind. One might even argue that this has not been wholly beneficial, and that one of the troubles about economic management during the last twenty years or so has been precisely this tendency on the part of both economists and officials to accept the soft option of the regular forecast with the consequent illusion that they could read off, as on a dial, the correct adjustment of the economy needed at any moment of time.

It is at this point that the question of the proper use of economists in policy-making arises. I approach this subject with some hesitation for reasons that will be obvious, but since it has received a great deal of attention lately, and since in the last resort Economics is only as good as economists, and economic policy as those who make it, I must clearly deal with it. The use of economists as economic advisers in government, or the increasing recruitment as permanent administrators of people trained in Economics is, of course, nothing new. What has created interest lately are two specific questions: on the one hand whether enough economists have been introduced into Whitehall and, on the other, whether those who have been introduced are properly used; in particular, whether their relationship with administrators and Ministers has been such as to give them the best chance to make an effective contribution. Criticism in both these regards has been expressed by a number of economists, including some who have had varied experience in recent years which has given them an insight into the government machine. Briefly summarized, the criticism of recent practice seems to amount to this:

1. Not enough economists have been introduced into Whitehall generally; more particularly, too many have been concentrated into one or two central departments instead of being used to 'stiffen' all departments concerned with particular sectors of the economy.

2. The economists who have been introduced into the 'machine' have been subordinated to the administrators, deliberately left in a backwater and, therefore, unable to bring a proper influence to bear on policy decisions.

3. This last criticism is closely linked with a criticism of an entirely different order, namely that of the difficulty which a Minister is said to find, particularly when there has been a major change in the administration, in imposing his will on the Civil Servants. It is argued that the Minister should equip himself with his own staff of advisers, sympathetic to his political point of view in a way in which regular Civil Servants cannot be.

4. That Civil Servants, both permanent and temporary, including presumably the specially imported advisers, should have much more contact with those outside official circles and be encouraged to debate with them the choices of policy.

5.   Finally, that there should be a considerable extension of the use of the committee procedure of Parliament, including the appearance before committees of Civil Servants, rather on the pattern of the Congressional Committees in the United States.

Let me say at once that I find some of the criticisms in this general area and some of the suggestions for improvement thoroughly worthy of serious and urgent consideration. I think, for example, that if more economists were available throughout Whitehall, they could make a very useful contribution in many Ministries, not only in the economic ones, such as Transport, and Power, or Technology and Trade,[1] but also in the Social Service Departments and in the Ministry of Defence, particularly if they were also as well trained in such matters as input and output analysis or linear programming as their American counterparts are. I also think that in recent years too many economists have tended to be drawn into central departments. This has not only starved other departments. There has been another unfavourable result. The role of the economist in central policy-making is still not very well established. It is likely, therefore, that diminishing returns will be reached as the number of economists grows. What this means is that the economists, when they are sufficiently numerous, will be left in a somewhat isolated group by themselves, thus making them feel that they have been shunted into a siding.

I am also fully in agreement with the idea that there should be much greater interchange of discussion between economists inside and outside the public service. There has been some progress in this direction but not nearly enough. Here the example of the United States can usefully be followed. In relation to the size of the economy there are relatively far fewer economists at the centre of government in the United States than there are here. On the other hand, they maintain the closest contact with those in the universities and research institutions or in private business, who were and will some day again be their colleagues. But what, above all, distinguishes the United States from us which I think is worthy of imitation is that the interchange of ideas across the boundary of officialdom is far less circumscribed by regard to official secrecy. While aware of some of the objections, I strongly support the view that forecasts, for example, should be made much more publicly and openly, as they have been in the United States, at any rate since 1961, so that they can become

---

[1] Now, in some cases, called by different names, but having the same functions.

the subject of informed debate.[1] But this is not all. With us the tendency is still for the relationship between Whitehall and outside research organizations to be at arm's length. Studies are commissioned by Whitehall on issues which are too long-term, or too academic to be thought appropriate for the crowded timetable of Whitehall. Only very rarely, as far as I am aware, are matters that might become the subject of very early government action discussed as freely, though often confidentially, with people outside the public service as they are in the United States. To one who has had the exceptional privilege of being present on one occasion at a meeting which the United States Secretary of the Treasury together with his principal economic colleagues regularly has with a very large group of university economists, the freedom of exchange of statistical data and forecasts and of the debate on policy is little short of staggering when compared with the habits of Whitehall. There are, of course, differences of a very far-reaching kind between the two systems of government which to a large extent supply the reason for some of these different practices—to these I shall refer again in a moment. But we clearly have some way to go yet in emulating America before we need fear that we shall find ourselves locked in a debate on constitutional change.

On the other hand, while I have much sympathy with the suggestion that the Parliamentary Committee system should be extended and that much greater use should be made of evidence by officials who would be subject to cross-examination, I must draw attention to certain difficulties in the way of carrying this very far. In the first place, the senior American officials whose appearance before Congressional Committees is most valuable are, of course, not officials in our sense of the word at all. They are political appointees whose tenure usually (though nowadays admittedly not always) terminates with a change in the administration. Secondly, as we all know, the relationship between the Legislature and the Executive in the United States is quite different from ours. The difficulty of a complete imitation of the American system is therefore obvious.

This difficulty can also be seen when we examine the suggestions that temporary appointments of a quasi-political character should be made. Many of these proposals are, I fear, totally misguided. An analogy with the French system of the *cabinet du ministre* is not possible because this, as is often forgotten, consists to a large extent of a

---

[1] Since this was written, a welcome beginning has been made in the financial statement accompanying the 1968 budget.

number of permanent Civil Servants and only here and there of 'in-and-outers'. In any event, the introduction of temporary advisers to a Minister raises two very difficult problems, one practical and one more fundamental. From a practical point of view it is not always easy to see what these advisers are to do or how they are to fit in with the rest of the political as well as the official machine. They would be subject neither to Parliament, as elected representatives of the people, nor to the constraints of the Civil Service. No doubt, at any one time a few of them can be absorbed, but it is very hard to see how a regular and extensive system of this kind can be instituted without calling in question certain traditional relationships between officials and their Ministers. I am not saying that it may not be desirable that these relationships should be called in question. What I am saying is that the existence of this issue is rarely recognized by those who advocate the changes of which I have spoken. Very few of them, for example, seem to have thought of the position of junior Ministers whose lot, particularly that of the Parliamentary Secretaries, is at the best of times not a very happy one. What is their position to be when new high-level advisers are brought in who do not belong to Parliament and yet do not have the still pretty clearly defined responsibilities of the officials? I can just imagine what some bright young man of Transport House or Central Office (who may well have got a First in PPE or the Economics Tripos), who has exposed himself to the hazards of a political career and who has managed to get into the House and obtain junior office, would feel if he is to be elbowed out by an 'expert' who has only temporarily forsaken the safe haven of his college. And what about the Minister himself—who may be similarly equipped academically? He has not only the officials but his Cabinet colleagues, his constituency party, the Parliamentary party, the sectional interests, the press, and the articulate outside experts to listen to anyway. What will he do with these new hybrid animals?

In fact, I think that there is a much more fundamental misconception here. Underlying it is the thought that a Minister's political objectives are frustrated by the bureaucracy; that somehow if Ministers were equipped with technical advice given by those who share their political convictions, they would be able to achieve what they aim at. I would not deny that the bureaucratic machine, like all old and well-established institutions, is very powerful and that certain attitudes of mind which it engenders—not political in the ordinary sense of the word let me hasten to add—are often found to constitute at least irritating, and sometimes very harmful, constraints on the innovator. But to suppose that some of the economic or political objectives that Ministers bring with them when they achieve office (and which are often extremely controversial even within the same political party) only require a few enlightened economists for their realization, betrays to my mind an astonishing naïvety about the world and something bordering on arrogance about the power of Economics. For obvious reasons I cannot relate this argument to some of the most recent controversies with regard to economic policy. However, we all of us have our favourite list of errors in British post-war policy and I am ready to name some items that I would insist on including in mine. I believe that much of the trouble from which we have suffered over the last twenty years can be traced to the excessively generous settlement of sterling indebtedness after the war, to the premature convertibility in 1947 which so quickly had to be abandoned, to the failure to recognize early enough the importance of the European integration movement and to take the lead in it when we were still powerful enough to do so, and to the excessively large defence programme of 1950/1. This is far from a complete list. I have picked out only items which are either wholly economic or which have a strong economic content. If you agree to even some of these as having been among the great errors of British policy in the post-war period, would you really suppose that the presence of another two or three dozen economists in Whitehall would have prevented successive governments from making them? Even another half-dozen Keyneses possessing his unique combination of distinction in Economics and in public affairs, would, as the Master's own occasional deviations of judgement show, have made little difference.

Or to take a more recent example—one which I dare take because it does not at present form a major part of the British domestic economic debate—the question of liquidity and of the proper organization of the international monetary system. There has certainly been no lack of expert advice both from within and from without national and international official machines. Indeed, this is an exceptional example of close collaboration over some years now between the academic and the official worlds. Yet this has not helped to achieve unanimity, let alone effective action—for the SDRs still remain to be formally put in place and activated. No, this has been another case of the sad lack of coincidence of the time and the place and the loved one. It is ironic to recall that when some years ago a

British Chancellor put forward a plan which involved a modest degree of pooling of reserves, this was promptly torpedoed by the United States, where at this moment similar plans are regarded as highly desirable—if only they could be got!

The truth surely is that the economic advisers who most loudly complain about frustrations by the bureaucracy would find themselves no less frustrated if they exposed their views, which are basically political, to the hazards of political debate, even within one and the same party.

So I conclude, sadly but I hope wisely, that the limits of Economics in terms of practical action are still very narrow, that beyond them lies the no man's land of Politics, and that it is not possible to get one's way on the cheap as it were, that is by fighting in that treacherous terrain only by proxy.

But improvements are possible: and economists, even at their most academic, can make an important contribution, particularly if they work together with other social scientists. A deeper study of the techniques—and implications—of micro-economic policy is clearly called for. At one extreme there is the question of the advantages and disadvantages of government stimulation of particular industries and, if advantageous, the techniques to be used. Here economic theorists, econometricians, business and financial economists, and political theorists can usefully work together. At the other extreme I might mention incomes policy where indeed micro- and macro-economic policy meet. I do not believe it is sufficiently realized yet how great the gap is between, on the one hand, the conception of national economic aggregates and the attempt to manipulate them through time and, on the other, the comparatively old-fashioned nature of both the means of economic policy available and the institutional framework within which they are exercised—a gap most glaring in the case of incomes policy. The first economist who develops a general theory (from the indications in Keynes) of how to make these—sometimes massive—changes in the pattern of resource allocation while having regard to traditional rights and aspirations, how to balance—in collective terms—the claims of different sections of the community as well as the claims of the present and future in an environment in which the democratic process itself makes sole reliance on market forces impossible, even if it were desirable, will, indeed, deserve a great prize!

In the field of macro-economic management itself, improvements are also possible. I suspect that some fundamental reforms of our tax system might give us, once made, a more flexible instrument for adjustment. Some of our procedures could also be made more flexible. Anyone who can devise a system which will give us the benefit of open discussion, which the American system provides, with the possibility for quick action inherent in our system but without the rigidity of an annual budget, will also have deserved well of the community.

There are, of course, dangers everywhere. The new micro-economic policies require sharp and constant vigilance in regard to the relation between the State and private interests. We do not need to panic and to fear the emergence of a corporate state; but we do need to be on our guard and to remember the still valid warnings of Adam Smith. Economists have much to do to work out the implications of new industrial structures on the right of consumers or competitors. On the other side, a better arsenal of macro-economic weapons will increase the risk of individual economists giving free rein to their special predilections. Even the most distinguished modern theorists are no more free from the temptations to erect great historical systems than other human beings. Let one of them evolve a theory of what slowed growth in Britain, and if he has enough influence on Ministers we wake up one morning to find that our haircuts cost us more!

In the sphere of the government machine itself, there is room for experimenting with new methods. The Civil Service will presumably soon have an opportunity to do so: and it is now widely accepted that we need greater mobility both within it and between it, the universities and business. Some reform of parliamentary procedure is already under way; and Ministers themselves can do much to improve matters. If they are excessively burdened by the machine and its enormous output of paper, as I firmly believe they are, the remedy is in their own hands. Here an ounce of courage and determination is often worth a ton of Whitehall reports.

Let me say in conclusion that it is in these directions that I would seek improvement, rather than by chasing the will-o'-the-wisp of installing the economist as a kind of modern philosopher-king. On this issue my vote goes, on balance, to Kant rather than to Plato. For he drew a distinction between the judgement of pure reason and the possession of power, the latter an inevitable source of corruption of the former. While I would not say that philosophers and kings should not meet—on the contrary, I would want them to do so more —it is as well that each should recognize the other for what he is.

ECONOMICS AND ECONOMIC POLICY SINCE KEYNES

The O'Brien Lecture 1971, delivered at University College Dublin on 14 May 1971. Published in the Report *of the Central Bank of Ireland for the year ended 31 March 1971.*

I should like to begin by saying that it is a great privilege to have been invited to give this lecture today to do honour to George O'Brien, who until ten years ago and for so many years occupied the chair of Economics in this University College. It is a special pleasure for me to do so, since it also gives me the opportunity to acknowledge a debt I owe him. It was a reading of his classic *Essay on Medieval Economic Teaching* that was in no small measure responsible for awakening an interest in me in the history of ideas, in the interplay between economic change and its reflection in the speculations of the human spirit, which has never left me. Accordingly, I have chosen to speak to you today on the most recent phase in the evolution of economic thought with special, though not with exclusive, reference to its bearing on economic policy, thus combining an old academic predilection with more recent practical preoccupations, first as a participant in the elaboration of government policy and now as one of its many passive recipients, or perhaps I should say victims.

I have chosen to link this brief survey of post-war economic thinking in its relation to economic policy with the name of Maynard Keynes. This great man, undoubtedly the greatest economist of this century, died almost exactly twenty-five years ago, ten years after the publication of his most revolutionary and influential work, *The General Theory of Employment, Interest, and Money,* and one hundred and seventy years after the appearance of the book that marked the birth of the modern science of Economics, *The Wealth of Nations.* To explain my choice of Keynes as the symbol of change, of the watershed in present-day Economics and to explain both his contribution and what has happened since he wrote, I must ask you to bear with me while I recall briefly the background of the evolution of modern Economics.

The first thing to remember is that however deep-rooted it may be in metaphysical speculation or in ethical principles, modern

Economics began as a severely practical science designed for the quite specific purpose of helping towards a better ordering of human affairs in the ordinary material side of the business of living. Yet classical political economy, as it developed in the fifty years around the turn of the eighteenth century, meant both a great intellectual awakening as well as prescription for policy. Adam Smith's great achievement was to have identified human labour (more generally we would now say economic activity) as the source of wealth and of its increase as against the fallacies of the primitive gold- and later trade-worship of the mercantilists who preceded him. This intellectual leap forward laid the foundation for quite precise developments in the field of policy: the dismantlement of remaining restrictions on trade—both in the sense of production and of commerce—of a spectacular widening of markets with a prodigious increase in the benefits derived from the division of labour, so that one hundred and fifty years later, Keynes could rightly say that all that had happened in, say, the four thousand years before the eighteenth century in regard to the standard of life was as nothing compared with what had happened since.

In some ways, Ricardo's achievement was even greater. He provided the intellectual basis for a vast extension of free markets into the sphere of international trade and finance. The machinery of central banking in both its domestic and international aspects as it exists almost to this day is largely rooted in his analysis and his policy prescriptions. Above all, his concern with the distribution of the national product between the various classes that contributed to its creation—land, labour and capital—provided the first coherent general picture of the total economy including the mechanism of dynamic changes in it through time. The mechanics of capital accumulation, of the absorption of technological innovation, the role of natural resources and the claims of labour, are all first and most illuminatingly analysed in his work.

I would argue that for well over one hundred years after the flowering of the classical school, the general pattern of economic thought remained essentially unchanged. For what did the changes of the nineteenth and early twentieth centuries amount to? True, there were some attempts, particularly on the continent where the modern economy was developing with a considerable time-lag, to lay stress on historical analysis, or, as in the romantic schools, to interweave mystical, political elements into economic analysis. There was, of course, the great blossoming of the marginalist schools in England, the United States and Austria towards the end of the century and the beginning of the present one which is sometimes regarded as a major new turning-point in Economics. I would admit that the emphasis on small changes of economic magnitudes at the margin, particularly when shorn of its original admixture of the psychology of hedonism or utilitarianism, introduced a valuable new technique particularly for studying specific prices and their movements. But it would be quite wrong, I believe, to claim that these technical improvements could even begin to rival the truly revolutionary change of one hundred years earlier. There was, of course, Marx. No one can deny him the title of revolutionary, though in a rather different sense from that in which I have used the term. Freed from his special view of history, which is at least grossly one-sided, and from a somewhat mystical sociology, his economics is very much in the tradition of Ricardo; and a good deal of it could stand to be looked at afresh and without that prejudice which the conclusions which he derived from it naturally evoke.

But from the point of view of understanding the economic process in the kind of society that was developing in the last hundred and fifty years in the western world, no fundamental changes occurred. By the twenties of the present century Economics had grown respectable, established and complacent. Theoretical refinements of specialists reared in the marginalist school and equipped with new mathematical tools abounded. Nor were controversies in the field of policy absent; but their scope was limited. This relative calm was rudely shattered by the First World War, by the hyper-inflations which followed it in so many countries, by the breakdown of the economic system as a whole in a considerable part of Europe, by the dislocations and disruptions of the international monetary system aggravated by, as it turned out, futile and destructive attempts to remedy them by a return to pre-war conditions that could no longer be sustained, by the Great Depression in the early thirties with its mass unemployment, the paradox of poverty amidst plenty, the renewed, and even more far-reaching collapse of the international financial mechanism and, finally, the ghastly social and political consequences to which this series of shocks to which our society had been subjected for nearly twenty years gave rise.

It was precisely at this point that the second great revolution in economic thought occurred, one that must forever remain linked with the name of Keynes. This is not the occasion to go into the details of his theoretical analysis. There are many path-breaking innovations here, foundation-stones on which a whole generation of economists have built. What is remarkable about the work of Keynes is rather the approach, the new way of looking at economic phenomena, at the working of the economic system. The surprising thing about this intellectual revolution when one looks at it in the perspective of history is that it was essentially (though this was probably not even fully perceived by its author) a rediscovery of the original approach of Ricardo and his school, namely a view of the economy as a whole, of the interrelation of the great aggregates of the system, private consumption and investment, public consumption and investment, that is government spending—the so-called macro-economic analysis—together with the elaboration of new concepts for denoting certain broad features of economic behaviour, such as liquidity preference, and the propensity to consume. Once again, the immediate effect—as was indeed the purpose of this development—was a highly practical one: to cope with the underemployment of human and physical resources which was the legacy of the Great Depression and to inculcate habits of thought and devise prescriptions for policy which would make the recurrence of this evil impossible. The main engine for changing attitudes was a kind of emancipation from the long-established predisposition to equate the impersonal behaviour of the total economy with the conduct of the individual or the single firm, and to derive policy guidance for the one from the cherished traditional precepts of the other. What is prudent in a single family can scarce be folly in the State, Adam Smith had argued, an argument that was already hard to sustain once Ricardo's pattern of the economic process had been elaborated. Keynes explicitly denied the proposition. He showed the importance which the national budget, that is the government's own decision on getting and spending, could have on the economy as a whole and on its various aggregates, analogous to the long-accepted influence of monetary policy which by determining the total availability of credit and the terms on which it could be obtained created a certain framework determining individual economic decisions. Henceforth, the drawing-up of the nation's budget could no longer be likened to the action of a prudent father of a family concerned solely with the financial solvency of his household. It came now to be seen as

B

the determinant of the level of economic activity as a whole, the full employment of resources, their overemployment, creating inflationary gaps or their underemployment creating deflationary gaps with appropriate consequences for prices, the real incomes of different classes of the community, consumption, saving and investment.

Those who have learnt to think about these matters in the generation since Keynes's death and to whom these concepts are commonplace, can hardly believe the sense of emancipation and understanding, bordering on revelation, that these ideas created in Keynes's contemporaries. Their spread was rapid not only in their homeland but elsewhere above all in the United States, and it is no exaggeration to say that since the end of the war they have held increasing and virtually undisputed sway over the minds of theorists and policymakers alike in the countries with our type of economic system.

As I have said, the original stimulus that helped to produce these ideas was the waste caused by large-scale unemployment; and so the first application of the new doctrine was to fight deflation primarily, though not exclusively, by fiscal policy. Deficit financing, public works and the like were the preferred means, and the American New Deal was the principal example of their successful application. In the international field, too, the Keynesian doctrines began to exert an increasing influence; and the growing collaboration between central banks that was a marked feature of the late thirties can rightly be regarded as the forerunner of today's international network of monetary co-operation which, however inadequate it may still be, certainly deserves a good deal of the credit for our having been able to weather some recent monetary storms.

But as I have also indicated the new theory was conceived of— though it took a little time to recognize it as such—as a general theory applicable in all circumstances and capable of yielding policy guidance for the avoidance of either of the two evils, unemployment or inflation. The greatest triumph for the New Economics was perhaps the fact that it became enshrined in important declarations of government policy and in legislation, notably the British Full Employment White Paper and the American Full Employment Act. However, as these very titles indicate, although lip-service was paid to the general character of the new doctrine, the preoccupation clearly was with only one form of disequilibrium, that of unemployment, the memory of which was still most vivid in the minds of the then ruling generation. Not surprisingly the New Economics has been accused of having a full employment and, therefore, inflationary, bias, and it is this belief which was later to give rise to some erosion of the supremacy of Keynesian doctrine. But to this I will revert later.

As far as the pure theory is concerned and the way in which it was integrated into the policy-making process, it should, however, be properly regarded as a general theory of economic stabilization. It is as such that it became the new orthodoxy, particularly in the Anglo-Saxon countries. This development was powerfully aided by two trends which, as is usually the case, it had itself helped to call forth: a greatly improved apparatus of statistical data and techniques and a considerable influx of economists into the machinery of government. It is a tribute to the far-sightedness of those responsible that even in the darkest days of the war, preparations were made for the introduction of these new techniques and the recruitment and organization of those who were to operate them after the war. National Accounts analysis, the collection and processing of statistics to provide numerical data for the Keynesian concepts, Gross National Product, private and public consumption and investment and so on, took a giant leap forward. So did the art of forecasting, at least in technical terms, I hasten to stress; and with it the elaboration of a systematic pattern of presentation of historical statistics, forecasting of changes in the main data on the basis of 'existing policies', as the technical term has it, judgements of the result in terms of the Keynesian inflationary or deflationary gaps; and then appropriate policy prescriptions.

The aim was stabilization, 'keeping the economy on an even keel' as it was so often called; and it is no exaggeration to say that a whole new industry—and, with it, a whole new literature—grew up around this activity of 'demand management'. Economics, and particularly Government Economics, has certainly been a growth industry these last twenty-five years; and there is already a large volume of books and articles, written by practitioners of the art—economists or administrators—as well as by outside observers.

It is undoubtedly the case, and will, in my view, be confirmed by history that this whole new movement has considerable successes to record. The transition from a war economy to a peace economy was accomplished relatively smoothly, certainly very much more smoothly than had been the case after the First World War. Reconstruction of war-shattered Europe was rapid and unaccompanied by depressions such as those of the twenties. International trade was restored and set on the road of an unprecedented period of expansion. Even in the international financial sphere, progress was not lacking. The elaboration of the great post-war institutions of the World Bank and the Monetary Fund owe much to the New Economics and to Keynes personally. Indeed, where they were deficient, and to the extent that the latter in particular remains inadequate today, it is because political impediments and intellectual time-lags prevented Keynes from fully having his way. The International Trade Organization which was to have been concerned with trade and employment together, and which would have completed the armoury of international instruments, remained stillborn for similar reasons and we had to make do with the GATT. Auxiliary motors had, therefore, to be employed, notably the Marshall Plan. But the very fact that this unprecedented act of international co-operation was possible—while it clearly owes much to the inherent generosity of America—is also a tribute to the progress of intellectual enlightenment in these matters. One has only to compare it with the mental attitudes that inspired the policy of reparations after the First World War to realize the enormous progress of understanding that had taken place.

Even after the first phase of post-war recovery the new form of macro-economic policy management seemed to be scoring many successes. Unemployment seemed to be banished, inflation intermittent and not too oppressive and production and trade seemed to be growing—though not uniformly in all countries, yet at a sufficiently rapid rate in the world as a whole. The experience of the fifties seemed to encourage a certain, apparently justifiable, ambition in policy-makers. If you were to ask what were the policy objectives which were then emerging, implicitly or explicitly, and which are today regarded as the prime tasks of wise economic state-craft, they could be listed under four headings: to produce a high level of economic activity and particularly reasonably full employment of labour; to sustain a reasonable rate of growth of the economy so as to absorb technological innovation and result in a continually rising standard of living, particularly of the poorer sections of the community; to avoid inflation, that is to say a rate of increase in prices in general that would significantly change the distribution of income; and finally, to preserve a smoothly functioning international monetary system.

The means by which these objectives were to be achieved were monetary and fiscal policy. The role of the former was fundamentally not new. It was in part a subsidiary instrument for the management of total demand. By reducing the volume of credit and making it dearer it could help to damp down economic activity and so contain inflationary pressures. Above all, it was especially designed to act upon (or support action upon) the balance of payments, and by the so-called domestic adjustment process help to keep a country as a member in good standing of the international financial system. While the means for exercising monetary policy have changed and have become more refined in response to the greater complexity of the credit system and the pattern and composition of international reserves, in essence the role of monetary policy remained until recently little different in kind from what it had always been. Fiscal policy, on the other hand, was the new instrument, and had to bear the brunt of stabilization policy in the manner I have already described.

I have said that these new methods of policy had achieved marked successes. Yet by the middle sixties considerable doubts about their adequacy began to appear. In Britain, where the New Economics had been practised with increasing technical virtuosity, there was also increasing awareness of the persistence of certain deficiencies in economic performance which made more and more people doubt whether the new policy and its chief instruments were adequate. Sluggish growth in periods of markedly increasing world trade and sharply rising gross national products in her main competitors and the constantly recurring balance of payments crisis accompanied by equally recurring bouts of stimulation and restraint—stop-go— began to shake belief in the total adequacy of demand management as then practised. In the United States, too, successes were seen to be partial only. Where employment was maintained and growth stimulated, inflationary tendencies appeared and the balance of payments began to deteriorate. When, as happened in the last two years, restraint—largely by monetary means—was imposed, unemployment on a substantial scale began to plague the economy without, at least reasonably quickly, either containing inflationary pressures, particularly of the so-called cost-push variety, or improving the balance of payments. In the United Kingdom the picture was again somewhat different: fiscal and monetary restraint in the last two years certainly did succeed remarkably well in restoring a healthy balance of payments, but this has not only been at the cost of substantial unemployment, but also without, as yet, a really decisive effect on inflation.

It is out of these disappointments, shall we say, with the continued efficacy of modern demand management, that a turning away from the full acceptance of the New Economics had its origins. Perhaps the degree of self-assurance which some of its practitioners had developed has contributed to the growth of these new doubts. The alliance between administrators, economists and statisticians, admirable though it is, has, perhaps, under the pressure of the requirements of the bureaucratic machine and the counterpressures of the political process, produced at times an appearance of complacency which may, in part, be responsible for the disenchantment which undoubtedly set in in the later sixties.

There were, of course, other factors at work; and to these I shall refer presently. But what I might call the 'endogenous' causes of dissatisfaction with the performance of the New Economics, have led in the first instance to some re-examination of the four objectives of policy which I listed earlier. What is increasingly questioned is whether their simultaneous achievement is in fact possible. Are they all compatible with each other, or are there 'trade-offs' between them, as our American friends would say?

This is a large area of debate and I cannot hope today to do more than scratch the surface. In the first place, we might exclude growth from our consideration, though I shall refer to it again in a different context later. While fiscal and monetary policy clearly have an influence on growth, it has long been recognized that there are many other, more deep-seated, causes, political, social and cultural, often with strong historic roots, which condition the capacity for growth of different societies at different times. We are left, therefore, essentially with the problem of reconciling high employment, absence of inflation and a healthy balance of payments. In regard to all of these, recent years have seen the revival of many old attitudes, though in new and more sophisticated forms, based on the implicit belief in the incompatibility of any two of these with each other. Thus a healthy balance of payments is sometimes said to be inconsistent with full employment except in a regime of flexible exchange rates. Similarly there is said to be a 'cruel' choice between full employment and avoidance of inflation, a dilemma graphically presented in the so-called Phillips Curve.

I cannot pause to examine these propositions; my purpose is rather to list them as examples to show that there is now considerable room for debate both on the choices of policy objectives as well as on the adequacy of the means for achieving them. If we do in fact have to accept that there are these dilemmas and that, as of now, we do not know how to resolve them, then in time the whole edifice built up on the work of Keynes may be threatened. Few people would be prepared to accept such a conclusion. In the first place, even if there are some incompatibilities, these could be stated in less extreme terms. It has long been argued for example that whether the Phillips Curve is a correct representation of reality in all circumstances or not, a degree of 'transitional' unemployment must be expected in a changing, technologically oriented society. Provided that this is kept modest, that through training programmes and a vigorous pursuit of policies of equal job opportunity and other means mobility of labour is kept high, and that the material hardships resulting from what unemployment there is are adequately alleviated, this need not be a blemish on our economy or our society.

Similarly, many modern economists would argue that it is possible to live with a modest degree of inflation. Social benefits can be scaled up, wage- and salary-earners compensated by responsive adjustments, savers protected by greater competition in capital and money markets, and pensioners subsidized. All this, it is said, would be cheaper than suffering the cost of the lost output caused by unemployment.

As for the balance of payments and the domestic adjustment process, if one rejects completely flexible exchange rates as being ultimately inimical to expanding international trade and smoothly functioning international capital and money markets, one is necessarily driven in the direction of still greater international co-operation, ultimately through the evolution of an institution equivalent to an international central bank—though it must be recognized that this inevitably raises the question of national sovereignty and the degree of explicit abandonment of it as against the already existing high degree of implicit abandonment—one is prepared to accept.

All this, as I say, concerns our policy objectives. But the doubts about the continued validity of the Keynesian revolution have also extended to the policy means. This has led in part to the advocacy of other, additional, policies; in part to the suggestion of a complete change of emphasis. As for the former, the two policies most often mentioned are, first, what I might call industrial policy and, second, incomes policy. Neither is fundamentally inconsistent with continued reliance on Keynesian analysis or the now traditional form of demand management. They are to be regarded as supplementary means, so, depending on the precise form they take, they could be thought of in different terms. They could be broadly similar to demand management, if they remain general, or very dissimilar, if they become detailed and specific. Industrial policy consists of various attempts more directly to influence industrial structure, management, and efficiency than is possible by fiscal and monetary means alone, since these operate only on the general market parameters. Incomes policy has been much debated and I need not spend a great deal of time on it. It can vary from the most general exhortation, through forms of voluntary restraint, to detailed statutory controls. The latter, of course, would clearly, in the limit, be incompatible with the maintenance of the market economy.

Another quite different form of reaction to Keynesianism, sometimes even regarded as a full-scale counter-revolution, is to be found in the monetarist school, often referred to as the Chicago school and particularly associated with the name of Professor Friedman. Its own principal author at any rate has described it as a counter-revolution. Not unnaturally those responsible for this rekindled enthusiasm for the monetary explanation of phenomena of instability in the economy and for their cure by monetary means, claim that it was primarily the inherent intellectual defects of the Keynesian system which led them to their views, and that they are able to support their conclusions by recourse to historical evidence. In the hands of an eminent economist like Professor Friedman, this way of looking at the problem undoubtedly acquires a good deal of plausibility. Nevertheless, some scepticism is in order. The historical substructure of the new monetarism, massive though it is, can, I am sure, be questioned. Indeed may I say parenthetically, I believe that eminent theorists of both the opposing schools (Professors Kaldor and Friedman, for example) should not be blindly followed when they forsake their deductive accomplishments and seek further achievements in the territory of broad historical insight for which quite other talents are required. Furthermore, whatever may be the theoretical and historical worth of the rediscovered quantity theory of money (a more sophisticated version of the old $MV = PT$ equation), it would never have achieved the vogue it has, if it had not been for the growing doubts about the practical results of the current methods of demand management of which I have spoken. More specifically, it was the supposed inflationary bias, the preoccupation with full employment—or at least the inability to banish inflation—of Keynesianism which encouraged the search for alternative policies. The value of the new monetarism must, therefore, also be judged by its practical results, actual or potential.

Briefly and necessarily crudely described, the theory of the new school amounts to this. The old quantity theory had stated that the amount of money in circulation multiplied by its velocity of circulation must equal the volume of transactions multiplied by the general level of prices. It followed that an increase in the amount or velocity of money had, in the absence of an increase in transactions, to result in an increase in prices, and so on. The new monetarism continues to stress that there is a correlation between the rate of growth of money and the rate of growth of money income with a time-lag which may, on an average, be of the order of six to nine months. The correlation in these rates of growth of income and money shows up first in output and only with a further time-lag of about the same magnitude in prices.

Thus, the rate of growth of money, if it is different from the rate of growth of output (as determined by real factors, such as technology, enterprise and capital formation) will open up gaps of an inflationary or deflationary nature; though largely in common with the earlier Keynesian theory, the monetarists trace these effects through a complex of changes in the prices of existing assets which are only later translated into effects on spending for the production of new assets or the purchase of current services in relation to the purchase of existing assets. Inflation is thus a monetary phenomenon, that is something produced by the money supply; and monetary policy, that is action on the money supply, alone can hope to cope with it. To be fair to the principal theorist of the school at least, he has consistently warned against relying too much on monetary policy. It is because Professor Friedman does not have much faith in the efficiency of what he calls a discretionary monetary policy (any more than in any other forms of deliberate intervention in the play of market forces) that he has advocated maintaining a steady, modest rate of growth of the money supply as most likely to foster a reasonable, though by no means perfect, state of economic stability, that is growth without inflation.

The theoretical arguments of the monetary school and the historical evidence by which it tries to support them have been and continue to be hotly debated. From my point of view today, the important thing to stress is that the practical effect of the emergence of the monetary view in relation to the acute dilemma in recent economic history between employment and inflation and the apparent inability of demand management by fiscal means to resolve it satisfactorily has necessarily been to urge policy-makers in the direction of greater reliance on the monetary instrument. There was never any doubt (and recent experiments in this regard have not contributed any new ones) that a strong dose of monetary restraint can sooner or later, the time-lag depending on many other factors, stop an inflation. But it does so only precisely because it reduces economic activity and creates unemployment. It is thus not a means of removing the choice between the two evils but only another and, I think, particularly violent method for alternating between them.

But I cannot at this stage go further into the intricacies of this debate. There are signs of other, and potentially more far-reaching, forms of discontent within the existing corpus of economics and its relation to economic policy to which I must refer before I bring this brief survey to a conclusion. The common features of the more fundamental questioning that is now prevalent in our present way of ordering our economic affairs can perhaps be stated in this way. It is by no means clear that the present economic structure dominated by large private corporations jointly with the government sector produces adequate results, either in relation to innovation in production or to the pattern of both public and private consumption. The roots of this discontent, of this questioning of existing institutions, of patterns of behaviour, of accepted mental attitudes, including analyses of the system, are in part similar to those from which the Keynesian revolution itself sprang. In part they are different and they go deeper. They have some family resemblance with the other discontents of the age: the rejection of the material culture, the irreverence towards anything that is established, the alienation of youth.

There are two forms in which this makes itself felt in Economics to which I think it is worthwhile to refer. In the first place there is scepticism about the efficiency of the industrial structure and concern about its relationship to the democratic political process. Much of the work that has been inspired by this attitude is associated with the name of Professor Galbraith. In a series of books on these topics, notably his latest, *The New Industrial State*, Kenneth Galbraith has, like that other, earlier American iconoclast, Veblen, enriched our understanding as well as our vocabulary and has certainly contributed to starting a whole new range of inquiry into the operation of oligopolistic large enterprises which are responsible for the major part of our industrial output. The creation of demand and the prefabrication of markets through oligopoly using modern mass-advertising techniques, certainly puts a different complexion on the notion of consumer choice and on the conclusions of neo-classical economics when they are based on a quite different sequence and relationship between, say, wants, demand, production and income. Professor Galbraith has also called in question the pattern of resource allocation which results from the manner in which the modern economy operates. His *The Affluent Society*, with its emphasis on the inadequate provision made for the production and consumption of public goods, the contrast between 'private affluence' and 'public squalor', has become a classic and the title of his book an important addition to the language.

This aspect of the newer economics, the questioning of the benefits to be derived from additions to the physical stock of certain goods, has sometimes taken a much more extreme form. A whole school devoted to 'anti-growth' now exists which goes to great lengths to probe the worthwhileness of life encumbered by the indiscriminate piling-up of the products of an undirected technology—a true Frankenstein monster. They argue that not only are the problems of pollution, urban sprawl, traffic congestion and so on made worse—if they are not actually created—by the blind pursuit of economic growth, but the actual quality of life of the individual is fundamentally impaired. What value, it is asked, is to be attached to a figure for the Gross National Product, say in the United States, which measures the escalating output of paper and packaging material (already twenty years ago as large as the whole Gross National Product of a smaller Western European country, such as Denmark, to say nothing of advertising, which is considerably larger), when its contribution to welfare may, because of the resulting waste disposal and pollution problem, be in fact negative. A distinguished Japanese economist, Professor Shigeto Tsuru, has recently analysed in some detail these factors which add to GNP but do not add to, or even subtract from, human welfare; and it is safe to predict that, while in a world in which poverty is still widespread, the contempt for material production is unlikely to sweep the board, more and more research will be devoted to the kind of issues which the anti-growth school has put in the centre of the debate. The attention paid not only by governments but also by big business to the problems of the environment is an indication of what is in store; and when we hear that anti-pollution measures in Japan are likely soon to involve expenditures running into billions of dollars, we can be confident that these problems of the newest of the new Economics are now well integrated into the general process of economic policy-making, even though it is not quite clear yet how they and similar questions of a socio-economic character such as ensuring adequate non-discriminatory job opportunities will affect the general body of economic theory.

Let me sum up and try and see what all this movement which has been going on for the last five or six years betokens. If we take first the whole corpus of Economics and economic policy as bequeathed by the classics and developed by Keynes and his disciples, the path ahead seems to me to be reasonably well marked. I have made it clear that I welcome the new scepticism about macro-economic management. It is, I think, wholly desirable that it should not be thought that provided the right data and forecasts are periodically fed into the machine, policy prescriptions as to how much should be 'put into' or 'taken out of' the economy could be read off as if on a dial. Nevertheless, we must not fall into the opposite, obscurantist, attitude which would deny all value to the new techniques. I shall expect further improvements in them but not of an order that would make economic stabilization virtually the function of an automatic pilot. So long as a fair measure of individual freedom of choice exists, so long will there be divergence on policy objective and imperfection of the results obtained by the policy instruments we already have, or the new ones we are likely to devise and amalgamate with the old. As for the monetarist counter-revolution, I would agree with those who expect it to peter out. This is not to say that monetary policy as such will disappear. It will continue to have an important part to play; and I do not foresee a sudden outbreak of unemployment among central bankers. More particularly in the field of international economic co-operation, especially in regard to the financial mechanism, is there a great deal more that can be done.

I would be less confident in predicting this kind of steady, unspectacular progress where the more radical attacks on received doctrine are concerned.

I believe that one gain, perhaps a modest one, that can be recorded with certainty is that we are now able to recognize and re-establish the limits of Economics and remove the excessive self-assurance, sometimes bordering on arrogance, which has tended to creep into economic administration. Curiously this arrogance has been fostered by, if it did not have its origins in, an ostensibly modest view of Economics and the economist, well exemplified in this quotation from Keynes. Writing in 1930, he said: 'But do not let us overestimate the importance of the economic problem or sacrifice to its supposed necessities other matters of greater and more permanent significance. It should be a matter for specialists—like dentistry. If economists could get themselves thought of as humble, competent people, on a level with dentists, that would be splendid.' I wonder if Keynes really believed this at the time he wrote it. It's hard to think that he did by the time he was applying the analysis of his *General Theory* to domestic and international policy from the vantage point of the British Treasury. In any event, whatever his views, it would be very difficult for anyone to sustain today that Economics could be likened to dentistry, both because it is less exact, and when the latter is well practised less effective than, dentistry, and also because today more than ever, the boundaries between the so-called material advance of mankind and its achievement of higher standards of welfare (in some transcendental sense) have become very blurred indeed.

It would be agreeable to believe that this foreshadows a new approach, perhaps another of these curious historical revivals on a new and higher plane: a return to a normative social science and an abandonment of the purely neutral 'value-free' Economics of the last two hundred years, though with full advantage being taken of the great technical advances that have meanwhile been made. Instead of Burke's lament about the passing of the age of chivalry and its replacement by that of the 'sophisters, economists, and calculators' we might then say with Professor Tsuru that the age of the calculators had passed and that of the humanists had begun.

But even if one could be confident about this, it would alas by no means be the end of our problem as far as Economics and the economist are concerned. For there would still remain the troublesome issue of their relationship to politics and the politician, the economist being concerned with the judgement of reason, the politician with power. And these, so one of the greatest philosophers of all time has assured us, do not readily mix.

THE WEALTH OF NATIONS 1776–1976

Published in Lloyds Bank Review, *January 1976*

According to temperament, all human history, perhaps especially the history of ideas, can be looked at in two ways. To some, it will be a continuous development without any break: a seamless garment. To others, it will be a series of seemingly unconnected but massive events, the haphazard appearance of great individuals responsible for gigantic leaps in man's imagination. For some, it will be a slow, laborious building of stone upon stone by many humble workers. For others, progress will be identified with Moses, Jesus and Mohammed, with Smith, Marx and Keynes, with Ptolemy, Newton and Einstein.

For the origin of political economy as a modern discipline, the first view can certainly be supported by much evidence. It is true that the classical system of economics associated with the name of Adam Smith, and the beginning of the era of industrial capitalism which it accompanied, had been in the making for nearly a hundred years before *The Wealth of Nations*. In the field of political and economic thought, North had inveighed against the remaining shackles of mercantilist ideas and restrictive regulations of trade: Locke and Hume, in philosophy, both general and political, had exemplified that liberal spirit that was later to find its clearest expression in the writings of the French philosophers: Petty had wrestled with the problem of value a century before Adam Smith: and the French Physiocrats had almost succeeded in building a self-consistent system of the circulation of wealth well before 1776.

Nevertheless, one would have to be peculiarly unimaginative, indeed insensitive, not to see the last quarter of the eighteenth century as one of the great watersheds in the evolution of human society. In 1775, James Watt, that strange, curmudgeonly genius joined with the worldly industrialist Matthew Boulton to make steam-engines by factory methods: as symbolic a partnership between science and business—and in as crucial an era of enterprise at that time—as could not possibly be bettered even it it had been contrived as fiction. Fourteen years later, the French Revolution unleashed forces of social and political change to transform society that were to go on working right up to the present day. In between, there was that annus mirabilis 1776.

And what a year it was! On 9 March there appeared *An Enquiry into the Nature and Causes of the Wealth of Nations*, by Adam Smith. Some months later (traditionally, on 4 July, though the precise date is in dispute among scholars) there was signed at Philadelphia the Declaration of Independence. It may seem odd, at first sight, to couple the two large quarto volumes of sober and intricate argument by a Scottish moral philosopher with the short, resounding call to arms of Thomas Jefferson. But the family connection is so powerful that it is right to begin by joining them in this bicentennial celebration.

The nexus is most obvious in those parts of the book in which Adam Smith discusses specifically colonial trade with America and the East Indies and, in particular, monopoly in that trade. Consider, for example, these passages: 'The monopoly of the colony trade, therefore, like all the other mean and malignant expedients of the mercantile system, depresses the industry of all other countries, but chiefly that of the colonies, without in the least increasing, but on the contrary diminishing, that of the country in whose favour it is established.' Or, 'to promote the little interest of one little order of men in one country, it (monopoly) hurts the interest of all other orders of men in that country, and of all the men in all other countries.' And in advocating voluntary separation of the American colonies from Britain, he says 'by thus parting good friends, the natural affection of the colonies to the mother country, which, perhaps, our late dissensions have well-nigh extinguished, would quickly revive.' Of Adam Smith, at least, Jefferson's complaint that the British brethren had 'been deaf to the voice of justice and consanguinity' was not true.

But, more fundamentally, the essential spirit that inspired Adam Smith was the same as that on which the new republic was to be founded. There is in both the appeal to the 'natural order' or the 'laws of nature'. The proposition that the pursuit of happiness is one of the inalienable rights of man is close to the whole approach of Smith's earlier work, *The Theory of Moral Sentiments*; and the principle that 'all men are created equal' is not far removed from Smith's view that 'the difference of natural talents in different men is, in reality, much less than we are aware of. . . . The difference between . . . a philosopher and a common street porter, for example, seems to arise not so much from nature, as from habit, custom, and education.'

In these matters, the relation between the individual and society and their respective rights and duties in the broadest sense, Adam Smith was very much in the spirit of the age. He believed, as the naturalist school of philosophy from the Greek Stoics to Hobbes and Locke had believed, that these relations were in large measure (though by no means exclusively) subject to the actions of natural forces which spontaneously produced a harmonious pattern and that the, largely unimpeded, operation of these forces would automatically best promote the interests of each individual consistently with those of others. It will be important presently to examine more closely the precise meaning of this doctrine, its application to the economic sphere and, in particular, the relevance of the conclusions drawn from it to the problems of today. But, first, a few words about the man, about his contribution to the science of Economics and about his role in the evolution of economic policy.

ADAM SMITH THE MAN

Adam Smith was fifty-three when his great work was published. By that time, this son of a Scottish Judge Advocate, who had been educated at the Universities of Glasgow and Oxford, had been a professor for thirteen years, during which time he published *The Theory of Moral Sentiments* and had travelled for two years in France as tutor to the Duke of Buccleuch, from whom he received a substantial pension. Soon after the publication of *The Wealth of Nations* he became a Commissioner of Customs, which he remained until his death in 1790. He was the first truly academic economist and it was from his time onwards that the progress of Economics becomes increasingly the result of academic work. His lectures during his thirteen years as a professor, partly through the medium of the closely-related *Theory of Moral Sentiments* (in many respects containing the philosophical foundations of *The Wealth of Nations*), were clearly elements in the process of evolution which culminated in the latter work. Dugald Stewart, Smith's early biographer, thought the lectures lost. Happily, this proved not to be so, for in 1895 Edwin Cannan was given to examine, and in 1896 published, a set of notes of Smith's lectures on Justice, Police, Revenue and Arms which contained much that was to be further elaborated in

The Wealth of Nations. And in 1958 Professor Lothian discovered, and five years later published, a set of much earlier lectures by Smith on Rhetoric and Belles-Lettres, which, though barely relevant to his economic ideas, give a fuller idea of the range of his interests and intellect.

An extraordinarily wide range it turns out to be. We already know from Dugald Stewart of his knowledge of languages and literature, ancient and modern, of his wide circle of acquaintances and friends among the outstanding minds of his time. These aspects of his personality are emphasized particularly by a reading of the Rhetoric lectures. He was a man of very wide culture: an eighteenth-century intellectual par excellence for whom the advances in economic reasoning were intimately linked with, indeed part and parcel of, speculations in political and social philosophy as well as in a large variety of other disciplines. (Smith may not in later life have been as interested in the natural sciences as were other contemporary thinkers, but it is perhaps relevant to note that it is reported that, while a student at the University of Glasgow, mathematics and natural philosophy were his favourite pursuits.) It may be a sign of maturity that two hundred years after *The Wealth of Nations* much of economics is not only more abstract, but often highly mathematical, and certainly not as accessible to the average educated reader as was and is Smith's opus. But it is certainly regrettable, and perhaps of even deeper significance, that not many of its practitioners can display the same width of interests and knowledge as the founder of the science!

SMITH'S PLACE IN ECONOMICS

The advances in economics proper associated with Adam Smith are so well known that a relatively short recapitulation should suffice. There is, first, the general approach and method of treatment. No one before Adam Smith had attained anything like the same level of systematic and consistent analysis in which, despite the regular use of examples and illustrations from the real world, a high degree of abstraction prevails. For the first time, economics becomes recognizable as an independent discipline, indeed as a science, self-conscious and self-confident; and while its affiliation to social philosophy is still clearly visible, it has now come of age and is ready to lead a life of its own. The plan of the work, the broad sweep of its reasoning, the skilful appeal, amidst intricate theoretical argument, to homely analogies the truth of which was universally accepted, demonstrate a mastery of the subject unequalled before and explain the immediate acclaim which greeted the book and the influence which it had on policy.

Although not entirely followed in subsequent economic treatises (notably Ricardo's *Principles*, the other pillar of the classical system) the structure of the book had a great influence on all later writers. Book One deals in the main with what today would be called static analysis: production, exchange and distribution. Book Two contains the more dynamic parts, the nature of capital and capital accumulation. Book Three continues the dynamic analysis and does so largely on the basis of historical and descriptive material rather than abstract reasoning. Book Four, entitled 'Of Systems of Political Oeconomy', contains the celebrated and devastating attack on mercantilism. It takes apart not only the individual devices of the mercantilist state, but criticizes the whole system in a manner which has not been surpassed to this day, though, no doubt, the examples used and the language in which the attack is formulated are presented in a more up-to-date manner in recent 'free-trade' literature. Book Five deals with the 'public sector', that is, as it was then defined. It contains both a detailed analysis of public expenditure and the means of meeting it: revenue from taxes and otherwise. It is here, perhaps, even more than either in the theoretical chapters on the nature of exchange and of markets or in those attacking mercantilism, that Adam Smith's theory of economic policy becomes clear and that the opponents of State intervention can find most ammunition for their views. In terms of the subsequent progress of pure economic theory, however, it is in the earlier parts of the work that the major contributions can be found. Here I would say it is not so much the theory of value that is path-breaking, for it has been shown that Smith had important forerunners, that much of the analysis is somewhat muddled and that it was Ricardo who was to give the specifically 'classical' theory its clearest expression. One could also argue (and I would be disposed to do so) that, in the light of the history of the subject during the last two hundred years, the dominant place which value occupied for so long at the core of economic theory was not wholly beneficial and that the shift of focus in recent decades is advantageous. It must, however, be remembered that the great attention paid to value by Smith stemmed from his desire to put at the centre of economic thinking labour as the creator of value, the division of labour as the means of making labour more productive (thus more creative of value) and the market as the means both of making division of labour possible and for determining its extent. This, indeed, was his greatest achievement and the imperfections in the elaboration of the theory of value weigh very little in the balance.

The other, related, great achievement was the emphasis on wealth as a flow rather than as a static fund. The very first sentence of the introduction sets a tone which is different from that of earlier writers or of the contemporaneous French Physiocrats:

> The annual labour of every nation is the fund which originally supplies it with all the necessaries and conveniences of life which it annually consumes, and which consist always either in the immediate produce of that labour, or in what is purchased with that produce from other nations.

It may be noted in passing that the next sentence carried the implication, as seen by Edwin Cannan, that the nation's welfare is to be measured as an average or per caput index rather than as an aggregate. Though it was some 150 years before the national income analysis and, later, the GNP measurement matured, here, in embryo is a decisively new approach.

There is, however, much more to be found in *The Wealth of Nations* that was new and was to prove of lasting value for economics. There is, for example, the analysis of wages and wage-differentials contained in the theory of net advantages and in the doctrine of non-competing groups which, though elementary now, is still an accepted part of the theory on the subject. There are, as I have already mentioned, the detailed critical discussions of tariffs and other restrictive devices in international and domestic trade which subsequent analysis has much refined but by no means displaced. There are also the celebrated four canons of taxation—equality, certainty, convenience and economy—which will evoke the emphatic, if wistful, agreement of every modern taxpayer.

But whatever its contribution to pure economic theory, the epoch-making character of *The Wealth of Nations* derives from its bearing on public policy. In this regard, Adam Smith was, as a later economist and historian of economic thought, Wesley Mitchell, recognized, 'one of the makers of modern history', his book being noteworthy above all for its criticism of 'the principles of a civilization which was passing', and for laying down 'the principles of a civilization that was coming into being'. To this aspect, I now turn.

PRESCRIPTIONS FOR POLICY

The essential character of Adam Smith's social philosophy from which, via his economic analysis, his prescriptions for economic policy are derived is simple enough. The whole of mediaeval society and in large measure that of early commercial and industrial capitalism had been based upon a complex system of rules and regulations, defining, often in meticulous detail, the rights and duties of individuals not only in regard to the wider aspects of human and social existence, but more particularly in the economic sphere. The mercantile system, especially, made the business of industry and trade one for regulation by the State either directly or through the delegated authority of guilds and privileged companies. This system was already in a process of rapid breakdown when Smith wrote. For new forms of production based on new technical inventions were demonstrating the incompatibility of old economic relationships with the new productive powers. The steam-engine, the power-loom, the spinning-jenny required a wider, freer and more flexible social and economic (and eventually political) framework if their potentialities were to be fully exploited.

In *The Wealth of Nations*, Adam Smith, though he did not begin with this, provided a brilliant critique of the absurdities to which the strict regulation of business activity under the mercantilist system led, culminating in the great demonstration of the doubly harmful nature of the colonial system (to metropolis and colony alike) and its political consequences, to be shortly most vividly exemplified by the Declaration of Independence. But it was not enough to show up the follies of particular restrictive devices and of the whole system of State regulation. Smith was a philosopher; moreover, the whole spirit of the age tended towards comprehensive explanations and 'system-building'. The attack on mercantilism had, therefore, to be based on a rational exposition of the superiority of a different economic system, and this, in turn, on a social philosophy which could be generally accepted as being in accord with the prevailing human understanding and with universal aspirations in these matters. Not surprisingly, therefore, the attack on mercantilism comes after the analysis of the virtues of a market economy and of the social philosophy with which it has a close family tie.

Smith believed, as had his teacher Francis Hutcheson, in the natural order. In essence, it means a belief in what is natural as against what is contrived. There is a natural order which if allowed to assert itself without let or hindrance would soon show its superiority over any order resting on artificially created man-made laws. It must be remembered that in *The Theory of Moral Sentiments* Smith had already expounded the mainsprings of human actions which in their balanced operation explain how a natural order can exist. They were: self-love balanced by sympathy, i.e. love of one's neighbour, the desire to be free, a sense of propriety, a habit of labour and a propensity to exchange. Let there be no interference with the free play of these forces and each individual will be 'led by an invisible hand to promote an end which was no part of his intention'. Applied to the economic sphere, 'it is not from the benevolence of the butcher, the brewer, or the baker that we expect our dinner, but from their regard to their own interest'. All the prescriptions, however recondite, for freeing domestic industry and trade and international commerce from direction and restriction ultimately stem from this simple principle. More generally, though he applied it in particular to the restriction of imports, Smith's basic approach was to equate economic statesmanship with the principles underlying prudent conduct by the 'master of a family'. These, he claimed, 'can scarce be folly in that of a great Kingdom'.

Perhaps because his natural order philosophy was founded on much the same pragmatic approach as that of the English utilitarian school generally, thus less 'mystical' than that of the Physiocrats in France (who were moreover handicapped by a similar 'mystical' belief in the superiority of agriculture), Smith became a more effective opponent of mercantilism and a more successful advocate of the policy of *laissez-faire*. With extraordinary rapidity his advocacy of the free market (to give the greatest scope to division of labour), of competition (which would always assert itself provided monopolistic positions were not supported by the State) and of unimpeded international commerce gained ground intellectually and helped the new industrial classes to achieve in large measure that emancipation from mercantilist shackles for which they were striving.

It would, nevertheless, be a mistake (which is often tacitly made) to think that *The Wealth of Nations* ushered in an era of unlimited *laissez-faire*—a golden age of economic freedom which was brought to an end by some kind of intellectual fall from grace. It is more than doubtful whether anywhere and for any length of time anything like a true system of *laissez-faire* has ever existed and whether it has been more than, according to taste, a chimera or a Platonic ideal towards which one is urged constantly to strive. This is not the place to trace the growth—which was not long delayed—of all the interventionist measures of the hundred and fifty years following Adam Smith. The fact is that interventionism of one kind or another has spread and that, with very limited exceptions indeed, both in duration and in geographical extent, the free market as Smith envisaged it has continued to be a distant ideal. Why this should be so is a difficult question which cannot be examined here. What seems to have become increasingly apparent is that the progress of universal suffrage and political democracy in the widest sense is incompatible with a *laissez-faire* economy, despite the fact that both went hand-in-hand in their infancy. What is more appropriate in this bicentenary year is to examine the relevance of those tenets of economic policy associated peculiarly with Adam Smith and *The Wealth of Nations* to the conflicting views on these matters held today.

ANY LESSONS FOR TODAY?

It is always tempting to try to guess what some writer of the past would say were he alive today. It is equally tempting to cull from his writings passages that seem strongly to support one particular point of view. But, apart from the well-known ability of those of evil intent to cite scripture, there are great hazards in yielding to these temptations. On the face of it, these hazards should be at a minimum where Adam Smith is concerned. The case he made for the free market and against intervention seems so obvious and so emphatic that it is natural for the extreme advocates of these views to claim him as a powerful ally. If the essence of the 'Keynesian revolution', which has so much influenced present-day economic thought, is to draw a distinction between what is rational economic conduct of the individual (or the individual enterprise) and the proper management of the aggregates of the economy by the State, would the man who equated prudence in the family with that in the kingdom not repudiate much of today's thought—and the action based on it? Or would he accept Keynes's own verdict (expressed in 1945 when defending the Anglo-American financial arrangements) that it was right to 'combine the advantages of a freedom of commerce with safeguards against the disastrous consequences of a *laissez-faire* system which pays no regard to the preservation of equilibrium and merely relies on the eventual working out of blind forces'? Would he agree that what Keynes aimed at was 'to use what we have learnt from modern experience and modern analysis, not to defeat, but to implement the wisdom of Adam Smith'?

No decisive answer to these questions is possible. There is a great deal to be found in *The Wealth of Nations* to delight the heart of any opponent of the 'Welfare State', of 'hand-outs', of public as against private enterprise or of the financing of public works out of the general tax revenue, to say nothing of import duties or other restrictions on trade. No doubt, on the evidence of Book Five, there is not much of present public expenditure (and the public sector borrowing requirement that goes with it) that would escape his criticism; though his reference to the Post Office as 'perhaps the only mercantile project which has been successfully managed by, I believe, every sort of government' and which produces 'a large profit' will evoke a wry smile in the modern reader.

Nevertheless, care is necessary in making these interpretations, quite apart from the fact that Adam Smith is not available to give evidence himself. In counselling care, I cannot base myself on much in Adam Smith's own words. There is hardly anything to be found except in the well-known cases of defence and education in which 'Authority' in the shape of the State or otherwise is explicitly allowed to do what unimpeded market forces might not, though there is a hint in one place of a derogation in favour of new developments that might not otherwise take place (a hint of the 'infant industry' argument?). On trade unions one would hardly expect any trace of modern thought; indeed in the quarter-century following *The Wealth of Nations*, the Combination Laws were made even more stringent than they had been before.

There are, nevertheless, passages which show that Adam Smith was not particularly confident about the beneficence of the aims of individuals when left to themselves. Landlords 'love to reap where they have not sowed'; and those who live from profits, who have a better knowledge of their own interest than the landlord has of his, have an interest which 'is never exactly the same with that of the public, who have generally an interest to deceive and even to oppress the public, and who accordingly have, upon many occasions, both deceived and oppressed it'.

But if we are to be, as I believe we should be, somewhat wary about invoking the authority of Adam Smith in the advocacy of an extreme *laissez-faire* attitude, this is not, and cannot in the nature of things be, on account of any specific disclaimer or qualification in

Adam Smith's work itself. He was a child of his time. His objective was aggressive: to destroy what remained—and a great deal did—of an antiquated system that put severe constraints upon the development of society's productive powers resulting from the ingenuity and venturesomeness of the new men who were building the new industrial age. In so doing, despite the more extensive use of the language of the natural law philosophers than was common among other English writers and despite many ambiguities, he was, I believe, in the main moved by a practical motive; and even he had, therefore, to defend his policy precepts by reference to the positive good they wrought (that is to say by the utilitarian principle) than exclusively by their conformity to a providential scheme of things.

Lionel Robbins—surely as sensitive as anyone can be on this point —has shown that the utilitarian (English) tradition (not as clearly visible in Adam Smith as in Bentham and Hume) regarded all laws and rights—indeed all social arrangements—as man-made and, therefore, to be judged according to their effects on human happiness—for the individual—was the supreme objective and every human institution was merely a means towards its achievement. Bentham, though most of his work was after *The Wealth of Nations*, epitomizes the utilitarian spirit and its liberal implications best. Yet Bentham, in both his political and economic writings, pours scorn on the undiluted natural law philosophy. It is perhaps symbolic that Bentham's *Fragment on Government* also appeared in 1776. And in that work, as indeed in many others, Bentham consistently took the view that the individual interest must be made to harmonize with that of others in order to produce the greatest happiness of the greatest number and that, as he said in another place, natural rights were 'simply nonsense'. It is perhaps not too fanciful to see in the special emphasis on the natural order that is to be found in Adam Smith, in contrast to almost any other of the great figures of the utilitarian and radical movements of the age, the need to establish economics as a science by making it rely on certain 'natural laws' akin to those of the natural sciences; to demonstrate a certain *Gesetzmässigkeit*, as the Germans were to call it, in economic phenomena, since, if this were absent, it would prove much more difficult, if not impossible, to regard economics as a scientific discipline. Such an approach would not necessarily rule out the intervention of human agency for certain defined purposes, supporting, or at times running counter to, the 'natural' course which economic tendencies might take. Indeed, Lionel Robbins has shown that the whole classical school was much less doctrinaire about the 'agenda' of State action than is often believed.

That Adam Smith, were he alive today, would be highly suspicious of those who are prepared to ignore the important part which 'the market' could play in the proper ordering of economic affairs, there can be little doubt. It is understandable that, given the widespread attack on the value of the market mechanism, many should be tempted, paraphrasing Wordsworth, to say 'Adam Smith! thou should'st be living at this hour: England hath need of thee'. But it is not likely, in my view, that Smith would endorse an exclusive reliance on market forces in all cases, particularly when the democratic process has put power into the hands of different groups to adapt the operation of these forces so as to favour sometimes one and sometimes the other group. We would certainly be praying for the presence of one whose good sense and broad humanity would be of inestimable value amid the shrill clamour of divergent views which are vying for our support. But we should, I think, do so without illusion. Undoubtedly, if he were alive today, Adam Smith would have some very crushing things to say about those who would deprive our economy of the benefit of a smoothly working market mechanism. But I believe that he would not be among those who would empty our mixed economy of all its interventionist ingredients. Above all, I suspect that were Keynes also alive today, those two great thinkers, whose principal works are one hundred and sixty years apart, would find much common ground in respect of the broad principles that should guide the management of the economy.

MARX'S *CAPITAL*—AN ASSESSMENT

A talk given on the Third Programme of the BBC on 22 August 1967. A slightly abbreviated version was published in The Listener, *23 November 1967.*

On 25 July, a hundred years ago, Marx signed, here in London, the preface to the first volume of *Capital*. On 16 August he wrote to Engels, his close friend and collaborator, that he had finished correcting the last proof sheet. Soon afterwards the book was published. There was none of the fanfare that would today accompany a potential best-seller: no advance serialization, no press conferences, no literary luncheons with signed copies. Nor did the author make a fortune; Marx lived the remaining sixteen years of his life much as he had done before: in great, sometimes in dire, need. Yet within a very short time the book had achieved a unique place in world literature. If Keynes was right in saying that 'the world is ruled by little else' than 'the ideas of economists and political philosophers, both when they are right and when they are wrong', he could certainly claim Marx as a good example. Fifty years after *Capital* was published, there occurred a revolution, led by men inspired by his ideas, which has been at least as far-reaching in its consequences as any in history. Today, there are still millions of our fellowmen who have come to accept Marx's ideas as the principles by which to order their lives.

There is nothing obvious about *Capital* to explain an impact on human affairs which puts it in a group of books that can be counted on the fingers of one hand. The first volume is long and full of difficult theorizing on a dry subject. The style, unless you are already a believer, or specially attuned to nineteenth-century post-Hegelian German prose, is somewhat off-putting. By the time *Capital* was completed, long after Marx's death, with the publication of three more volumes, the whole usually bound in eight, it presented a very daunting task indeed to even the most industrious student. It has often been thought unreadable. Keynes himself thought it 'turbid'. He might well have called it 'turgid', too. It seems pretty well established that only a very small proportion of the millions who swear by it have actually read it. Shaw once claimed to be the only man in England to have done so. Even he, when he was seen reading it in the British Museum, had by its side the score of *Tristan*; and it is by no means certain that *Capital* commanded more of his attention.

So we have here an astounding paradox. To explain it is not made any easier by the fact that the problem of Marx and Marxism has rarely been approached dispassionately. This is itself something of a paradox. For although Marx was concerned essentially with political action, he always protested that what he was aiming at was to discover the laws of social development in the most objective and scientific manner possible. His socialism and his economics, he claimed, were scientific, not 'utopian' or 'vulgar'—his favourite terms of abuse for those with whom he disagreed. As I hope to show you in a moment, both in time and in logic the relation between his political views and his economics is almost exactly the opposite of what he claimed. And it is this, perhaps, which has been responsible for the violence of the views both of his supporters and his opponents.

Let us then see first what the economics of *Capital* amounts to. It is, of course, not easy to summarize this enormous work in a few words; all the more so, since like all books that have acquired the authority of scripture it has been subjected to the most elaborate exegesis by interpreters of many shades of opinion. However, very simply put, the main structure of the theory is clear enough. The material world in our type of society consists, from an economic point of view, of a mass of commodities, things that are bought and sold. A commodity has use value, its significance to the man who is going to make use of it in a material sense, that is, consume it, or use it for further production. It also has exchange value, which is what it can command in exchange, its price. I must ignore the intricacies of the analysis in Marx and in earlier and later economists, of these concepts and go straight to what for Marx was the crucial point, namely the role of labour in this world of commodities. Under capitalism, labour (or, more precisely, labour power as Marx called it) is a commodity like any other. The labourer has to sell it in order to live; the capitalist buys it and combines it with machinery and raw materials in the process of production. He gets its use value. But he pays for it a price which is determined by its exchange value; and that, like all exchange values, depends on what Marx called the socially necessary labour time to produce it. Putting it in more conventional terms at the risk of violating strict Marxist terminology, what it amounts to is this. What has to be paid to the worker will be no more than is necessary to enable him to produce the physical or mental output for the period for which he is hired. Naturally, this includes what he needs to reproduce his kind. Also, its amount will depend on historical circumstances, the conventional living standard, the strength of trade union bargaining and so on. But whatever it is, the value of the output which the capitalist secures will be greater than the amount of his outlay. Labour can and does produce a surplus product, that is over and above the products that make up its own subsistence needs.

Leaving aside certain further sophisticated, at times even metaphysical arguments, there is so far nothing very startling in this statement. The whole progress of mankind has depended and will continue to depend on human ability to produce more than its subsistence needs, something that can be the basis for accumulation and greater, and more complex, production in the future. It is at this point, however, that the most important and characteristic feature of Marxism comes in. Marx goes on to say that since, under capitalism the surplus product is the property of the capitalist, it becomes, in his hands, surplus value, the source of his private profit and of his accumulation of further capital which can then become the means for creating further surplus value and so on. The theory of value thus leads Marx to a theory of exploitation.

Even so, there is still nothing wholly novel in this. There were many, particularly among the English economists who followed Adam Smith and Ricardo, who had developed the classical theory of value in similar directions.

But here Marx introduces yet another characteristic element, his dynamic theory of how capitalism must evolve. This is a particularly intricate part and in simplifying it, I run even more danger of criticism from the faithful. The source of surplus value is labour power; therefore, says Marx, what the capitalist lays out to hire the worker—what he called his variable capital—is the only part of his capital that can procure surplus value for him. But as capitalism develops, labour productivity is increased by a greater relative use of plant and machinery—the constant capital, giving rise to what Marx called an increasing 'organic composition of capital'. In other words, though variable capital increases absolutely (which it must do if there is to be continuing accumulation), it will decline relatively to the total of capital employed. This, in turn, means that while population has to grow to keep pace with accumulation, the total labour force employed—that which is put to work with the capitalist's variable capital—will tend to diminish relatively. Thus is created what Marx called the 'industrial reserve army'. Its existence has the effect of exerting pressure on wages when the demand for labour is low; and it prevents wages from rising unduly when the demand goes up. In short, says Marx, as capital accumulates and wealth increases, the conditions of the working class become more precarious. This is his celebrated law of the 'increasing misery' of the workers under capitalism.

But all is not well with the capitalist either, for as the only source of surplus value, namely variable capital, declines (relatively, at least), the process of accumulation becomes itself precarious, as shown by recurring and ever more violent crises. Capitalism, thus must eventually become so grossly incompatible with the further development of production that it must give way to another system. The organization of society on the basis of private property in the means of production and of private appropriation of surplus value must give way to one in which there is common ownership of the means of production.

This, then, is Marx's economics. It is interesting to speculate whether Marx would have had the influence he has if he had written nothing but *Capital* and had produced this prediction of the ultimate fall of capitalism exclusively on the basis of the economic theory contained in that book. I think myself that he would not. The prospect of a 'rising organic composition of capital' a 'falling tendency of the rate of profit' or even the theory of the 'industrial reserve army' would hardly have formed powerful rallying cries for a revolutionary movement. Even if they could have brought themselves to read *Capital* from beginning to end, the vast bulk of Marx's followers would not have made much of it. I believe that if we wish to understand the appeal of Marx's economics and fathom the secret of the success of *Capital*, we have to read not it, but a book which Marx wrote nineteen years earlier, when he was only thirty: *The Communist Manifesto*. There we have his sociology and his theory of history, both of which provide the doctrine and the slogans for his politics. There we have the challenge of the opening words, the spectre of Communism that is haunting Europe; and, at the end, the ringing appeal to the workers of all lands to unite. *Capital* is really a gigantic rationalization, a supposedly scientific underpinning, which Marx developed after he had already made up his mind.

For the young Marx, as a good Hegelian, there had to be an all-embracing explanation of historical development, a unique engine of social change. This is a common enough desire among historians and philosophers, and it was particularly strong in the nineteenth century. For Buckle, it was climate, for Turner, writing about America, it was the frontier. For Marx it was classes—classes defined in relation to the changing material conditions of production. Again highly simplified, his view of history runs like this. At the base, that is, as the ultimate determinant of all social phenomena, there are the material powers of production that exist at any given time. To put them into operation human beings band together in certain social relationships which are appropriate to the state of development of these productive powers. On top of the social relations is erected a superstructure, first of political and legal institutions and, beyond them, of ideas and modes of thought. Essentially these relations must be seen, according to Marx, in terms of property; and so defined they create a certain class structure. As the material powers of production at the base change, so the class structure, which initially helped to ensure their most effective use, becomes inappropriate and has to be replaced. This usually involves revolution, since it can only be accomplished by destroying the political and legal buttresses of the existing class relationships. Eventually ideas, too, are changed.

The Communist Manifesto presents this theory in its clearest form. There, all history is described as a procession of class struggles. Slave and slaveowner, serf and feudal lord, capitalist and proletarian, these are the chief actors on Marx's stage of history; their struggles the motive force of social change. The process cannot come to an end until all classes are abolished, and it is the historic role of the modern working class to bring this about by abolishing private property in the means of production. Once this has been done, economic relations will cease to take the form of different classes with opposing interests. Thereafter, history will proceed through a dynamic different from that of the class struggle.

This, then, is the Marxian view of history: a materialist version of the unfolding of the Hegelian idea; an extreme example of that historicism which, thanks to the attacks of writers like Professors Popper and Berlin, has in our own day lost much of its appeal. This is not to say that emphasis on the economic features of history or on the opposing interests of different social groups has not been a very fruitful one in modern historical research. But what we have in Marx is something all-embracing which demands complete acceptance of an exclusive view of historical change. The economic theory of capitalism, to which *Capital* is devoted, is designed to infuse this particular historical vision with a sense of inevitability. What Marx tried to do, once he had made up his mind that capitalism had to be destroyed, was to show that the seeds of this destruction were contained in the very cell of capitalist society, the commodity, and in the development which it must inevitably undergo.

What we have to judge is, thus, a unique combination of a philosophy of history with an economic analysis specially devised to support it. If there were only the economic analysis it is doubtful whether there would be more than antiquarian interest in the intricacies of *Capital*. Most of the mining in that quarry has been done by those wishing to prove a thesis—for or against. Professor Samuelson, the eminent economist, some years ago, attempted a more objective appraisal. He gave Marx credit for some originality, calling him, *inter alia*, 'a not uninteresting precursor of Leontief's input-output analysis', a description not designed to endear its author to the faithful. But he also observed that the economics is the mere cap of Marx's iceberg. In terms of modern economics, either as far as the understanding of a complex industrial society or its effective management is concerned, Marx has indeed little to offer. His most significant prediction has not been fulfilled. The progressive misery of the working class has not come about. Even at the beginning of this century additions, revisions, re-interpretations had to be made by his followers to cover up the increasing lack of realism of this concept. First it was made to mean a relative rather than an absolute growth of misery. Then, when this would not serve, Lenin's theory of imperialism was called in aid. Colonial exploitation, this stated, postponed the fall in the rate of profit and enabled the capitalists to bribe the working class in the imperialist countries with a share of their gains, thus creating an aristocracy of labour. It is highly doubtful whether this theory ever contributed to an explanation of the problem of colonial development. What is certain is that today, after the passing of empires, it has lost all relation to reality. Nor has it anything to offer to the great contemporary problem of the relation between the developed and the less developed countries, the rich and the poor. Indeed, a distinguished modern economist, Professor Joan Robinson, who has approached Marx's economics with considerable sympathy, had to say in this context that 'the world-picture has slipped out of the frame of Marx's argument'.

Marx is even less relevant to the practical problems of managing a modern industrial economy. Here Keynes, in a letter to Shaw, in 1935, before the publication of his *General Theory of Employment, Interest and Money*, rightly forecast that he himself was writing a book that would, as he put it, 'revolutionize the way the world thinks about economic problems', while in Marx, he thought, there was 'nothing but out-of-date controversializing'. It would be foolish to pretend that there is not still a vast amount of poverty, misery and economic mismanagement in the world. But that there has been an improvement in both the understanding and the management of the developed societies—both capitalist and socialist ones, cannot be denied. And this improvement owes a great deal more to Keynesianism, and to the related national account analysis with which we are now so familiar, than it does to Marxism.

But what of the other and more significant aspect of Marx: his theory of history? It is in this, as I have said, that the real secret of his appeal must be sought. And here his own intellectual development is perhaps our best guide. We find him undergoing a remarkable transformation. In the only extant letter to his father, written when he was 18, he shows himself as an unsure youth, his breast, like Swift's, lacerated by savage indignation, searching violently for guidance through the maze of problems and ideas which he had encountered at the university. Thirty years later he had become the cocksure writer of the preface to *Capital*. In this interval the revelation had been received and it had been enshrined in doctrine. Looking at this development, I conclude that the first and most potent ingredient in the attraction of Marxism is that it offers the certainty of dogma. Offensive though this might be to true believers and to Marxists alike, I must, therefore, class it with the religions. Like them it not only gives certainty of a final destiny but it imposes upon the follower a duty to make his own contribution to this end and it lays down a clear line of conduct. 'The philosophers', quotes the inscription of Marx's tomb at Highgate, 'have only interpreted the world in different ways: the point is to change it.' This then is the kernel of a militant faith. Like others, its initial appeal tends to be mainly to the young. Like others it has readily bred bigots and fanatics; and it has, in the end, increased rather than diminished the sum total of human misery which, at its origin, it had set out to abolish.

Whether Marx willed this result or whether his was the role of the sorcerer's apprentice is ultimately not important. If we give him the benefit of the doubt and look upon him only as a man of ideas and of scholarship, we cannot deny him a place among the greatest political philosophers. He was a patient observer with an exceptional ability to absorb facts and to engage in the most abstract speculation. He was moved by human suffering and he displayed a sweep and audacity in this theorizing which are very rare indeed. But, in the end, he offers those hungry for the bread of enlightenment no more than a philosopher's stone designed to supply ready-made answers to all the most baffling problems of the human condition. Here, too, therefore, I would say that his legacy is essentially harmful. For where such complete certainty is prescribed, inevitably an anti-rational outlook is bred. As Lecky, writing in Marx's own lifetime, so rightly said of all anti-rationalism, 'it encourages a spirit of blind and at the same time wilful credulity' which is 'diametrically opposed to the spirit of inquiry'. Our final judgement must, therefore, be that it is inimical to that attitude of mind which alone can make possible the progress of human understanding.

C

II.

MONEY, BANKING AND INTERNATIONAL FINANCE

THE IMPACT OF ECONOMIC POLICY ON THE FINANCIAL SYSTEM OF THE UNITED KINGDOM

The first Mercantile Credit Lecture, delivered at the University of Reading on 24 November 1970.

I consider it a great privilege to be able to give the first of these annual lectures in Economics, endowed by the Mercantile Credit Company, and I should like to thank the University Authorities for the honour they have done me in inviting me to do so this evening. To be the first has, perhaps, the disadvantage that one has no precedent to follow, no established pattern on which to rely. On the other hand, one has a certain freedom of choice which will perhaps not be quite so fully enjoyed by those who come after. In choosing to speak on a subject in which economic and financial, technical and theoretical, descriptive and analytical elements are inextricably mixed together, I have followed a personal inclination; for owing to the accident of a somewhat variegated yet essentially uniform career, I have managed to maintain an interest in the academic aspects of Economics through a later experience in the domain of public policy as well as through my present concern with matters lying within the activities of the financial community, that is, in the private business sector.

I do not wish my title to be taken too literally. Clearly, a comprehensive treatment of this large subject is not possible within the compass of this lecture, and I will, therefore, have to be selective. I have also avoided leaning too heavily in the direction of theoretical sophistication, or getting lost in highly intricate technical detail, but have rather indicated, I hope reasonably clearly, what seem to me to be the main problems which should concern us in this general area.

I should begin by defining the two terms of my title. As regards economic policy, I am in the first place concerned with what is nowadays called macro-economic management. My working definition of it is the sum total of the actions of the Authorities—that is government and those agencies, such as the central bank, whose activities are largely determined by government—which set the framework within which our economy, private and public, operates. This management is generally designed to ensure that the economy achieves what are nowadays—rightly or wrongly—widely accepted objectives. These are a high and steady level of economic activity (including employment of labour), and a reasonable rate of growth of the economy as commonly measured. The achievement of these objectives is also required not to conflict with, indeed to make more likely of accomplishment, certain broad social objectives which are also widely accepted at present, at least in the richer countries of the world, namely a rise in the average standard of living and a steady improvement in the conditions of social justice. Moreover, they are also supposed to be achieved in a manner that is consistent with membership in an international trading and financial system which imposes certain obligations, the most acute reminder of which is the state of the balance of payments and of the exchange rate of the currency. I do not pause to consider either the value judgements implicit in these objectives or the possibility—which is certainly not self-evident—of reconciling them one with another. I merely recite them in order to recall the deeper sources from which policy actions spring.

It follows, particularly from the last of these, that there can be outside policy influences at work; and indeed in relation to my present theme I shall need to refer to at least one of these, the effect of the changes in the US balance of payments in recent years, and of the consequent American measures, on the state of our financial structure.

Economic policy also includes the more detailed actions and regulations in the financial field designed to give effect to some of the macro-economic policies to which I have referred; or, at any rate, to underpin them.

I thus leave out of account—though not because they are unimportant—a large number of policies, particularly in the social or foreign policy areas. There is, however, one to which I propose to refer at some length at a later stage, namely the prospect of British membership in the European Economic Community. This is not merely a bow to topical interest. Although the problems involved in our potential membership of an evolving economic union of Europe go far beyond the sphere of economic policy in the ordinary sense of the word, they will clearly have a profound effect on that policy and, therefore, a major influence, *inter alia*, on the future structure of our financial system.

As far as that system is concerned, definition for my purpose does not present any great difficulty—I mean simply the chief types of financial institutions, and their relations with one another, which, between them, compose the sum total of the credit and capital markets of this country.

Like all living organisms, the structure of these markets has not stood still and, at first sight at least, the City looks a very different place from what it did when Bagehot wrote his *Lombard Street* nearly a hundred years ago. Yet one feature has continued to be characteristic of it, the high degree of specialization between its various component parts. Of course there have been some changes due to the evolution of the system itself, but the main categories of business done and of the institutions that do them have shown a good deal of inherent stability. The most important changes that have occurred in the last decade or two have been brought about largely by certain developments of economic policy, themselves caused by the need to adapt the British economy—and British society as a whole—to the post-war world. Broadly speaking, the basic principle of this policy has been to manage total demand by means of various 'mixes' of fiscal and monetary measures in the light of changing forecasts of inflationary or deflationary gaps, usually measured by reference to the relation between a forecast and a desired balance of payments performance.

I cannot pause to examine this principle or its operation in detail but I would like to recall two points that have, in the most recent period, been of special significance for the financial system. The first thing to note is that largely under the influence of increasing pressure of our international obligations, this country, in common with most other industrialized countries, has come to abandon direct action on the trade balance, and indeed, with the exception of travel expenditure, on current transactions generally. Consequently, direct action on the balance of payments has been concentrated on the capital items, and since 1964 this has been done with a high degree of severity. My second point is the following. The general background of economic policy in the post-war period has been one of almost continuous inadequacy—at least relative to the demands made on it—of our balance of payments performance. The underlying tendency of demand management has, therefore, had to be a restrictive one. Of course, changes in the balance of social or diplomatic factors as against strictly economic ones have produced some variations in the degree of restrictionism; and one should also record for the sake of completeness that the full rigour of demand management has been moderated by what we might call the 'election cycle'.

Nevertheless, the basic factors that matter as far as the conduct in the last few years of business by the financial community is concerned, remain clear enough: a hold over total demand fluctuating in its tightness and exerted by means of varying applications of fiscal or monetary measures combined with control over capital movements. Thus, in the last few years the City has had to operate almost continuously against the background of the Authorities' aim to control the volume of domestic credit and, through the exchange control regulations, to conserve our foreign exchange resources.

It is not my purpose here to attempt to disentangle the causes that have led to certain structural changes in the general manner in which finance for business is provided, or to assess how far any particular part of official policy such as the restriction of credit available from the deposit banks has been responsible for the growth of what has been aptly called the secondary banking system. A complex of causes has been at work, among which may be mentioned recurrent deficits in the balance of payments, a reduced call by government for finance from the banking system, and the vastly increased demand for outside finance from the private business sector. The fact is that the outstanding feature of the sixties has been the growth of this secondary system composed of the accepting houses and other merchant banks, overseas banks and foreign banks, as well as the considerable increase in the size and importance of finance companies providing mainly consumer credit. A whole series of 'by-passes' of the main part of the banking system—which is, of course, most readily subject to control by the Authorities—have arisen, ranging all the way from 'involuntary' credit exacted by strong buyers from weak sellers, to the growth of money-market broking firms, the short-term borrowing by Local Authorities through Negotiable Bonds and to the great increase in the use of Sterling Certificates of Deposits. I do not propose to go into the intricate technical details of all these new ways of meeting the financial requirements of industry and trade, which, of course, the Authorities have steadily and with a fair measure of success brought within the ambit of credit control.

At the 'long end', that is, in the capital market, there have also been new developments directly brought about by legislative or regulatory changes, quite apart from the changes in the general

climate for the provision of long-term capital caused by fluctuations
in the level, or forecast level, of economic activity, by inflationary
expectations, and so on. For example, the introduction of Corporation Tax and Schedule F in 1965 helped to bring about a shift from
equity to debt or quasi-debt financing, an increase in the popularity
of the convertible debenture and the virtual disappearance of the
preference share. The imposition of capital gains at first had an
adverse effect on the gilt-edged as well as the straight industrial
debenture market, while the exemption of gilts from capital gains
in 1969 has changed the balance adversely to the industrial debenture.

However, the developments to which I want to direct particular
attention are those that stem from measures, here and in the United
States, concerned with the balance of payments, namely the emergence of the Euro-dollar, or better, Euro-currency market, and the
Euro-bond market.

It is no coincidence that in the early sixties when the decline in
the role of sterling as an international currency became marked, the
banking institutions in the City of London began their activities in
the Euro-currency market which presented an alternative source of
finance. Until 1967, relatively few UK companies paid attention to
this emerging financial market. In that year, however, the Authorities took more deliberate steps to change the position by making it
possible for UK companies to borrow foreign currency.

Since then, there has been a very substantial development in this
field. Between December 1967 and May 1970, a period in which the
Bank of England maintained strict control of domestic credit by
quantitative ceilings placed on sterling advances and acceptance
credits, these sterling credit facilities expanded (within the official
limits) as follows:

1. Advances by London Clearing Banks rose 16½ per cent, from
£4,862 million to £5,663 million.
2. Advances by Merchant Banks, Overseas and American banks
in the UK increased 21½ per cent, from £1,039 million to £1,264
million.
3. Acceptance credits granted by non-clearing banks increased
8 per cent, from £458 million to £495 million.

In contrast to the fairly modest annual rate of increase reflected
in these figures, loans in foreign currencies to UK companies and
institutions increased during the same period no less than 136 per
cent, namely from £279 million to £660 million.

These currency loans were mainly arranged for three purposes:

1. UK companies obtained currency loans to finance exports from the United Kingdom, generally on short term, that is, from three to six months. To the extent that the exporting companies invoice their foreign sales in the currency borrowed, they of course eliminate any exchange risk; but even companies whose exports are traditionally invoiced in sterling have taken advantage of the availability of currency loans. During a period of tight credit, London banks have been able to grant such currency loans, as these are not subject to credit restrictions.

2. A second category of currency loans for UK residents is represented by the amounts borrowed in foreign currency, mainly US dollars, by UK companies for the finance of fixed investments outside the sterling area, for instance to establish subsidiaries abroad. Such loans must generally be obtained for a period of at least five years. The foreign investments in question can normally also be financed with currency bought in the investment currency market (premium currency). A great number of companies have, however, been reluctant to pay the premium at which investment currency has been trading over the last few years, which has ranged between $17\frac{1}{4}$ per cent and 55 per cent. By borrowing the currency to finance the foreign investments, the UK companies have the opportunity to repay the loan out of earnings from the investment, and the loans can in any event be repaid through investment currency at the end of the five-year period.

3. A third significant category of currency borrowing by UK residents has been the large credits arranged by syndicates of London banks to investment trusts and unit trusts which utilize these loans to finance their portfolios of foreign securities. Here again the object is to avoid paying the investment currency premium, at any rate for the time being.

London is today the undisputed centre of this Euro-currency market, the total volume of which is now estimated at $48,000 million. The merchant banks, the American banks and the foreign branches of the Joint Stock Banks have all played an important role in this development. A great number of new banks, among them subsidiaries of Joint Stock Banks, have been formed or transformed in recent years for the specific purpose of participating in this market. A number of these banks have also been established to grant medium-term credits. The number of London branches of foreign, particularly American, banks has risen steeply and of the latter there are now well over thirty.

Thus the successive periods of the credit squeeze have encouraged borrowers who cannot borrow sterling (both non-residents and residents) to borrow foreign currency instead. Similarly the banking community has been encouraged to develop currency lending. The branches of the American banks to which I have referred are now the biggest operators in this Euro-currency market. While they have used their Euro-dollar deposits in the first instance to finance their corporate clients, more recently a striking feature of this business has been the recourse which the head offices of these banks in New York and elsewhere in the United States have had, sometimes to a very high degree indeed, to these funds of their branches, since they are not limited in the interest rates they can pay by American domestic restrictions, the so-called Regulation Q. Thus, at times, the Euro-dollar market has been used as a mere adjunct to the New York money market, often to the discomfiture of European money markets.

Perhaps even more striking than the development of this Euro-currency market has been another one resulting from the persistent US balance of payments deficits in the sixties, which led to a marked restriction of the ability of foreign borrowers to obtain capital in New York, as well as of US companies to export capital from the United States to finance direct investment abroad. Combined with the restrictions on the access of foreign borrowers to the London Capital Market and on UK companies' direct investment abroad, these conditions have led to the emergence of an extremely important international Capital Market, of which London is, once again, the main centre. The following figures, which are in millions of dollars, reflect this development. In 1963, the amount raised by public issues was 164, in 1964, 795, in 1965, 1,164, in 1966, 1,138, in 1967, 1,884, in 1968, 3,075, in 1969, 2,731, and 1970 in the first 10 months, 2,040. The total over the whole period amounts to 13,000 million dollars. The variety of currencies, of borrowers and of instruments in this market is also noteworthy. The vast bulk, some 9,500 million, have been denominated in dollars. But there has been a very substantial volume in Deutsche Marks, as well as some in other currencies and in so-called European Units of Account. There have been straight bonds and convertible bonds, bonds with fixed and with variable rates of interest; and more recently medium-term (five to seven years) notes or syndicated bank credits have been used as well as long-term bonds in the true sense of the word. There has also been a large variety of borrowers. While in the early phase

US Corporations and their overseas subsidiaries predominated, more recently there have been many UK, Continental and other (including Japanese) companies; there have been various Governments, State-owned enterprises, Local Authorities and international bodies, such as the European Coal and Steel Community and the European Investment Bank. In all this very voluminous new business, the institutions of the City of London have played a major part; and much of the remarkably satisfactory showing of the 'invisible' items in our balance of payments is directly and indirectly due to this fact.

Thus, the performance to date of the financial system can be judged to have been reasonably satisfactory; in particular it has shown itself not only adaptable to new circumstances which have often at first been adverse, it has to a considerable extent been capable of taking advantage of change so as to evolve new forms of organization and new techniques and, thus, to advance more than the economy as a whole. Does this encourage a high degree of confidence for the future? To answer this question, one needs to make a number of assumptions about the likely shape of future changes on different levels of generality. An exhaustive study is clearly not possible now. I will confine myself to looking at the way in which the financial community might be influenced by policy changes of three kinds. First, I assume no fundamental change in the surrounding framework, but only changes that might result from the forces already at work and discernible today. Second, I assume a change in the general balance of our economic policy management in the direction either of an easing of credit restrictions or of a much greater reliance on the monetary than on any other instrument of policy. These two are not easy to separate and I shall therefore, have, in part, to consider them together. Third, I consider the consequences of British membership of the European Economic Community. The choice of these three somewhat disparate sets of factors is, of course, quite arbitrary, but they seem to me to be among the most useful for setting out what are likely to be some possible directions of change and the most acute problems each would produce.

As far as the first of these is concerned, the main question, I suppose, is whether the high degree of specialization, the highly variegated structure of financial institutions and the business they each do, are likely to survive changes in economic policy and conditions, including some which may historically have been responsible for the present pattern of institutions or types of business. Among these

I would include the effect of a major change in two of the chief factors with which the financial community has had to live for some years. First, the recurring crises in the UK balance of payments, leading to a régime of strict control of capital movements as well as a general climate of credit restrictions with only moderate fluctuations in their severity; and the second, the persistent deficit in the US balance of payments since the early sixties, leading to large accumulations of dollar balances outside the United States, and accompanied by a stringent US programme to regulate outward capital movements.

A study of the effects of possible future changes in domestic credit restriction is complicated by the fact that the financial community, like any other sector of competitive business, is subject to certain dynamic changes of its own, responding to broad changes in industrial structure, or to demographic and many other changes, rarely directly traceable to or even to be correlated with changes in policy. If we take the chief characteristic of the City of London, for example, its own, highly complex brand of specialization, it is by no means easy to disentangle independent changes which one might foresee from those which might follow changes in economic policy. Forecasts of the former are largely influenced by personal beliefs or preferences. Among these I would mention, as examples, the size and number of clearing banks, their relation to industry, that is the short-term credit and long-term capital needs of industry, and with it, therefore, the relation of the clearing banks to the merchant bankers. Then there is that of the latter, for example in regard to new issue business, to the stockbrokers; and the question of the future of consumer credit which has so greatly expanded in scope and complexity, partly with and partly without the clearing banks.

It is clear that these matters are, even without any additional assumption about policy changes, not only highly complicated, but also highly contentious. Thus if one also supposes—perhaps unrealistically at this moment—an easing of the credit restrictions which have in the recent past been so largely responsible for the growth of a parallel money market and for the emergence of new forms both of deposit-taking and of short-term credit-giving alongside the traditional activities of the Joint Stock Banks, forecasting becomes very hazardous indeed. In general, I would expect the disappearance of the reasons which have led to the growth of new forms of pseudo-deposit banking, to cause at least a partial reversion to the earlier pattern since this is a field in which the Joint Stock Banks must be more competitive once quantitative control of credit is eased; though it would, perhaps, be legitimate to assume also that something like a reasonable long-term capital market is then restored, so that the traditional distinction between the needs for different types of finance can once again emerge. I would, therefore, regard those forms of finance based on deposit-taking in which a relatively modest margin between interest rates is the source of profit, and which can flourish because of the non-availability of normal bank lending, to be particularly vulnerable to any, even partial, return to 'normal' credit conditions.

On the other hand, there is some comfort here to be found for some of those affected, for example the merchant banks. For if the process of easing of credit is accompanied by a recovery of the capital market, as I have assumed, some of the clearing banks' best customers would at last be able to consider funding their bank advances; and so, as the clearing banks returned to their traditional role of providing short-term credit for a larger and more varied clientèle, the merchant banks would have a more active new issue market to look to. This, of course, presupposes that the Joint Stock Banks will not push further the efforts, as yet isolated, to get into the new issue business, perhaps on the basis that if they have sustained a client for a long period with overdrafts, they should be responsible for securing long-term finance too. This is not the place to debate such a proposition in detail; I would only state my own view that these are different functions requiring different kinds of specialized knowledge and experience. This seems to me to be equally true as far as the relation between stockbrokers and issuing houses are concerned. If one is to develop the business of the other, a reverse process cannot be excluded. Though at a time when there is an agonizing reappraisal on this very score going on in Wall Street, it would I suppose be wiser not to encourage radical change in either direction. It is even more hazardous to make predictions where consumer credit institutions are concerned when we are shortly to have the benefit of the findings of the Crowther Committee. Whatever may be the recommendations of that body (and it is to be hoped that they will tend to make more logical as well as simpler the legal regulation of this business) there remains the question of the wisdom of continued reliance, as in the recent past, on direct regulations of the terms of consumer credit as a major instrument of economic management. If it is true, as has been said, that governments tend to deal with the urgent rather than with the important problems, it is even more the case that they tend to grab the nearest weapon at hand and not necessarily the one most appropriate to the task. It would, therefore, be unrealistic to suppose that any government would readily abandon the use of, say, hire-purchase regulations, so handy an instrument particularly in a country in which the annual budget (or some equally portentous variant of our traditional spring rite) plays so large a part in economic policy-making. But awareness seems to be spreading of the doubtful wisdom of singling out for special attention certain sectors of industry, and the financial mechanism that has grown up with them, regardless of their relevance to the broad objectives of economic policy as a whole. This is a particular example of a mechanistic attitude in these matters which may even have had the effect of widening rather than narrowing the amplitude of economic fluctuations.

Another set of considerations is raised by the possibility of a period of reasonable balance of payments stability here (which would presumably be a concomitant of a period of easier credit), particularly if it should also be accompanied by a material improvement in the American balance of payments. A more or less simultaneous easing of capital movement controls here and in the United States may be thought, in the first instance at least, to have opposite effects. The former could be expected to lead to an increase in the business of the City both directly and indirectly concerned with the financing of all types of overseas investment, at any rate by British companies and perhaps by certain Commonwealth borrowers. I am, however, not at all sanguine that this will happen to any significant degree in the near future, and despite the continuing massive external deficit of the United States I think it much more probable that easements on capital outflow, such as a reduction or even the abolition of the Interest Equalization Tax and some easing of the controls of the Office of Foreign Direct Investment will happen there. It is sometimes thought that such a development would overnight destroy the thriving international capital market that has been built up in Europe, of which London is the centre, and to which I have referred earlier. There would undoubtedly be a period of readjustment, though the highly expert knowledge which European houses have of this business should stand them in good stead and should enable them to follow some of this business at least to New York to the extent that this might be necessary. It is to be hoped if that time comes that American investment bankers will remember that they have found a ready welcome in Europe in recent years and have worked in close partnership with their European opposite numbers in the development of the new Euro-market.

Perhaps a further, more general word might here be added about the appropriateness of the City's structure to the likely needs of the future, particularly as this has recently been called in question in certain quarters. It will not surprise you, in the light of what I have said earlier, to find me somewhat sceptical about the injunction that the City should do as others have done. It would be foolish as well as presumptuous for us to tell the French, for example, that the involvement of their *Banques d'Affaires* in industry is excessive, or to impress upon the Germans that their striving for *Universalbanken*, that is commercial banks which do every kind of financial business under one roof, leads to something less than complete efficiency; even if one felt that both their systems might create a lack of resilience which could be troublesome in difficult times. History certainly provides many examples which could be made to sustain such a contention. But we must remember that these Continental systems are adapted to the particular conditions in those countries, especially of the capital market, and are the result of a certain historical development, economic and political, which any undergraduate is taught in his first year. But by the same token, it is odd to hear in our own country the market economy extolled while at the same time the financial structure is criticized which, having emerged from a quite different historical background, is based on a highly developed capital market and a series of the most refined money markets to be found anywhere in the world. These have given rise to, and have in turn been sustained by, a large number of highly specialized institutions. While I can understand that a certain ideology might lead one to justify the abolition of the IRC, I do not quite see the logic of its also justifying a clamour for the City to run industry!

I do not wish these remarks to be taken as indicating the slightest degree of complacency. The structure of the City has undergone much change even in the one hundred years or so since Bagehot wrote his classic description. But this change has generally been in one direction: to create new markets and new financial instruments to cope with an ever-changing and increasing variety of needs, domestic and international, each served by specialized institutions. This process will undoubtedly continue and the lines of demarcation between the classes of business which the different sectors of this financial community do will also undoubtedly change. Where size and massiveness of resources count, as in the 'retail' banking business of the deposit banks, the trend towards bigger units with greater emphasis on service to the retail customer has certainly been inevitable and may continue. But there are many areas of finance in which size is not the chief criterion; those for example which require, as it were, made-to-measure service to the corporate customer or the investment client or to particular classes of borrowers who can be best served by specialist organizations. I would be the first to say that one cannot be confident that the broad pattern of the City's specialization will continue indefinitely. But it would be highly imprudent, in my view, deliberately to seek to change a supple and resilient system which has stood us in such good stead. For if we are to move towards the 'universal' bank, we shall find others, in the countries of the Common Market, with a longer experience of this form; while if size of resources is to be the sole criterion, we may not find it so easy to compete with the American giants. What I have said does not, I repeat, preclude changes of demarcation and, even less, alliances between different types of institutions both within the UK and internationally. But it is precisely here that it is highly desirable for us not to destroy a unique asset which we could bring into such alliances.

It is in this connection that I should like to refer to another factor which might affect the structure of the London financial community, namely the apparently spreading fashion to emphasize monetary policy within the total economic armoury. The theoretical case for and against the new 'monetarism' is being actively debated at this moment and I do not propose to enter into this debate in any great detail. On the most general level of economic theory, I find it, like the case for floating exchange rates, an example of an excessively mechanistic outlook and, therefore, in the deepest sense irrational. It represents an instance of the never-ending search for the simple cure-all so beguiling and yet so dangerous, particularly in anything relating to the problems of society. May I also say that the juxtaposition of 'monetarism' to 'Keynesianism' seems to me very odd when one remembers that Keynes was the author not only of the *General Theory* but also of the *Tract on Monetary Reform* and the *Treatise on Money*.

More particularly as far as the balance of policy for the present juncture in our affairs is concerned, I cannot resist the temptation to say something about monetary policy in the present fight against inflation. Let no one suppose that monetary policy is an easy option. I do not mean by this that a strict monetary policy is difficult to effect, true though that is. But one must realize that monetary policy involves very serious economic consequences before one can hope that inflation will be contained by it.

A strict monetary policy means rising interest rates and less credit. Any hope that it might be possible to keep a tight hold on the money supply—to quote the fashionable phrase—without accepting the implication for interest rates, is illusory, since it is just through changes in the relative rates of return on assets, real as well as financial, that monetary policy works. The higher cost and the lessened availability of funds will make capital expenditures by companies, both for fixed investment and for stock-building, seem less worth while. I realize that the disincentive effect of rising interest rates is lessened if the rate of price inflation is seen to be rising at the same time. Nevertheless, if monetary pressure goes on mounting, then the point must come when general business confidence is affected; and once expectations start being revised, the direction of the economy could be very quickly altered.

When real demand begins to grow by less than productive potential, unemployment results. The rise in unemployment, and the concurrent development of buyers' markets, should help to reduce inflation, though current developments here and abroad have not made me confident that one could forecast what extent or what duration of unemployment might be necessary to achieve this purpose.

But if the aim of a tight monetary policy is to cure inflation by means of raising unemployment one would want to ask whether there are not better ways of curing inflation than by purposely wasting resources, particularly at a time of low growth; and even if it were argued that a much larger margin of unemployment was a necessary evil, which I do not, would it really make sense to achieve this degree of deflation by placing the main reliance on monetary measures?

Some people seem to think that monetary policy could be used to counter inflation without involving this traumatic development. They hope that monetary pressure will act directly upon employers to make them less prepared to meet inflationary wage claims, and that thereby one could get a general decline in monetary expansion, wages and prices simultaneously without any necessary increase in unemployment. This seems to me to be oversimplified. The outcome of wage negotiation depends on a lot of factors, and it is not clear why the impact of monetary pressures should change the balance of bargaining power between unions and employers directly. It will do so indirectly if monetary pressures weaken the markets for the industrialist's goods sufficiently, so that he is likely to face greater difficulty in passing on wage increases in higher prices. But this brings us right back to using monetary restriction to cut expenditures, and, subsequently, to increase unemployment. Indeed, it is this threat of unemployment to the worker, as well as the implication of lower profit margins to the industrialist, that in theory at least finally makes the policy bite upon wage negotiations. It is, I suppose, possible to imagine that the adoption of a more restrictive monetary policy could so change expectations about future prospects for inflation and for the markets for labour and for goods, that inflationary wage settlements would subside spontaneously as it were without much increase in unemployment having to occur. All I can say is that those who believe that will believe anything; so long as it has a happy ending.

But I would add something which is more directly germane to my theme. As must already be evident from the general line I have taken, I have grave doubts about the wisdom of the kind of extreme monetary pressure which is sometimes advocated from the point of view of the financial structure itself. There are both theoretical and practical differences in the way in which fiscal and monetary policy become effective. Much of the former operates directly on different forms of demand, and if contraction or expansion are desired, the consequences can often, though by no means always, be foreseen. In the case of monetary policy, the operation is indirect, often highly indirect. It involves increasing or relaxing pressures on highly specialized intermediaries by changing directly or more often indirectly the terms on which they operate in their different markets. They then have to transmit the impetus thus received through their own mechanisms. This makes the effects of any particular monetary measure much less predictable. It would be interesting to speculate what a 'monetarist' might have forecast, say, ten years ago about the consequences of monetary policies. Would he have foreseen all the changes in mechanism, techniques and institutions which have been called forth by monetary measures and have led to a considerable distortion in the originally desired and expected effects of these policies? But the adaptability of our financial institutions is not unlimited. So far they have had to adjust to, shall I say, relatively 'normal' types of restriction. The burden which some people now wish monetary policy to carry, that is to say, the major burden in dealing with a cost-push inflation (even if not yet complicated by a demand-pull one as well) and, therefore, the burden which they would thereby impose on the financial system may be too great to be sustained by that system without lasting damage to its efficiency.

Finally, I would like to give you a few reflections on the question of Britain's entry into the European Economic Community in relation to some of the matters I have discussed. This subject, as I have said earlier, is of a different order from the other policy developments so far mentioned. There are issues involved here, of an economic, social, political and even cultural character, which are of transcendental importance, and the purely financial ones, when looked at narrowly, would certainly seem insignificant. Nevertheless, they are not unimportant in themselves and they have important implications; and to look at them may help to illuminate the wider problems. I leave on one side the question of how the City will be affected by our membership in a customs union, that is, an organization which has no trade barriers within and a common external tariff and an increasingly common commercial policy to the outside world; or the other question of the effect of a common agricultural policy with common financing arrangements. To deal with these would amount to rehearsing all the hotly debated short-term economic arguments for and against our entry. I propose to confine myself to two main points: how the City will fare in this Community on the basis largely of present policies; and what effect the proposed monetary arrangements in the Community will have on the shape of economic management, as now practised by us, and, in particular, on its financial aspects.

Like much else that is said about British membership of the EEC, by both supporters and opponents, the effects on the City are usually described in emotional rather than analytical terms. Thus membership is thought on the one side to involve the loss of a great deal of business to continental financial centres and their institutions; while, on the other side, great benefits, in terms both of private profit and the national balance of payments are expected. The truth is likely to be much less dramatic, though even in the short run more in the direction of gain rather than loss. There is no reason whatever to expect London's pre-eminence as a financial centre to be impaired, let alone lost, simply as a result of our membership. The qualities which are required for the role of an international financial centre may be historically rooted in a certain abundance of resources

—in this case capital for domestic and overseas investment; or in a certain predominance of trading position or even in political and strategic power. But its maintenance depends, in a relatively free economic world, on the continued existence of certain outstanding facilities, that is of specialized institutions and highly developed skills. These take a very long time to build up and can, for quite some time, resist even the most persistent efforts to destroy them. But there is no evidence that their maintenance is dependent on the particular factors that have given rise to them. Indeed, the contrary seems to be the case. It is no longer possible to say, as Bagehot did, that 'England is the greatest moneyed country in the world', though perhaps his dictum that the term 'London Banker has a specially charmed value' may still be true. Certainly, in a period in which our share of world trade has declined and the transactions function of sterling with it, in which sterling's reserve function has been steadily reduced (from nearly one-quarter of world reserves little more than a decade ago to about 8 per cent now)—and is moreover underpinned by the Basle agreements, when outward capital flows have been severely restricted (to say nothing of the fact that the dispatch of a gunboat to the Yangtse or of a cruiser to the river Plate is no longer available as diplomatic support); while all this has happened the City has greatly extended its international activities and, with them, its earnings. And this, furthermore, in a time of recurrent and sometimes violent economic and financial crises. During this period also, other centres in countries which have enjoyed a more tranquil economic climate, more steady growth, and generally stronger currencies, have not noticeably enhanced their relative positions. There is no evidence that either Frankfurt or Tokyo is just about to take over London's international financial functions.

But, by the same token, it would be wrong, I believe, to suppose that membership of the Common Market will suddenly open up vast new opportunities beyond those already present and to some extent already exploited. The chief benefit to the City institutions would come from precisely those developments which might, in the short term, be burdensome for the UK balance of payments, namely those associated with freer capital movements within the Community and with the rapid approximation of certain of our taxation and foreign exchange provisions, which today complicate some of our international business, to those of the Community. Looked at purely from the point of view of the City, therefore, a very rapid progress towards complete monetary union would be highly desirable. But on the wider implications of such a development I shall have something more to say in a moment.

If the City stands to gain (though perhaps in the short term not very substantially) from entry in the EEC, what is the position of the Six? It has been argued that they will derive much benefit from our inclusion. I would agree that our financial skills and mechanisms are indeed a major dowry that we would be bringing into such a marriage, though it may take some time for it to be fully exploited. The facilities of the City are, of course, already largely available to, and used by, various sectors of the economies of the Six. Nevertheless, some institutional and perhaps, even more, psychological obstacles remain. If these are overcome—and here again full monetary union would be an advantage—the financial needs of the Six would have at their disposal to the fullest extent the existing and potential facilities of a truly international financial centre.

I have referred to the significance which progress towards full monetary union would have for the financial activities of an enlarged Community. It is at this point that this discussion merges with that concerned with the effects of the Community's efforts in the monetary field on the problems of economic management. Forecasting here is made extremely difficult by the uncertainty which surrounds the practical intentions of the Six. To describe the present state of the Community as no more than a customs union with a complicated and highly protectionist agricultural policy tacked on to it is, no doubt, something of a travesty. But the undeniable lack of accomplishment in other fields has goaded the more active spirits concerned with European integration to attempt a major leap forward by means of a new development in the monetary sphere.

The method first expounded to achieve this end sketched out with complete rigour—and this, in my view, was as it should be—the basic conditions of a monetary union, namely rigid, or virtually rigid, exchange parities between the members. Today, after two reports by a committee under the chairmanship of the Luxembourg Prime Minister, this position has been considerably attenuated, and any connoisseur in these matters, when reading the latest Werner Report, will easily identify those highly negotiated passages which reflect the customary attempt to do justice to two diametrically opposed views. At any rate, while we do not yet know exactly what commitment governments will take towards the Werner Report, we can see that the report does two things on a pattern already well established within the Community. It sets out an ultimate objective with a deadline—the end of this decade—attached to it. And it maps out the steps towards reaching the ultimate end. It does so in fair detail as far as the first step is concerned (the next three years), and rather more sketchily for the next. Whereas the original conception seemed to require an early implementation of monetary union in order then, from above as it were, to force the pace of economic union, the present proposals envisage a more simultaneous progress on both fronts, but with monetary integration still assigned the more active role. The relation between the two is most easily seen on the basis of the original, and more ambitious proposals. For virtually rigid exchange parities require automatic and potentially massive balance of payments support for a member in difficulties. This, however, is inconceivable—to me at least—without commitments by the members for the equally automatic adoption of measures in the field of what is technically known as the 'adjustment process', that is, measures of economic policy—fiscal, monetary, and perhaps other—which could be very rigorous and far-reaching indeed. It is impossible to see how this is to be accomplished by the normal means of inter-governmental consultation and harmonization even of the more intimate kind which the Community is at present endeavouring to practise. As far as monetary policy is concerned, nothing short of concerted action involving detailed technical measures in regard to interest rates, credit policy and exchange rate policy *vis à vis* the outside world will really do, if the initial commitment to fixed parities is to be met. But to say this is in fact to say that the whole panoply of monetary union would be required: a single (or federally structured) central bank, perhaps a single currency (though this is not indispensable if the separate currencies are genuinely freely interchangeable at fixed parities). If this is so, then one must visualize the need, not far behind monetary union, at least of common fiscal policies; and these would certainly involve much more progress in political control over the executive organs of the Community.

It is true, as I have already said, that under the latest proposals, this stringent pattern has been abandoned and a certain parallelism has been laid down. Moreover, recent reports suggest that even the present proposals are not entirely welcome to some of the member Governments of the Six. It is not my business to speculate here on how this debate will end or whether a very gradual approach in matters which go so very much more to the heart of national sovereignty than does the creation of a customs union, is really feasible. As far as we in this country are concerned, it seems to me extremely important that these wider implications should at least be recognized and fully understood. As to the desirability of going all the way into monetary, and, through it, economic union, much wider interests than those of the City—which, as I have said, would certainly benefit—must be taken into account. For my part, I would only make two personal observations. First, that to me it would hardly seem worth while to attempt to engage the vision and the energies of this and future generations, to say nothing of suffering the considerable short-term economic cost of entry, if this enterprise is to remain confined within its present narrow limits. If, as I believe, it is worth joining in the effort to build a European Economic Community, it is so only if we accept its more distant economico-political goals and, beyond that, are in fact prepared to work actively to reach them.

My second point concerns the question of the substantial abandonment of sovereignty that is involved even if we confine ourselves only to the monetary sphere. An immediate point to be made here is that in practice sovereignty in these matters is already severely limited for most, if not all, countries by their membership in an international monetary system, and by the necessity, which has been demonstrated over and over again, for all of them to have the active co-operation and help of their fellows while accepting the necessary constraints on their freedom in regard to economic management without which this cannot be forthcoming. But there is a further point here, namely the feasibility and desirability of pushing further and formalizing this close interdependence on a regional European, rather than on a wider basis. The answer to this question will, I think, depend on the view one takes, first of the likelihood of such a development on a wider basis in the direction of making the International Monetary Fund more nearly an international Central Bank, as originally proposed by Keynes and as recently advocated by the former Chairman of the Federal Reserve Board, Mr. William McChesney Martin. The recent activities of the IMF and the quality of its reports, for example in relation to greater flexibility of exchange rates, and the apparent readiness to make increasing use of the mechanism of the Special Drawing Rights, do encourage one to think that hope on this score is not as unrealistic as might have appeared only a short time ago.

On the other side, a European Monetary Union will have a currency (whether on a unitary or on a federal basis) which would have great international importance and might well acquire a reserve currency function unless by that time progress has already been made towards a World Central Bank. There arises therefore the question whether the creation of a European Monetary Union would be helpful in regard to strengthening the international monetary system and encouraging the closer worldwide monetary integration which seems to me to be essential in the long run. This is not an easy question to answer, but about one aspect at least I would venture an opinion. I think that an affirmative answer is much more likely if we are members than if we are not, provided, of course, that we make our own view on the relation between the regional and the worldwide systems clearly known. I say this not because I believe us to be specially unselfish or to be endowed with a specially enlightened vision, but simply because our experience and our interests in international finance have worked and must continue to work in that direction.

I have in the latter part of my remarks roamed fairly wide and perhaps wandered somewhat from my main theme. My excuse is that it would give quite the wrong perspective if I had merely emphasized this or that regulation of the amount of instalment credit that can be granted, or this or that provision of the Finance Act which, combined with the foreign exchange regulations, makes certain types of foreign business more cumbersome than they might be. In the end the scope and structure of our financial system will depend, like all the rest of the UK economy, on the manner in which the broader issues of economic policy are resolved. If this is done in a way that avoids mechanistic reliance on this or that panacea or only on the emotional impulse provided by ideological slogans; if it is the right mixture of realism and imagination, prudence and courage, then the financial system will have no difficulty in continuing to do its job.

INTERNATIONAL CAPITAL
MOVEMENTS PAST, PRESENT, FUTURE

*The Per Jacobsson Lecture 1971, delivered in Washington, DC on 26
September 1971. This text was circulated before the lecture. Additional, oral
remarks follow at the end.*

I deeply appreciate the honour which the Per Jacobsson Foundation
has done me in inviting me to give this lecture today. I feel bound
to add, however, that to undertake to write a paper on an international financial topic in 1971, around the time of the summer
solstice, for delivery around that of the autumn equinox, requires a
degree of recklessness that may lead to immediate expulsion from
the fraternity of bankers, whose outstanding quality is, or at least
ought to be, prudence. The officers of the Foundation, recognizing
this hazard, were kind enough to give me a few weeks' grace. This,
however, proved a mixed blessing, as every day brought new
pronouncements from the authorities, new interpretations of what
these meant, and new rumours of what they really intended to do, as
distinct from what they said; and new disturbances in financial
markets.

This audience, containing so many bankers, will, therefore,
appreciate why my acceptance of this invitation was coupled with an
option to supplement what I say in my paper with additional observations which may differ considerably—and perhaps in part completely contradict—the views here expressed. For who is to be sure
what events the next few weeks will bring, including in 'events' the
unforeseeable acts of governments!

There are other reasons for approaching this subject with some
hesitation. Two formidable panellists are to initiate a discussion of
the subject of this paper. They have both considerable practical
experience of the problems with which it deals and they have both
fairly recently pronounced on it: Henry Fowler, less than a year ago
in Tokyo, and Wilfried Guth earlier this year, in Geneva, on the very
morrow of the most recent monetary crisis; and they have each expressed quite decided views. This audience contains some of the most
eminent among both the poachers and the gamekeepers in the
monetary forest, if I may so refer to them, as well as distinguished
monetary theorists. The subject itself, for some unaccountable

reason, evokes strong emotions. Floaters and fixed exchange raters, monetarists and fiscalists, interveners and *laissez-faire*-ites, those whose greatest desire is to have more autonomy in national economic policy-making and those who are deeply devoted to the international monetary system: all seem to find in the present developments in international capital movements support for their own particular theories. Indeed it is true to say that if one wants to plunge at once into all those most complex problems in monetary economics: balance of payments equilibrium, the domestic adjustment process, the role of exchange rates, the proper policy mix for economic stabilization and, even, the role of international institutions, it is difficult to think of a better springboard than the subject of this lecture.

It is not surprising, therefore, that it also has a very long and distinguished history, from Ricardo through the controversies after the Napoleonic wars to Keynes and the post-Keynesians. One can fill a respectable section of any economics library with discussions of international money flows. And in the last ten years—perhaps more particularly in the last twelve months—it has become virtually impossible to pick up any publication in this field that does not discuss the Euro-currency market and its real or imagined misdeeds.

There are, moreover, considerable limitations in dealing with a monetary subject as such. Not only does money, as has so often been observed, throw a veil over real phenomena, but monetary policy is often invoked to perform tasks beyond its capacity. If I may quote some words from a little-known publication, the *Irish Banking and Currency Report* of 1938, which were almost certainly written by the man in whose honour these lectures were instituted, Per Jacobsson, I commend to you the following: 'Some of the greatest difficulties of monetary policy arise from the fact that it has to be pursued in an environment largely conditioned by political and other non-monetary factors. . . . It is quite clearly unreasonable to expect all mistakes committed in the political and economic field to be neutralized by monetary action, however wisely pursued.' I am sure these words will find a loud echo in the breast of many a central bank governor today.

In this situation, it would be rash to suppose that one can say much that is new or say it in a way that would contribute light rather than heat. One can, of course, always pose more questions, though one should remember Charles Colton's saying of one hundred and fifty years ago that 'the greatest fool may ask more questions than the wisest man can answer'. What, however, I think may be particularly helpful is to try to bring some order into the debate. Here I take as my inspiration what I once heard Josiah Stamp say: 'If we have to have minds like ragbags, let us at least sort out the rags.'

CAPITAL MOVEMENT IN THE NINETEENTH CENTURY

My title suggests that I have divided the subject, like ancient Gaul, into three parts. They are, however, not of equal length and weight; and on some of the aspects of the problem, I have had to intermingle past, present and future.

As far as the past is concerned, international capital movements would certainly repay renewed study both in their theory and in their actual evolution. For example, Jenks's *Migration of British Capital*, Cleona Lewis's *America's Stake in International Investment* and Jacob Viner's classic, *Canada's Balance of International Indebtedness*, are, I suspect, rarely read nowadays, but certainly should be. I want to refer only briefly, both to the theory and the history of the subject, primarily as an antidote to some of the present-day attitudes which tend often to regard every problem as unprecedented, while at the same time being only too ready to derive policy guidance from somewhat primitive theories of the past which developments of recent decades have made inadequate. There is some comfort to be got from realizing that our present discontents as regards long-term capital movements or flows of 'hot money' are not unique but have been experienced many times before, and this can at least teach us to keep them in perspective. It is also salutary to be reminded that some of our reactions to current phenomena may spring from half-remembered lessons of first-year textbooks in Economics that were perhaps not wholly adequate to what was happening in the real world even at the time when we imbibed them.

The general theory of international economic relations, embracing the theory of international trade, of capital movements, and of the international monetary mechanism, has an ancient and honourable pedigree and is perhaps the most solidly established part of general economic theory. In its basic elements it is probably the least changed since the two hundred and twenty years when David Hume first expounded the theory that became the foundation for the explanation of the relationship between the influx and outflow of the precious metals (or reserves, as we would say today) and the domestic price level; and the hundred and fifty years since Ricardo first elaborated the theory of the division of labour into one which also explained the fundamental reasons for international trade. As for the first, during the relatively limited period of a half-century or so, when the pure gold standard held sway and the specie points (the equivalent of today's 'bands') determined money flows, the total acceptance of this international system was best demonstrated by the fact that it was referred to simply as 'the mechanism'; though with hindsight one can see that there was a hint of potential impermanence in the fact that it required the observance of certain rules of the game for its proper functioning. As for the origin and direction of international capital movements, the explanation was also fairly straightforward. Comparative advantage determined the international division of labour; natural endowment and institutional arrangements determined the accumulation of capital. The two combined would create export or import surpluses which would be compensated by long-term capital exports or imports, thus usually closely linking trade and capital flows, as Roosa has recently reminded us. It should be noted, however, that many of the empirical studies, for example that of Jacob Viner, show that even a long time ago, triangular, and even more complicated relationships, between trade flows, long-term capital movements, and the movement of short-term banking funds were by no means uncommon.

It is not my purpose here to trace the changes that have taken place in the corpus of economic theory on this subject, or to describe in detail the stages through which international movements of capital—long and short—have actually gone in the last hundred years. Generally speaking, the theory has been a steady adaptation of the classical doctrine to actual changes in institutions and practices which have, in turn, been due to changes in the relative position of different countries, the reasons for which must be sought in profound demographic, technological, social and political factors. What, I think, even the briefest review of the last hundred years or so makes one realize is, first, how far the 'textbook' description of a smoothly working international monetary system is an idealized pattern that was both relatively short-lived in its pure form and, above all, underpinned by certain political or institutional factors which were the prerequisite for the system's operation. Thus Per Jacobsson, in the report I have already quoted, after pointing out that it was roughly the period of 1850 to 1910 which marked the heyday of the pre-First World War gold standard and that this was a period when more peaceful international relations were maintained, goes on to say: 'The *de facto* predominance of London in the short- and long-term money markets provided a centre of stability for the world credit structure which enabled the pre-war (that is pre-1914) system to work with a high degree of smoothness and reliability.'

Similarly, Keynes, writing in 1930, says: 'During the latter half of the nineteenth century the influence of London on credit conditions throughout the world was so predominant that the Bank of England could almost have claimed to be the conductor of the international orchestra. By modifying the terms on which she was prepared to lend, aided by her own readiness to vary the volume of her gold reserves and the unreadiness of the other central banks to vary the volume of theirs, she could to a large extent determine the credit conditions prevailing elsewhere.' It is thus important to remember—and I say this in no spirit of chauvinism or nostalgia, but purely as an objective aid to understanding—that what made the old gold standard system work was perhaps as much the existence of an '*Aequilibrium Britannicum*'—alongside a *Pax Britannica*—as its own inherent virtues.

The other point that a study of the history of this subject brings very forcibly to mind is the relative speed with which, shall we say, the surrounding data of institutional and national realities change. I shall refer to the more recent examples of this later, but even in the nineteenth century there are some to be found. It is as well to remember that in the forties, when the American Federal Government was in a less favourable credit position than some of the states, it is reported that the Paris Rothschild told an agent of the US Government: 'You may tell your Government that you have seen the man who is at the head of the finances of Europe, and that he has told you that they cannot borrow a dollar, not a dollar'; and Barings were only prepared to raise money in London (at 3 per cent) if the Federal Government would assume the state debts.

Yet by the seventies, with the passing of the frontier and the beginning of the great industrial upsurge in the United States, the situation changed. America began to be not only a powerful trade competitor, but a great potential exporter of capital, and cries of the 'American Peril' and of the 'American Invasion' were almost as loud as they have been at times in the last two decades. So let us remember these quite sharp turn-arounds when we try to diagnose problems and prescribe remedies based on the experience of half a decade or less!

THE POST-WAR WORLD

The developments of the first fifteen years of the post-war period are sufficiently fresh in everyone's memory to require little detailed recapitulation. It may, however, be worth while to note briefly some of the main background changes that must be borne in mind in examining the most recent developments. These points are all obvious ones; they are listed here for the sake of emphasis only. The first is that, since the war, international financial arrangements have been conducted under the aegis—even though they have unfortunately not yet been dominated by—new institutions: the Bretton Woods machinery. Long-term capital movements, at least between developed and developing countries, have to a certain degree been influenced by the operations of the World Bank. The régime of exchange parities, the provision of world liquidity and the relation between balances of payments and domestic policy have been carried on under the aegis of the Fund, aided by the 'auxiliary engines' of the Group of Ten, Working Party Three, and the increasingly close cooperation of central banks both in terms of consultation and in terms of practical mutual assistance. It is, however, to be noted that the Bretton Woods machinery was deficient. Not only did it lack— through American unreadiness to participate—an institution that would explicitly have brought together international and national economic management problems, the International Trade Organization (ITO), but it almost explicitly excluded capital movements from its purview. This was an interesting example of the difficulty of reconciling the preoccupation for freedom of national policymaking with membership in an international system. Keynes himself in his original proposals for a Clearing Union, after arguing the case back and forth, concluded that 'the universal establishment of a control of capital movements cannot be regarded as essential to the operation of the Clearing Union, and the method and degree of such control should therefore be left to the decision of each member State'. One must remember—and this is something of a paradox —that this conclusion was reached within the framework of an expectation of a Clearing Union that would have been much more like a World Central Bank—with a single universal reserve asset— something very different from what the Fund has been, at least up to now. It would be interesting to speculate whether Keynes would have wanted control of capital movements to have remained the prerogative of national authorities had he realized at the time of the original proposal that the Clearing Union itself would not conform to his complete vision.

The second important point to recall is that at the end of the fifties, convertibility among the major currencies had been achieved and that this greatly encouraged a much enlarged flow of capital across national boundaries. This is a development to which many have drawn attention, not least Per Jacobsson himself who, almost exactly ten years ago, in his 1961 report on the work of the Fund, spoke of the 'growing freedom for the international movement of funds' and the fact that this had 'created new problems which the world has not had to face since the start of World War II'.

This easing-up of capital movements, both long and short, led, as might have been expected, to a contradictory sort of development. For as one 'eases up', new practices are generated, new markets arise, new institutional arrangements are formed, and many of these changes are irreversible. This means that whenever the need arises— or the Authorities think that the need arises—to restrain the freedom which they, themselves, have called forth, they find themselves faced with new and unforeseen pressures. In other words, they cannot simply 'return' to the situation that existed before.

Another more general point to be recalled in this connection is the changed relative position of different countries, and, indeed, the mutations which these, themselves, have undergone. The post-war period began under the overwhelming influence of the economic strength of the United States. The dollar shortage and the fear of its persistence was the overriding feature of the international economic scene; and the 'scarce currency' clause of the Fund's Articles, in-spired solely by this fear, remains as eloquent testimony to the transitory nature of what appeared to be the most solid of historical data. Keynes himself had second thoughts; his 1946, posthumously published, article on the US balance of payments foreshadowed some of the changes that have occurred, though even he would have found it difficult to forecast either the facts of the US balance of payments as they have developed during the last decade or, even more, the attitudes to which they have given rise in many places to the dollar.

Another most important background fact of the post-war period that must be constantly borne in mind is the changed attitude of governments—and of the governed—to the level of economic activity. In the perspective of a century, the greater concern of the 'Authority' with the level of employment of resources, and therefore with the economic process has, no doubt, developed gradually and as a result of a complex of pressures and changing ideas. But as far as the last twenty-five years are concerned, the acknowledgment of responsibility of government to maintain a high and stable level of economic activity and the development of new techniques of economic management, together with a greatly advanced statistical apparatus to enable these techniques to be employed against an assessment of facts, must be accounted as little short of a revolution. The relevance of this factor to our present theme, that is to the international financial system, is not difficult to see. Throughout the inter-war years there were occasions when the dilemma between the desiderata of national policy and the requirements of an international trading and financial system appeared very acute: when Britain returned to the Gold Standard or during the Great Depression, for example. Already in 1930, Keynes had written that the international monetary system 'requires that the main criterion of banking policy of each member should be the average behaviour of all the other members, its own voluntary and independent contribution to the final result being a modest one'; and, then, of the difficulty of being a member of an international system 'and to preserve at the same time an adequate local autonomy for each member over its domestic rate of interest and its volume of foreign lending'—prophetic words indeed! As we have seen, the Bretton Woods system sought to remove this dilemma by allowing controls on capital movements. But what was not sufficiently realized twenty-five years ago was the extent to which the management of aggregate domestic demand for the purpose of a high and stable level of activity was to develop into a universally practised and highly sophisticated art, nor the extent to which monetary as well as fiscal policy was to be employed in its service. The relationship, therefore, between not only the objectives but also the means of domestic economic policy and the mechanism governing the stability of the international monetary system was to be profoundly altered.

The sixties were ushered in by a return to convertibility of the currencies of most of the major trading countries and with it, greatly increased possibilities for the international movement of short-term funds. The period was also dominated by a change in the position of the United States. The traditional and large foreign trade surplus gradually disappeared and this was compensated for by increasing capital inflows. The dollar greatly enhanced its position as a transaction currency, while its use as a reserve currency came under some pressure as a result of the turn-around in the US balance of payments. The underlying trend of the decade was for world trade to increase sharply under the impetus of liberalization, currency convertibility, technological advance and population increase, and with it, both capital requirements and the movement of long-term capital across international boundaries. The growth of the multi-national corporation was both a product and a cause of these developments. Its spread created a new surge in the volume of direct investment. Portfolio investment, too, despite remaining restrictions, found ways of increasing to a vast extent, thus enabling many to participate in the greatly enhanced level of activity mirrored—though sometimes grossly distorted—in the general upward trend of equity values.

The growing use of the dollar for financing international transactions, against the background of currency convertibility and the emerging United States balances of payments deficits, also led, as already stated, to a sharp increase in the volume of short-term money flows. The consequences of the great increase in long- and in short-term capital flows were twofold. It led to the creation of new markets for the accommodation of supply and demand, the Euro-bond and the Euro-currency markets, and it made even more remote and indirect than it had been before, on the one hand the relation between trade flows and long-term capital flows, and, on the other hand, that between the normal means of the domestic adjustment process and the requirements of international balance. While this phenomenon has become particularly marked most recently, it is not a new one. Throughout the sixties, we find examples of countries being in imbalance on their international payments not only because of changes (positive or negative) in their international competitive position—to which the traditional domestic demand management remedies would be applicable—but also because of long-term capital movements having strong, historical or institutional origins, but no longer thought appropriate and, therefore, subjected to control; and, finally, also due to short-term flows caused by confidence factors, superimposed on more basic deficiencies, or brought about either by short-term inequalities in the trade-cycle position of different countries, or, indeed, provoked by monetary policy measures imposed as part of the programme of demand management itself.

A future historian of the decade will find many curiosities to wonder over. The ups and downs of the United Kingdom, of France and of Italy are among them. But so also are the changing positions of the United States, Germany and Japan. In none of them are the main factors such as the domestic economic situation, the fundamental position in regard to international competitiveness, or the measures taken either in the area of domestic credit policy—with their marked effect on short-money flows—or in regard to the control of inward and outward long-term capital movements, always easy to relate to each other. Above all, I think a review of those years should have the effect, once again, of instilling in one a proper sense of caution not to regard as a lasting feature any individual country's position in the 'league table' of stability-performance in the balance of payments, and therefore to eschew solutions which are implicitly based on the assumption that such positions will continue for a long time.

THE EURO-BOND MARKET

At this point, I propose to describe the salient features of the two markets that have developed in the last ten years or so to organize the flows of long- and short-term capital to which I have referred, before going on to examine the most recent activities in them, particularly in the short-term market, which have given rise to a certain amount of concern. First, then, the long-term capital market. Until the last war, there were only two large capital markets for international borrowing: London and New York, to which might be added Switzerland as a more modest one, though with a decided tendency to grow after the war. For obvious reasons, London, though possessing the traditional skills and institutions, could not, after the war, provide funds for foreign lending out of domestic capital formation. After the balance of payments crisis of 1964, impediments to both direct and portfolio investment by British investors other than in the Sterling Area were increased, and even the last named became subject to control. Continental capital markets which, even before the war, had not played the same role that London and New York had done, remained, again for obvious reasons, mostly closed to non-resident borrowers. New York, therefore, remained after the war as the only really large market for foreign governments, international institutions or foreign corporate borrowers, as well as the main outlet for international, i.e. non-US originated investment funds. These funds, including European funds, available for international investment were considerable, and, even in the first few years of the sixties, attempts were made to mobilize them for international issues arranged in Europe rather than in New York. But the total of such issues remained very small, amounting to only about $150 million per annum on the average, until 1963. That year saw the beginning of a series of policy changes in the United States resulting from her worsening balance of payments situation, which cumulatively had a profound influence on the development of the international capital market. In July of that year, President Kennedy, noting an increasing outflow of long-term capital (from $850 million in 1960 to an annual rate of nearly twice that in 1963), introduced the Interest Equalization Tax. This was followed later by a Voluntary Balance of Payments Programme designed to discourage these outflows, and later still by a mandatory programme designed to restrict them severely.

As a result of these measures, the development of an alternative market for bringing together the large and still growing volume of international funds seeking long-term investment and borrowers seeking capital proceeded swiftly. The fact that this market has to a very large extent been centred in London is easily explained, first by the fact that the traditional skills of London's merchant banking houses, supplemented by a number of American investment banks which established themselves in London, were available to take advantage quickly of the new opportunities; and secondly by the helpful action of the Authorities, for example in halving stamp duty and, above all, in allowing once again the issue of bearer bonds.

In the last eight years, while the market has undergone a number of changes and fluctuations, it has, on the whole, shown considerable growth. From a total volume of $164 million in 1963 it grew to the remarkable total of over $3,000 million in 1968, the peak year. After that it declined somewhat to approximately $2,500 million per annum in the next two years. During the first seven months of this year, it has already reached over $2,100 million, the total over the whole period being $15½ billion. These figures relate to internationally syndicated issues only, and do not include foreign bonds in the narrow sense. Within these totals, there have been interesting developments regarding the type of bonds issued, the denominations in which they are issued, and the types of borrowers. As regards the types of bonds, the two main classes have been straight and convertible bonds, and the proportion between them, not surprisingly, reflects the changing fortunes of stock markets, in particular Wall Street. Thus, the volume of convertible Euro-dollar bond issues rose from $227 million in 1967 to $1,735 million in 1968, to drop back again to less than half that figure in 1969, and to $189 million only in 1970, with slightly less than that figure so far in 1971.

Another, somewhat different aspect might be mentioned to illustrate again the variety of this market, namely the experiment made with floating rate bonds, i.e. bonds in which the rate of interest varies every six months, being linked by a fixed margin to the inter-bank six-month lending rate in the Euro-currency market. These bonds, of which there have not been many, have not unnaturally been regarded primarily as banking instruments, of interest to the banking community, and their maturity has tended to be considerably less than that of long-term bonds. Unless interest rates were to drop to levels which now seem highly unlikely, it is probable that these maturities will remain limited to seven years or so and thus form a type of borrowing in between the medium-term bank credit and the long-term bond proper.

An interesting feature of the long-term market has been the fluctuation in the currency in which the bonds have been denominated, reflecting changing views concerning the strength of different currencies. At first, they tended to be almost exclusively dollar bonds, though already in 1963 some were in European Units of Account, which remained a small but fairly steady denomination right through the period, to be joined in 1970 by a small volume of issues in European Currency Units. There have also been at times issues denominated in two currencies, e.g. sterling and Deutsche Marks, allowing the investor a certain option in regard to subscription, payment of interest and repayment of principal. I need not go into the technical intricacies of these various multi-currency formulae, which have also been employed in medium-term bank credits. The important thing to note about them is not only that they are a vivid demonstration of the liveliness of the market and a tribute to the inventiveness of the financial institutions operating in it, but also that they have been devised as means for overcoming investors' hesitation, stemming from uncertainty about potential exchange parity changes. The formulae are complicated and provide varying degrees of assurance to the investor while carrying different degrees of risk for the borrower. It would, however, not be extravagant to see in them, limited though their use has been, proof that the market is often ahead of the regulatory authorities in creating its own safeguards in circumstances in which otherwise the whole capital-raising activity might have to be severely curtailed, to the disadvantage of lender and borrower alike.

Thus the flexibility and adaptability of the market has shown itself primarily in its change from time to time in the choice of currency in which a loan has been contracted. While the dollar has through-out remained the most important currency, for reasons which have already been touched upon, other currencies have been used from time to time. Already in 1964, Deutsche Mark issued accounted for just under 40 per cent of the amount raised in dollars. In 1965 the proportion was 50 per cent, but it fell off in the following two years. By 1968 it was back to one-third of the dollar amount; in 1969 it rose to about 65 per cent (or 40 per cent of all issues) to fall back to about one-third in 1970 and to the same proportion so far this year. To these must be added in the last year or so, some, though much smaller amounts denominated in Dutch guilders.

In judging these developments, a number of separate, sometimes contrary, factors must be borne in mind. The surge of issuing activity in Deutsche Marks was, of course, largely the result of the rapid rise in German reserves, itself a consequence of the weakness of the dollar, before revaluation in 1969. This led the German authorities to encourage the export of capital and this coincided with the desire of many investors to find securities denominated in 'hard' currencies. On the other hand, the German authorities maintained a careful supervision of the volume of all borrowings organized on behalf of foreigners in Deutsche Marks. A committee formed of the principal issuing banks with close contact with the Bundesbank, operates a queue system which determines the issues—foreign and domestic—to be authorized each month, and this has operated and continues to operate most effectively. It is conceivable that, without this control, the volume of Deutsche Mark issues would have risen from time to time to much higher levels in response to the desire of borrowers for funds which could only be obtained in terms of a 'hard' currency obligation, though it is reasonable to suppose that the market would then have been subject to the fluctuations, to the occasional periods of indigestion, to be cured by fasting, which the dollar market has experienced. At the same time, it is noteworthy that once the Deutsche Mark was revalued in November 1969 there was considerable selling pressure on these bonds, thus demonstrating that they were in part used as a safe haven for hot money which could not be placed short-term owing to the German Authorities' regulations designed to discourage short-term inflows.

The advantages of this relatively new, yet already substantial and highly developed market are not far to seek. As far as borrowers are concerned, their variety is itself a testimony to the services which the market is rendering. The most cursory glance at the list is illuminating. It includes Governments, Municipalities, Governmental agencies such as public utilities, international organizations and corporations which are household names all over the world. Many little-known, smaller corporations, particularly in new industries, engaged in advanced technology, have also been enabled to secure long-term capital resources through this market and, in the process, have become more widely known internationally, while themselves becoming acquainted with the international financial community. Many purposes have been served by the capital raised in this way and it is no exaggeration to say that much new development from international highways, pipelines and North Sea exploration to international joint ventures and mergers, might, at the least, have been more difficult to accomplish if it had not been possible to make use of the facilities of this market.

As for the investor, the service to him is less easy to demonstrate, since the identity of those who buy these bonds is not readily discoverable. Unlike domestic public issues, these internationally syndicated ones are sold (or placed) by a selling group of banks, including (but not exclusively) the underwriters of the issue. Institutional investors in many countries cannot subscribe to issues denominated in currencies other than their own. Nevertheless, many internationally operated unit trusts and investment funds have invested in these bonds in recent years, as have certain international insurance companies in respect of their 'free' funds and the pension funds of large international companies. However, the bulk of the investors are private individuals; and it is widely thought that this gives to these bonds generally a much greater stability of holding and less sensitivity to relative interest rates and currency uncertainties than is, naturally, displayed by the banks or international companies that operate in the short-term market. What seems clear is that the Euro-bond market has managed to tap resources of investors in various parts of the world which might otherwise well have stayed in the short-term pool and not only remained unavailable to those in need of long-term capital but also added to the volume of potential short-term flows.

More generally, it can be said that the market has reached a certain maturity which justifies one in saying that it has added an important new dimension to the international financial mechanism. It is clearly a far cry from the earlier movements of capital of the nineteenth and early twentieth centuries, when the link between trade flows was still strong and when not only direct export and import movements but also traditional commercial and marketing patterns, no less than political and linguistic ties as well as the concentration of financial skills, largely determined the character and direction of these movements. The Euro-bond market represents a more perfect market in the economic sense, in that the motive forces behind supply and demand are now wholly generalized; it is a market in which where capital is needed and where capital can be got are the decisive factors.

This, of course, is not the whole story; and the emergence of such a market—in pure culture, one might say—serves to highlight some of the problems to which the movement of capital, internationally, gives rise. In the first place, the new issue market itself, despite its great flexibility, has shown moments of disturbance. While the issue of bonds denominated in Deutsche Marks is, as we have seen, under careful supervision which has worked extremely well, as have the much smaller, but equally supervised markets in Swiss francs and Dutch guilders, the dollar-denominated market is completely uncontrolled; and it is this market which has on a number of occasions in recent years shown itself to be extremely sensitive to pressure from potential borrowers who rushed in only to find the market evaporate as the result of mistaken judgment concerning interest rates, availability of funds or the investor's reaction to currency uncertainties. This sort of problem could be resolved, or at least greatly alleviated, by the institution of a measure of self-regulation, as suggested by Sir Siegmund Warburg, whereby the principal issuing houses would organize a queue system similar to that operating in Germany, Switzerland and Holland, backed by the support of the central banks and stock exchanges concerned.

More difficult are the questions that have been raised by some, for example, Roosa, of the relationship between capital flows and the balance of payments problem in conditions in which these 'autonomously generated' flows take place through the intermediary of an international market. As far as nationally originating capital movements are concerned, the Authorities in all the major countries have continued to regard them (with the full support of the Fund) as proper objects of supervision in relation to national policy concerning the balance of payments. Thus the United States and Britain have maintained control on outward investment, and Japan has operated a queue system for Japanese borrowers wishing to tap foreign capital markets. These measures are taken alongside various domestic policy measures in the interest of curing a surplus or a deficit of the balance of payments. But in the present state of our knowledge it is by no means clear what their actual effect is, particularly whether, in imposing impediments to long-term flows, resort to medium- and short-term markets by both borrowers and lenders is not encouraged and the problem thus simply shifted to a different part of the system. While much attention has been devoted recently to the problem raised by short-money flows—to which I shall turn presently—very little has been done to study the consequences of longer-term capital movements and the attempts to influence them, often in response to relatively short-term variations in the balance of payments situation, the assessment of which itself rests on an understanding of relationships between the different items and of their statistical presentation which is, as yet, by no means perfect. It may be that the growth of world liquidity, more assured through the introduction of Special Drawing Rights, will help to resolve this problem and make it less necessary to seek to influence relatively short-run balance of payment fluctuations by action on the long-term capital account. What is clear is that this subject requires much more detailed and internationally co-ordinated study than it has so far received. Meanwhile, the international capital market has provided an invaluable new piece of machinery and one may well agree with the judgment of the Bank of England that 'under more stable conditions it may reduce disparities between national markets in the demand for and supply of capital' and given that 'the international demand for long-term capital seems likely to grow rather than diminish' the market 'could ease the task of mibilizing the capital required to sustain economic progress throughout the world'.

THE EURO-CURRENCY MARKET

At this point I turn to the question which has recently been uppermost in the mind of anyone concerned with international finance, namely that of the international movement of short-term funds. This, again, is no new problem, for 'hot-money' flows have been known and much debated in the inter-war years, as well as in the earlier post-war period. What has happened is that the volume of funds now capable of rapid movement has vastly increased. This, incidentally, is exactly the phrase used by Keynes when, over forty years ago, he spoke of the difficulties created by movements in the 'short-loan' fund as he called it, and which he estimated to be at the end of 1929,

£1,000 million, a figure which may seem less than terrifying by comparison with the Euro-currency market (if, *pace* Professor Machlup, I may still so call it for convenience) now estimated at about $60 billion.

So much has recently been written about this market (or perhaps one should say banking system) that it will be sufficient for our purpose to recall only a few of its salient aspects—some accepted, some still highly contentious. I would like, however, at the outset, to stress again some general points to which I have had occasion to refer before. First, we must never lose sight of the fact that the phenomenon of short-money flows is not new. What I have just quoted from Keynes is part of a lengthy analysis of short-term flows due to the existence of a highly mobile international short-loan fund which occupies many pages in the *Treatise on Money* and which includes, *inter alia*, an elaborate discussion of possible means for limiting these flows, in order to reduce the possibility that domestic policies might be frustrated—the very subject to which so much attention has been devoted in recent months. The second point is once again not to overlook the speed with which the situation changes. It really is not very long ago—two years at most—that the westward flow of funds was so great and sudden as to create serious fears of a renewed dollar shortage, making recent improvements in European balances of payments precarious and driving up interest rates in Europe to great heights even where domestic policy made this inappropriate. There were many then in Europe who urged the United States Authorities to adopt measures—which in fact they did—to stem this flow, if only in their own interest, so as not to risk having American tight-money policy frustrated. In fact, this westward flow, that is, the liabilities of US banks' head offices to their branches, rose in 1969 from $6 billion to $15 billion, only to fall back to less than $6 billion by April of this year, at which point the eastward flow greatly accelerated still further for a variety of reasons, to which I will refer later. It is clear that any consideration of the operation of the Euro-currency market and its relation to the speed and mutability of short-term flows cannot be separated from a whole complex of other considerations, including the domestic stabilization policy-mix in different countries (with its effect on interest rates) as well as on the relation between domestic policy and balances of payments. It is, therefore, highly unwise to jump to conclusions as regards the causes of the observed movements.

As regards the market itself, it is clear that a good deal of further study—based on more abundant and carefully analysed statistical material—is needed before we can hope to know as much about it as we do about the operation of a domestic banking system. Professor Machlup last year sketched out the framework of concepts and theory which would need to be filled out for this purpose. Until this has been done, I would think it rash to deal with the problems of the Euro-currency market too readily by analogies drawn from domestic banking operations. This applies particularly to the vexed question of the extent to which this system is as capable, or perhaps even more capable, as a domestic banking system to create credit, since legal requirements or traditional practices that control the relation between reserves and liabilities domestically are here absent. It may well be that this capacity is considerable; Governor Carli has lent his very great authority in support of this view. But what is perhaps more immediately important, but at least as difficult to discover with certainty, is the extent to which this capacity has actually been utilized; that is, how far the existence of this mass of funds has added to the total world supply of credit. There is a presumption that it has, though there must be doubt as to how significant this has been in relation to the total. Above all, as Milton Gilbert has done well to remind us recently, the effect on total credit supply to non-bank borrowers will depend very largely on the direction of the short-term flows rather than on the total size of outstanding deposit liabilities denominated in foreign currencies as reported by the Bank for International Settlements or, for London, by the Bank of England. The westward flow in 1969 probably tightened credit more outside the USA than it eased it inside; while the recent eastward flow seems to have had the opposite effect, i.e. of easing credit more outside the USA than it contracted it inside.

Another feature which has been much discussed in connection with the size of the total market and its credit-creation capacity, has been the placing in the market of balances by Central Banks and the Bank for International Settlements (BIS). While this is substantial, though not overwhelming in relation to the total—Gilbert has estimated it earlier this year at $10 billion out of $60 billion, of which one-third was from the BIS, and the Central Banks of Switzerland, and the other countries of the Group of Ten—it is probably more significant that it has more than trebled in twelve months, as against an increase in the total volume from $44 billion to $60 billion. There are perfectly good explanations for this development: apart from the general growth of world reserves,which would create a predisposition for these placements to rise, the same relative interest rate movements which caused an eastward flow also shifted the relative attractiveness of holding these balances in the Euro-market rather than in the United States.

What, however, this increase in official placements has done is to intensify interest in the question whether the market should be controlled, while, at the same time, appearing to offer at least one means of doing so, namely restriction of these official placements. What is undoubtedly the case is that the flows of recent years and months would have taken place even if the Euro-currency market had not been in existence. Fundamentally, these flows are not different in kind from earlier ones, particularly those in the inter-war years. One can, however, assert that, as a result of certain institutional changes, the ease with which these flows take place has been much improved and the speed of response to the underlying factors and, therefore, of the changes of direction have been much accelerated. Among these changes must be listed the greater spread of the international establishments and activities of banks, including particularly of American banks in the London market, and the much more considerable funds which corporations, particularly larger, multi-national ones, now have to manage. Altogether the greatly enhanced alertness now demanded of those who have large funds of money to manage, be they of pension funds, of investment trusts, or of the disposable funds of international companies, has been responsible not only for the enormous increase in the international short-loan fund of which Keynes spoke, but has also caused operations in it to have become the concern of many more, and more diversified, interests than in the past.

Nevertheless, the factors that influence their activities have remained fundamentally the same. The reason for short-money flows are, as they have always been, relative rates of return as between long-, medium- and short-term employment, as well as between these relative returns in different centres, together with the relative security of these funds in the different placements. Under the heading of security must be included factors that denote not only that of outright political risk, but also the possibility of the imposition of restrictions on the movement of funds, i.e. exchange control and the risk of changes in exchange rates. In a well functioning market, all these various elements should be compounded in two rates, the rate of interest and the forward exchange rate. The Euro-currency market has organized transactions of this kind in a more perfect manner (in the economic sense of the word) than had ever been done before. It can truly be regarded as the best organized market of any in existence today, exhibiting all the textbook characteristics demanded of one. It has had the effect of combining and integrating all the major money markets of the world and making their reactions to each other's movements virtually instantaneous.

It is at this point that the problem of the relationship between the needs of domestic policy and the response to international movements once again arises. Under the gold standard system this problem was automatically resolved, so long as the rules of the game were observed, in favour of the requirements of the international monetary system. The gold points acted as the triggers which caused inflows and outflows of precious metal, i.e. expansion or contraction of the domestic credit base; and the central banks responded immediately by an expansion or contraction of the volume of credit. This simple mechanism had become suspect already in the circumstances of the inter-war years, if only because of the improbability of different countries finding themselves at the appropriate relative position in the business cycle and, therefore, at just the right point to suffer an externally imposed credit expansion or contraction. The increased responsibility of government for the level of economic activity, now universally accepted, has made for increased awareness of this problem and, therefore, greater sensitivity to the irksomeness of being exposed to 'dictates' from outside which may seem to run completely counter to what are judged to be the proper domestic policies. Thus, in one period the credit base, in so far as it is affected by conditions in the Euro-currency market, may be sharply contracted because American banks are drawing in funds from this source, while, at other times, European monetary authorities may find their reserves suddenly and substantially swollen, though their judgment of their own situation makes expansion of credit the opposite of what is needed.

It is not surprising, in these circumstances, that more and more thought should have been given to the measures that might be used to avoid these undesirable effects. Generally, this has taken the form of asking whether, and by what means, the Euro-currency market should be 'controlled'; or, as the question might be more appropriately phrased, as to whether it was desirable and feasible to diminish these flows and/or to offset their effects on the domestic situation where this seemed called for. In one sense it is surprising that this question should occupy the centre of attention. It is not long since it was believed that increasing freedom of international capital flows was likely to facilitate the balancing of international payments, i.e. that such flows would generally be equilibrating. There are two reasons for the change in attitude: first, that the maintenance of exchange rate parities is no longer regarded as a fixed datum to the extent to which it used to be when post-war convertibility was first achieved; second, that a coincidence of economic cycles and of domestic rates of inflation and deflation in different countries is recognized as much more improbable than it seemed at one time. When to these are added the further facts: first, that countries differ (and that there are also sharp differences within countries) on the proper policy mix for domestic stabilization, in particular what importance is to be attached to monetary policy; second, that the significance of the impact of capital flows on the domestic credit volume or their relation to the other items of the balance of payments varies from country to country; and third, that the short-term flows have become very large indeed, one can readily see why the earlier hopes have proved vain.

Before I examine the arguments for and against intervention of one kind or another into these capital flows, there is one somewhat different aspect of the existence of a Euro-currency market which needs to be looked at. It is not strictly relevant to the questions with which we are concerned here, but it has been discussed in recent months in connection with various suggestions for controlling the market; that is the problem of how far the Euro-currency market has encouraged departure from traditional banking standards in regard to the requirements both of liquidity and of proper criteria of creditworthiness of borrowers. As to the second of these, factual information is, for obvious reasons, not easy to come by. While there have been some disagreeable experiences, the number of spectacular failures has so far been limited. Nevertheless, many people of very great experience in these matters are apprehensive because of the extremely rapid increase in the volume of transactions in this market, of the great multiplicity and variety of ultimate borrowers, and of the greatly increased number of intermediaries whose experience in this field may be inadequate, particularly as ability to establish the precise creditworthiness of the borrower may in any case be less than is desirable. It is sometimes thought that the rapid spread of new, and expensive to maintain, branch offices may lead to so aggressive a pursuit of new business as to impair the care that should normally be exercised in these matters. As I say, it is extremely difficult, if not impossible, to establish the facts. But, in any event, even if all the fears are justified, it is hard to see how they can be translated into arguments for control, in addition to those which, as we shall see, are often adduced in the interests of national policy. Even if measures of supervision could be devised, the purpose of which would be to underpin the skill and judgement which experience, including bad experience, should provide, these would be even more difficult to apply in an internationally harmonious manner than those designed for wider policy objectives.

As regards the question of liquidity, as the Governor of the Bank of England has pointed out in a speech earlier this year, the analogy of domestic banking and of the role of a 'lender of last resort' must not be taken too far. The dangers to liquidity (apart from that which arises from the failure of a non-bank borrower and its possible chain reactions) are related to the degree of matching of maturities of liabilities and assets. Here, the position of non-dollar (or non-Deutsche Marks) banks may be somewhat different from those whose normal, domestic transactions are in these currencies; and more careful practice in regard to mismatching (which in the absence of standby facilities, depends for its success on the unfettered continuance of the Euro-currency market) may, therefore, be in order. The Bank of England, as is well known, maintains a periodic survey in this regard as far as the London market is concerned. But here again, it is hard to see how 'control' could improve the position: indeed the possibility of restriction could, precisely for the reason just given, quickly have a highly inhibiting effect on transactions and lead to a rapid shrinking of what is still widely regarded as a most advantageous development on the international financial scene.

CONTROLLING SHORT-TERM CAPITAL FLOWS

In order to analyse effectively the arguments for controlling short-term capital flows in the interest of wider policy objectives, I propose to ask, first, to what extent the fear of inappropriate influences arising from these flows on domestic policy is real, or, put in another way, what are the limits of tolerance for these inflows and outflows. In the first place, it is perhaps worth reminding oneself that there is by no means always a clear correlation between the state of the domestic economic balance and capital flows. The latter may be provoked by factors unrelated, or only distantly related, to the basic international competitive position of a country. Furthermore, the existing machinery in a country for stabilizing inflows or compensating for outflows may be more or less effective. Thus the argument that inflation is exported or imported by means of short-term capital movements, requires a good deal of qualification. Not many, I imagine, would argue that the inflation from which Britain is still suffering has been induced by the inflow of reserves during the last twelve months or so, or that the outflow of funds from the United States during the same period has significantly diminished inflationary pressures. The correlation depends clearly on exactly what the domestic situation is, in particular, if it is inflationary, whether the inflation is one of demand-pull or of cost-push; and in the second place, on what measures the Authorities can and have taken to reduce the effect of capital inflows and outflows on domestic credit policy.

Quite another question is the extent to which the Central Bank is prepared to see its reserves diminished or swollen as a result of short-term flows, regardless of whether and in what way this may, or need, affect its domestic policy. In the past this question has usually appeared most acute in the case of a country losing reserves. As Keynes put it, the problem 'is likely to prove more severe and intractable in the case of a debtor nation than in the case of a creditor nation because it is easier to lend less in an emergency than to borrow more'. Though, more generally, it has long been recognized that the correction of short-money flows, even where it is closely related to an underlying payments imbalance requiring correction, is not easy—the high mobility of international lending contrasting sharply with the low mobility of international trade in the short term—while it may be inappropriate where this close relation does not exist. More recently, the problem has appeared more acute from the point of view of the country gaining reserves through a heavy inflow of funds. The problem then becomes one of the willingness to accumulate a certain reserve asset. At the present time this question is inevitably linked with the role of the dollar and cannot be further pursued without at least some reference to this problem. To clear the ground, let us for a moment leave out of account the position of the US balance of payments, the question of how far its persistent deficit has been responsible for the greatly increased volume of international capital movements and for the doubts that have arisen regarding the dollar's continued fitness to serve as the key currency and, therefore, as an asset which creditor countries would be willing to hold in unlimited quantity as once they were willing to hold gold. We will revert to these questions after we have looked further at the alleged responsibility of the Euro-currency market for frustrating domestic policy, in particular, for 'exporting inflation', as well as the various means which have been proposed for controlling the market.

First of all, it should be clear that it is wrong to look at the Euro-currency market rather than at the forces that determine the volume and direction of flows through it. It is as if one looked at a conduit pipe rather than at the alternating pumps that determine the flows through it. We have already looked at the forces that are responsible for these flows: interest rate differentials (and the policy decisions that influence these) together with expectations regarding exchange rates. We have seen that we cannot assume that the relation of foreign borrowing and lending to the management of the total volume of credit is the same in all the major countries concerned, nor can we assume that each country will always be in an appropriate relationship to the others as regards the economic cycle so that inflows and outflows will be responses to the needs of expanding or contracting the credit base. Nor can we assume, *pace* the monetarists, that the role of credit policy is the decisive one in this process, nor, even if it were, that it would be so regarded in each country. The reality is, of course, very different. It would be a bold man indeed who undertook to quantify precisely the degrees by which the rates of inflation in say, the United States, Germany, Britain and France had differed at any one moment of time during the last twelve months, or the shares of difference of the origins of these respective inflations, or the weight of the different elements in the economic policy mix in each of them; and who would derive precise guidance from such an analysis for what should be the proper levels of interest rates in each of these markets (as well as their relations to rates in the Euro-currency market) and, finally, for the extent to which short-term money flows should have been acceptable.

Simply to enumerate these various factors is enough to demonstrate the formidable task that awaits anyone who wishes to impose controls on short-term flows that would in some way harmonize the diverse policies that various monetary authorities follow which, even if their objectives are fundamentally the same, namely economic stabilization, may be based on quite different appreciations of the various factors that I have listed, even if one ignored the intrusion of different political pressures. Thus, as I have said before, it is not possible to achieve clarity regarding the problem of short-money flows, let alone agreement on policy, without some clarification of the domestic policy mix, that is, on the emphasis to be placed on fiscal as against monetary policy or indeed other measures of economic stabilization such as incomes policy, a subject on which opinion both academic and governmental is still in a considerable state of flux.

There are various ways that may be used for dealing with disturbing capital flows. First, there are measures to offset in the domestic economy the capital flows that give rise to major reserve changes; second, there are those that would prevent reserve movements by the use of official borrowing or lending operations; and third, there are ways of influencing the private short flows themselves by varying the incentives that give rise to them. It is the third group of measures that has most actively been discussed recently, and various devices have in fact been tried in one country or another from time to time. These include banking regulations relating to net position *vis-à-vis* non-residents regardless of currency, or in foreign currency *vis-à-vis* residents and non-residents alike and combinations of these. Maxima and minima may be set; or reserve requirements may be imposed which may be different for domestic liabilities than for those to non-residents. Interest rates may be set at differential levels for foreign depositors; non-banks may also be subjected to regulations which would generally have to be on the transactions themselves, and would, therefore, make it practically inevitable that it should be based on a comprehensive exchange control embracing current as well as capital transactions. Finally, there are various fiscal measures that can be adopted to change the relative incentives for capital flows. All this, apart from analytical questions, raises formidable difficulties, particularly where control of intermediaries, i.e. banks, are concerned which can usually find a non-controlled 'haven' from which to operate.

There is also the possibility that the use of monetary policy, in particular interest rate policy, might be directed more to international, rather than national policy objectives, leaving fiscal policy to take the burden of the latter, a point of view that has been urged by some economists, in particular by Professor Mundell; but the fiscal instrument is seldom sufficiently flexible. No clear conclusion for or against control of the Euro-currency market is possible now, in my opinion, but no one can help but be impressed both with the difficulty of applying the various measures and with their limited effectiveness when applied. I, for one, remain highly sceptical and I agree with the view of Sir Leslie O'Brien that 'the danger of concentrating attention of the Euro-currency market is precisely that it distracts attention from the real causes of international maladjustment'. Without by any means eschewing short-term measures to offset some of the disturbing effects of these flows, it is on these real causes that I believe attention must continue to be kept.

There is, however, one other area that must be examined since, as we have seen, capital flows are also influenced by expectations regarding exchange rates, while, at the same time, the attitudes to them of central banks are determined not only by their real or supposed disturbing effects on domestic economic management, but also by the central banks' willingness to hold certain reserve assets. At the present time, as I have said, this means dollars. Indeed, while interest rate differentials can usually be regarded as the main initiating cause of capital flows, they have often quickly had superimposed on them exchange rate uncertainties; and these have then become the main force maintaining or even accelerating the money flows.

The problem of the US balance of payment deficit, of the dollar as a key currency, and of central banks' willingness to accumulate dollar balances, has been a feature of the international financial situation for nearly a decade. Its specific linking with the problem of short-term money flows (and, not altogether relevantly, with the Euro-currency market) is, however, rather more recent. As a result, discussion of the role of the dollar and of the US balance of payments has once again been clouded by emotion, as it has on one or two other occasions in recent years. But that is the one thing it should not be. It is not easy, but essential, to consider the matter dispassionately and in perspective. While I think the phrase 'benign neglect' which has been suggested as the watchword for a US balance of payments policy is unfortunate (and even the less emotive 'passive policy' is ill-chosen), I would myself regret even more a policy of 'hysterical anxiety'. The facts, though clouded by changing statistical presentations, are not particularly obscure. The United States has had a varying deficit on her balance of payments for several years. While in recent months, some concern has arisen over the trade balance, in general the US deficit on the 'official settlements' basis has been relatively moderate in recent years and has indeed shown surpluses in 1968 and 1969. The basic deficit which is, no doubt, a better measure of long-term overall performance has been fairly persistent and considerable for most years since the mid-fifties, but the reasons for this state of affairs and, in particular, how far it amounts to a 'fundamental disequilibrium' in the sense of the Articles of the

International Monetary Fund, require careful analysis. Leaving aside aid programmes and military expenditures, the main causes of the basic deficit are to be found in a shrinking of the technology gap to America's disadvantage and in massive outward long-term capital flows, until the mid-sixties at any rate. On the other hand, differential rates of inflation are by no means a proven source of the deficit: indeed, when measured by price movements, the United States enjoyed more prolonged phases of stability during this period than many of her competitors. It is, therefore, very doubtful whether the longer-term imbalance in America's international payments was by itself sufficient to cause questions about any 'overvaluation' of the dollar even though the dollar may not have fully met the four conditions for a smoothly functioning key currency which Wilfried Guth has recently referred to. Indeed, it is widely acknowledged that the US deficit has had some beneficial results in enabling many other countries to rebuild their reserves and, thus, in general to have acted as a source for supplementing world liquidity before the introduction of the Special Drawing Rights.

In this connection one must also remember that, if on a number of occasions in recent years the United States had attempted to correct its balance of payments deficit either by the restrictionist means to which some other countries have had recourse or by a more drastic domestic deflationary policy designed radically to improve her international competitive position, it is far from certain that this would have been welcomed by those who have been most emphatic in their strictures on America's balance of payments performance.

More recently, as Dr. Burns and Mr. Volcker have pointed out, there has been superimposed on the more lasting deficit, a sharp fluctuation as regards short-term capital transactions. These, rather than the underlying balance of payments deficit itself, have been responsible for triggering off the recent disturbances and doubts.

It remains important, nevertheless, that the United States should tackle, and be seen to tackle, the underlying deficit, though, if I have understood the advocates of a so-called passive policy right, I would not disagree with the view that, provided means are found for avoiding excessive short-term flows or at least their self-perpetuating enlargement, improvement of the underlying deficit should be a by-product of the right domestic policy. It is clearly essential for the economic health of her trading partners no less than for her own, that the United States should, as soon as possible, achieve much higher levels of economic activity with a substantial reduction of inflationary pressures, by whatever changed mixture of old policies or the adoption of new ones, such as in the field of prices and incomes, this can be brought about. How soon such a development would be reflected in an improvement in the underlying balance of payments cannot easily be predicted, but to the extent that it was it would deprive the short-term flows of one possible source of encouragement; and it is reasonable to predict that success on the domestic front would soon, even by itself, dispel the doubts that have nourished the massive money flows of recent months. It is also desirable that world liquidity should no longer have to rely to the same extent as hitherto on the American deficit but be consciously and increasingly based on the use of SDRs with a view to encouraging continued progress towards the emergence of a single, universally acceptable and internationally controlled reserve asset.

But it must yet again be emphasized that restoration of a better balance in America's international payments would not completely remove the risk of short-term capital flows going too fast and too far for the stability of the system, as Dr. Burns has said. If we rule out, as I have done, as neither desirable nor feasible, some general, overall 'control' of the Euro-currency market, then we must look for other means of removing that risk. Some have already been tried. Certain unilateral moves in the field of banking regulations such as those employed in the United States have helped, so long as the flows did not reach flood proportions due to the operation of the confidence factor. Similarly, the imposition of certain restrictions on foreign borrowing by the Bank of England may have moderated the flows somewhat. Certain debt management operations by the United States Treasury, and special issues by the Treasury and the Export-Import Bank designed to 'mop-up' funds have probably also reduced the total volume in the market, as has the decision by the BIS not to place any further funds with it.

But, in essence, these measures are, at best, palliatives. Even in the relatively well-understood area of interest rate differentials which are the basic cause of international movements, they cannot hope to overcome the sharp fluctuations that are due to divergent national policies. There are two equally difficult sets of problems on which further progress will be necessary before one can hope to see much prospect of improvement. In the first place, there will need to be much greater agreement than there is today on the role which interest rate policy should play in domestic economic management as compared with its part in the stabilization of the international monetary system. I have already touched upon this issue at a number of points, and there is nothing else that I would add except that I welcome the signs which I detect of greater readiness in a number of countries to make more use of prices and incomes policy, in the present conditions of cost-push inflation. I hope that those who have been sceptical in the past will not hesitate to change their minds for fear of inconsistency. As Alvin Hansen said, 'A man may wear an overcoat in winter and a straw hat in summer without being charged with inconsistency.'

The second question is that of the international harmonization of interest rates, to which a solution of the first problem could make an important contribution. Attempts made hitherto in this direction, apart from routine and unpublicized central bank consultation, have not been notably successful. I confess to some doubt whether much more can be done in the absence of progress, first, on the question of exchange rates (of which more in a moment) and, second, on the subsequent and much wider question of the evolution of the international system towards a World Central Bank.

As I have said, while interest rate differentials are usually the predisposing cause of short-term money flows, they would normally tend to be self-correcting, unless they are strongly combined with, or followed by, uncertainty regarding exchange rates. For this then leads to movements which are totally unmanageable by normal means, because they are the result of a crisis of confidence. When such movements occur, and in particular when they affect the relations between the key currency, the dollar, and the rest, as they have done since May of this year, the whole of the international monetary system is thrown into disorder and short-term money flows are seen as the outward signs, rather than as the causes of maladjustment. Attention then turns, as it has again in recent weeks, to exchange rate policy, both as a means to overcome a temporary crisis, as well as to make the system more lastingly sound. Naturally, all the old debates concerning the dollar and the official price of gold are revived in a specially acute form and I do not propose to enter into these now, having made my own position clear on many earlier occasions. Similarly, the advocates of a completely flexible system of exchange rates have professed to derive considerable support from recent events. This is not the time or place to go into this question. I cannot, however, refrain from saying that I find it hard to follow those who say that the exchange rate is 'a price like any other' and should therefore be left to 'find its own level'. Even if the dollar were to be excluded from this principle (though I do not quite see the logic of this), I doubt whether the prices of sterling, the yen or the Luxembourg franc are really no different in kind from the prices of a packet of cigarettes, a bushel of wheat or an oil refinery.

There are various devices, however, that might be used, ranging from forward exchange rate intervention, through dual exchange rates for current and capital transactions (the latter too often wrongly identified with 'speculative' ones), to greater exchange rate flexibility within wider margins.

Of these, the second and third have been most frequently considered in recent months. They differ from each other substantially, in that one involves control, while the other does not. Controls will tend to be uneven in their incidence and unnecessarily hampering to individual transactions. There is, basically, the conceptual difficulty of distinguishing capital and current transactions except on a basis which is arbitrary and which such experience as there is has shown would in practice mean that control would quickly involve some current transactions as well. Even if one ignored the intellectual and practical difficulties of segregating these payments, experience has also shown that a system based on such segregation will work only so long as the discrepancy between the two rates of exchange remains small. As soon as it becomes substantial for any length of time, the problem of evasion becomes troublesome and efforts to deal with it would quickly lead to more and more extensive exchange control.

The use of wider bands of exchange rate fluctuations around parity is not based on any attempt to classify transactions. I leave out of account here the argument that is advanced in favour of this device, namely that the possibility of wider fluctuations would assist to produce a more smoothly functioning balance of payments/domestic adjustment process mechanism; and furthermore that, because it would accustom everyone to the possibility of greater swings than hitherto, it would make changes of parities less 'political' and, therefore, traumatic. For our purpose, the advantage claimed for wider bands is that they tend to make expectations of further exchange rate changes in one direction weaker, the more the rate actually moves in that direction. This will have an equilibrating effect on short-term capital movements. It is not entirely clear why this should be so, and the experience in this regard from floating exchange rates is not, perhaps, entirely relevant; but it may be that, provided the whole system of exchange rate parities is generally regarded as reasonably stable for a considerable time ahead, the greater freedom of manoeuvre of the Authorities in adjusting their intervention policy will encourage the equilibrating tendencies in capital flows rather than their escalation. The proviso is, however, extremely important; and there is the further point that it is not *a priori* clear how wide the margins should be to produce this beneficial effect. Announced margins should not be wider than those the Authorities intend, in fact, to enforce, nor should they be too narrow for the equilibrating tendencies to assert themselves.

But it should not be forgotten that greater flexibility also has disadvantages, since some of the flows themselves contain self-correcting equilibrating forces and one would not wish to discourage these by the possibility of wide exchange fluctuations. This may theoretically be less of a danger in the case of long-term capital movements than in medium- and short-term ones; but in practice, especially as the result of the great strides made in recent years in refining the operations of different markets and their interrelation, one must be prepared to see considerable disturbance created by exchange fluctuations, the net effect of which may be a general discouragement to international capital movements, desirable and undesirable ones alike. Similarly, some price in terms of discouragement to international trade itself may also be involved.

The paradox about wider bands, thus, is that they are unlikely to produce the good effects which are claimed for them unless they operate against a background of general stability of the whole system, while the greater that stability is, the less will wider bands be needed. Nevertheless, of all the specific measures suggested, moderately wider bands may be the most useful, at least in a period of transition to a better general system.

In the end, however, despite the understandable search for relatively simple, limited and quasi-automatic solutions, it is difficult to escape the conclusion that, at this stage in our economic evolution, a much more general attack on the problem of international financial stability is the crying need. As we have seen, even in the calmer days of a hundred years ago, the system was sustained by what I called an *Aequilibrium Britannicum*. The attempt, in recent decades, to underpin the Bretton Woods system by an *Aequilibrium Americanum*, while it has considerable successes to its credit, has proved inadequate essentially because, in the conditions of the world today, a broader base is required. A prerequisite for at last creating this is an atmosphere in which different views, based on national interests— whether real or illusory—are not to be equated with virtue or vice.

Of course, if divergent policies are immediately made objects of moral obloquy, progress will be non-existent. As far as being moved only by enlightened concern for the well-being of the whole system, we should assume that all countries have an unblemished record. And as far as the pursuit of sensible policies to this end is concerned, it is as well to assume that all countries live in glass houses. Unheroic though this may sound, it is unfortunately the case that nothing other than continued and more intimate international co-operation can produce the right result. Even most of those who believe in *nostra*, like universally freely floating exchange rates, will admit that for such a system to function, more rather than less international co-operation is required not only in the international field itself, but ineluctably as we have seen, in regard to domestic policy also. The lesson to be learnt from the history of the last twenty-five years is not that the Bretton Woods system has broken down, nor to indulge regrets that those primarily concerned were not ready after the war to knit the world economy more closely together. It is rather whether they are ready now.

THE TEXT WHICH FOLLOWS IS THAT PRESENTED
ORALLY BY THE AUTHOR

It gives me great pleasure indeed to be appearing here under the chairmanship of Randy Burgess. He may not recollect it, but I remember vividly the first time I met him. It was when I first came to the United States as a Rockefeller Fellow, very many years ago. I was armed with a list of introductions from Josiah Stamp, whose son I am glad to see here today. And the first of these introductions which I used was to a young but already very eminent commercial banker in the city of New York, Randolph Burgess. And since then, I have been fortunate enough for our paths to have crossed quite frequently, particularly when he and I were both in the public service.

As for the man in whose honour these lectures have been founded, I cannot claim to have known Per Jacobsson as intimately as many of those who are present here today. But it was my good fortune to see a great deal of him from time to time, and more particularly during the Marshall Plan. And I have very clear recollections of early breakfast meetings with him in his hotel in Paris, or of late-night nightcaps in Montmartre bistros. He combined in a unique fashion three great qualities—fine theoretical understanding of the international monetary mechanism fortified by keen appreciation of the practicalities of finance; warm sympathy for the problems of individual countries, but subordinated to concern for the well-being of the international commercial and financial system as a whole; and, above all, fearlessness in expressing his views.

Happily, these qualities, as vital today as at any time since the war, are once again combined in the present distinguished holder of the post of Managing Director of the International Monetary Fund, who for reasons that are well known to all of us cannot be present this afternoon, and is engaged, I hope, on much more fruitful occupations.

I spoke in my paper of my hesitation in broaching this subject. And as the distance, both in space and time, between the Oxfordshire Chilterns and the Great Hall of the International Monetary Fund has diminished, hesitation has turned into trepidation. For we are on the eve of an annual meeting of the Fund which is taking place after what must surely be accepted as the most climactic development since the Fund was created.

I have prepared an inordinately long paper for this occasion. I am fully aware of it. But knowing that it would not have to be delivered, I felt it right to provide a fairly detailed background to our discussion.

It will be evident to you, even if Randy Burgess had not told you so, that my paper was finished before the announcement by President Nixon of the August measures. Re-reading my paper, I do not feel— and I hope this is no sign of complacency—that as a result of these measures I would need to change anything that I have written. But clearly, something must now be added.

No one, I am sure, would wish for progress in human affairs, whatever they are, to be the result of sudden convulsions or of crises. Nevertheless, when these do occur, as they have, they can be useful if they enable us to distinguish, as is perhaps difficult in more tranquil times, between the essential and the inessential. They can help to clear the air.

For my part, I would hope, for example, that one result of the events of the last six weeks or so will be to remove the exclusive concern that was evident before, and against which I have argued in my paper, I hope convincingly, with the Euro-currency market as such. I hope that at least one lesson we shall learn from the present monetary disorder is that fundamental factors are at work and have therefore to be dealt with, rather than to concentrate on the surface phenomena to which these give rise.

Again, to take the same example, I have given various arguments in my paper for taking the view that so-called controls of the Euro-currency market are undesirable. Since then, the number of measures that affect the free flows of short-term funds has grown. But I remain unrepentant in thinking that, so far from making more fundamental remedies less necessary, they have had the opposite effect. A universal system, for example of dual markets, seems to me, even if it were feasible, to be highly undesirable.

This is not to say that there may not be occasions when the monetary authorities, finding themselves in an extremely difficult situation, may not need to resort to measures which restrict the freedom of short-term capital movements, measures of the kind to which I allude in my paper and which I don't propose to go over again here. But if they do, I do hope we won't fool ourselves into thinking that these are good in themselves or that they are anything but the most superficial symptomatic therapy.

It is as well, I think, for the authorities to remember the old Horatian tag—though you drive Nature out with a pitchfork, she will still find her way back. And that way, some of us know, will lie through various control-free Ruritanias.

The emphasis which I have tried to place on interest rate differentials, and the forces which determine them in each country, including the differing significance attached in the various countries to monetary management, and on expectations concerning the stability of existing exchange rates, together with the forces that determine these, seems to me to have been fully justified by recent events.

I myself, more than ever, am convinced that in the long term flourishing international capital and money markets, the advantages of which I am sure are fully accepted by everyone, depend for their continuance as a beneficent force, rather than as one of disturbance, on, first, greater progress in the harmonization of domestic economic policies, and second, the underpinning of the stability of the international monetary system.

In the longer term, moreover, these two objectives are really one and the same.

I have given sufficient indication, I think, in my paper, of my own views on these objectives, which I profoundly believe should ultimately lead to a World Central Bank as the guardian of a single international reserve asset, sustained neither by the nineteenth-century *Aequilibrium Britannicum*, of which I spoke in my paper, nor by the *Aequilibrium Americanum* of the last twenty-five years, but by a true *Aequilibrium Universale*.

However, it is not on these longer objectives that I want to dwell in my brief remarks today.

As is clear from my paper, it is all very well to start off by talking about international capital movements, long or short, but one is inevitably, and very soon, at that, obliged to deal with the whole range of current international monetary problems. This means, particularly after the August measures and the various international discussions that have taken place and are still taking place since, that one must talk about the present currency disorder.

This is not easy.

Having spent a very large part of my life in the service of government, I am particularly keenly aware of the hazard of saying anything publicly at a time when difficult and delicate negotiations are going on. Nevertheless as I speak only for myself today, and this is an occasion when the speaker, I think, can regard himself in Shakespeare's words as a 'chartered libertine', I will give a few personal views on the events of the last six weeks and their consequences.

In the first place, I am bound to say that I have enormous sympathy for the position of the United States, the pressures that the Administration was under, both nationally and internationally, and for the need it felt for bold decisions. Particularly as far as the international side is concerned, it seems to me to be hardly for those who have been lecturing the United States for so many years on the need to put its house in order to complain about its decision finally to do just that. One might express regret at the tardiness of these decisions. One might feel that had they been taken earlier, they might have been less radical and troublesome. One might disagree with some of the individual items in those decisions. But the determination as such, both to set the US economy back on the path of growth without inflation and at the same time to bring the deficit in the balance of payments under control, should surely evoke nothing less than the warmest welcome.

As I said in my paper, it is essential for the economic health of the world that the United States, in common with so many other countries, including my own, should quickly achieve much higher levels of economic activity with a substantial reduction of inflation.

It would be presumptuous for me today to comment on the domestic parts of the measures taken here to this end. But I for one am delighted that the Administration was not deterred by possible charges of inconsistency to make some moves on the prices and income front.

When it comes to the decisions in the international field, their consequences must naturally be subject to debate. But so also must be the reactions of other countries, both in word and in deed.

For my part, I find that the decision to 'close the gold window', which necessarily entailed a decision by a large number of countries no longer to endeavour to maintain the fixed parity of their exchanges with the dollar, to have been entirely correct.

I would emphasize, as should be clear from my paper, that I am strongly opposed to floating exchange rates as a normal régime. But in certain circumstances it becomes inevitable as an interim measure. And this is clearly very much the case at present.

I am less convinced that in strictly economic terms the imposition of a ten per cent surcharge on imports was essential. And lest it be thought unseemly on the part of one who in 1964 had to explain to the American Administration—I may say with some success—the virtue of the British decision to impose such a surcharge, I must point out that the circumstances were different, in that Britain was at the time trying to maintain its parity, while the United States was effectively producing a devaluation of the dollar.

More important, there must surely be considerable doubt whether in a situation in which the international competitiveness of the United States has declined, owing to a relative deterioration of productivity over a number of years, the provision of further protection to the domestic market in this form, as well as by other devices, is likely to be a corrective in the medium and longer term. Experience elsewhere does not support such an expectation. However, I can quite see the political factors, both domestic and international, behind this particular decision.

I also have very great sympathy with the view which, if reports are to be believed, is being held by the US Authorities, namely, that the present situation requires a fundamental reform of the international monetary system rather than a hurried patching-up of some sort of agreement. Many of us have long argued that fundamental reforms were becoming increasingly necessary, and therefore we must necessarily agree that every opportunity should be taken, such as the present situation, to press on with these.

However, these are, as we all know only too well, matters that are not easily resolved quickly. The experience of the discussions on improving the methods for providing world liquidity and in the process creating the beginnings of what would eventually become the basic reserve asset, which led to the creation of the Special Drawing Rights, does not make one sanguine that progress can be achieved in a short time.

Furthermore, the inclusion of other problems in the field of aid and defence burden-sharing, if these are really meant to be tackled concurrently, can hardly be looked upon as improving the prospects for an early overall long-term solution. I myself would be much happier to think that these matters will be dealt with seriatim rather than all at once.

What, then, must we hope and work for?

My own feeling is that the present state of affairs in the international financial system must not be allowed to continue much longer. True, life has a habit of going on, and markets and individuals and institutions operating in them tend to adjust themselves even to the most disorderly situation.

But there is already evidence of the inhibiting effect which this is having on international economic relations. And it would be totally wrong to think that if this present situation is not remedied soon, it will simply stay as it is. It will certainly deteriorate further through the spread of further restrictions of exchanges, both commercial and financial.

At a time when so many countries are trying to reactivate their economies, not yet having fully conquered inflation; at a time when great developments, both public and private, are needed, in the field of, say, oil exploration, extraction and transport, or in the provision of a better social and economic infrastructure in a large number of countries, even in the rich, developed world; and when these are crying out for huge capital resources, the prospect of a gradual shrinking of capital markets must be truly terrifying.

At the same time, it is naturally highly desirable that whatever early agreement is reached in the monetary and trade field, it should be in the direction in which the longer-term reform in the international monetary system is being sought.

Suggestions, for example, which I have seen attributed in the newspapers to the distinguished Italian Finance Minister, Sr. Ferrari-Aggradi as well as, of course, to the Managing Director of the Fund himself, certainly recognize this essential link. Nevertheless, I am particularly anxious to see an early agreement for the re-establishment of exchange parities *vis-à-vis* the dollar at levels which command credibility. I expect that this will now have to be combined with a greater margin of fluctuation within support points, though I have shown in my paper that I for one do not regard wider bands as the great remedy that some people do. I do not myself consider that there is any cogent economic case for including in such a realignment the modest increase in the official dollar price of gold which is advocated in some quarters. I can see that this might have some significance in terms of bookkeeping for central banks.

The more sophisticated arguments which I see are now being used in favour of this proposal, although seductive, seem to me to be drawn from quite a different universe of discourse; namely, from a régime appropriate to a situation in which there is a single reserve asset already in existence and accepted, and from a consideration of how this asset, as a yardstick, is to be related to all the currencies that will be linked to it.

I am not yet convinced, though I am open to persuasion, of the relevance of this proposal to a solution of the interim-period problem of parity realignments designed to secure a better US balance of payments performance, including a discouragement of sharp fluctuations in short-term money flows.

Thus, essentially this particular proposal seems to me still to be political rather than economic. And while that may in no way diminish its importance, we must remember that in politics usually there is some political element on both sides of the argument. Still, if this one measure really made all the difference between an early agreement on parities and continued deterioration, I for one would naturally not oppose it.

However, I would strongly hope that an early realignment of currency parities would be accompanied by the withdrawal of the ten per cent surcharge and of the other new protectionist measures of the United States. These seem to me to be the minimum elements for immediate action.

It is also, I think, essential that they should be accompanied by agreements which will make the new pattern of exchange parities, as I have said, one commanding a high degree of credibility as to its viability for a reasonably long period ahead. To this end, some action must, I think, be taken in regard to dollar balances, as has been advocated by a number of people, including, I think most recently, by Bob Roosa.

Whatever may be the arguments which the United States may see in favour of adopting a purely waiting attitude while other currencies float, mainly upwards, and whatever may be the arguments for more rapid progress towards the elimination of the dollar as a reserve asset and its replacement by a single, universal, internationally acceptable asset à la Special Drawing Rights, it cannot be in anybody's interest in the meantime to allow confidence in the dollar to continue to be eroded without limit. It certainly cannot be in the interests of the United States for this to happen, however much she may desire an immediate upward movement of certain other currencies.

Lack of confidence in a currency can be extremely dangerous and beyond a certain point impossible to control, particularly when it begins to affect one's own nationals.

Moreover, however much we may all want to see a new reserve asset, the dollar is bound to continue to be the principal transaction and intervention currency.

I believe, therefore, that some action in regard to dollar balances in parallel with a realignment of parities is essential.

It is vain to hope that one can at one stroke find parities that will reflect all the varying factors that, in theory, go into the determination of relative exchange rates—factors such as relative competitiveness, probable relative rates of inflation over time, and so on—to such a degree of accuracy that they will lay to rest all anxieties or hopes which lead to what are called 'speculative' movements—particularly if large short-term balances of the major currency overhang the market. These must, therefore, be consolidated in one way or another.

Indeed, in the light of the remarkable turnarounds which we have witnessed in the last twenty-five years in the relative fortunes of so many countries, there is some danger that parities chosen under the impact of an immediate crisis may be very much out of line with the likely development in relative international productivities and international competitiveness that we are likely to witness over the next few years. And I must say that some of the figures that I have heard mentioned, without authority, of course, give me a certain amount of anxiety in that regard.

I do not think that I need say anything much about what should constitute the longer-term improvement of the Bretton Woods system, which one would hope could also be proceeded with, though necessarily at a somewhat slower pace. Happily, there seems, in theory at least, to be a fair measure of agreement on much of this, though no doubt there will be sharp disagreement when it comes to deciding the rate at which a new reserve asset should be installed. And much as I would like to believe it, I cannot see that degree of international pooling of decisions on matters such as domestic monetary policy without which, I fear, we shall never be free from the risk of recurrence of crises, to be just around the corner.

These matters, we must remember, are not decided by economists or financial journalists writing from their secure fastnesses. They are not even decided by bankers, who are, of course, subject to the vagaries of the market—though we must remember that in many an economist and in many a financial journalist there is a politician hidden, wanting to get out. They are and must be decided by politicians, who are subject to the at least as hazardous vagaries of the electorate. Long acquaintance with politicians over many years has taught me that while they are only rarely much better than other people, they are hardly ever worse. But their priorities and their time-horizon are necessarily different. It is no good, therefore, trying to turn them into economists or bankers. The most important thing I believe one can say to them in the present situation is what I mentioned in the concluding remarks in my paper. When it comes to doing the right thing in international economic matters, none of us has an unblemished record. We all live in glass houses. And we know what people who live in glass houses should not do.

E

III.
THE BRITISH ECONOMY

OUR PRESENT DISCONTENTS

Based on an address to the London and District Society of Chartered Accountants on 4 December 1968. Published in The Accountant, *7 December 1968.*

I want to confine myself mainly to economic and political matters, and also I must be a little careful how strictly I interpret the word 'present', not only because of the long years of discretion imposed upon a Civil Servant but also because now I have to mind out what the 'Old Lady of Threadneedle Street' may think. So I shall try and say something rather general about the background to our present difficulties.

GOOD OVERALL PERFORMANCE

Contrary to popular belief, the British economy has really performed remarkably well in the twenty-three years since the end of the war. Indeed, if you look at the performance in absolute terms, be it leadership in certain highly advanced technological industries, be it the reconstruction after the war, be it in terms of ensuring for its population a higher and more widely shared standard of living, in all these matters the absolute performance is good. This is so even in terms of foreign trade and financial strength. I remember when I was an undergraduate, one of the things I first learnt about our foreign trade was that since 1857, or thereabouts, there have been very, very few years indeed in which we have managed to have a surplus on visible trade, and for more than a century our deficit on visible trade has been more than compensated for by our invisible earnings, the earnings of the 'Square Mile' and the income from overseas investments.

I remember when I worked under Sir Stafford Cripps in the Treasury in the immediate post-war period, we would have regarded it as a remarkable achievement for the early seventies if we had managed by that time to double our exports and to cover a very much larger proportion of our imports with exports. Well, we have achieved that particular objective long since, and I think from that point of view again the economy deserves good marks. Take our financial condition. We ended the war with practically all our foreign investments gone, and look at us now. I do not know what the latest figures are, but I imagine that we are certainly next only to the Americans in the volume of our foreign investments. I suppose they must be something of the order of between £15,000 million and £17,000 million. Now that is no mean achievement in twenty-three years.

Whey then the moans and the groans? Why are we unhappy and discontented? Why do governments fall from time to time over economic issues? I think the answer is simple—at least the first answer is simple. It is not the absolute performance of the economy that matters but it is its relative performance, and I do not mean by that only its relative performance in terms of some international league table, but rather more in terms of the tasks which we collectively in one way or another through the mysteries of our democratic process have imposed upon it.

These tasks were very formidable when the war ended. There were not only the immediate tasks of making good the ravages and the wastes and the loss of construction in the wartime period itself, but there was the making good of the whole substance of the economy after four years or more of very exhausting struggle. There were certain social aspirations that had to be fulfilled. They were widely shared at the end of the war—if you cast your minds back, you will, I think, agree that they were very widely shared aspirations. May I say parenthetically that what we have done in this field is by no means out of line with what other countries have done. We must not think that we are the only ones that have a Welfare State, because most of the other countries have achieved progress in that field as fast, if not faster than we have.

Above all, on top of all that, what we have to remember is that we set ourselves the task of maintaining in the post-war years a posture in defence, in foreign policy and in terms of the international monetary mechanism which had been established in quite different circumstances a hundred years or so earlier, and without any thought to the possibility of maintaining that posture in the changed circumstances. This, I think, is most clearly seen in what has happened to our balance of payments in the post-war period.

LIST OF ERRORS

You can see it in another way, too. I daresay that each one of us has his own favourite list of errors of government policy in the post-war period. I will give you some of mine, if you like. I think, for example, the terms on which the sterling balances were settled just after the war were excessively generous. I think that the attempt to restore convertibility of sterling in 1947 was premature, largely, I may say, under American pressure which we should have withstood; and the retreat from this premature convertibility which took place within a few months of it happening, if you remember, was, of course, much worse than if we had never attempted it at all. I think the failure to recognize the strength and the significance of the European integration movement, as first seen in the Schumann Plan, and not to jump on that bandwagon and to get hold of the reins, if that is the correct image, was another great error of post-war policy which, of course, continued for something like ten or fifteen years thereafter.

If you look at these, is there some common feature? Is there something you can detect in all these that could give us a clue as to why these errors were committed? I think there is. I think we have to come back to the point I made earlier—nearly all these stem from an uncertainty, not about what to do today or tomorrow, what to do about this item of taxation or that, whether to have investment allowances, or whether to have tax allowances in respect of investments and so on and so forth. They stem from a much deeper uncertainty about our posture in the late twentieth century. We were moving this way and moving that way, leaning towards the United States at one time, leaning towards Europe at another, preserving perhaps far too long the illusion that the Commonwealth over and beyond sentimental and political ties had really lasting viability as a special economic concept.

You may well remember the concept of the three rings with Britain standing at the centre of three circles, at the intersection of the Commonwealth, Europe and US. Looking back upon it, I think this was probably one of the gravest illusions because really to stand at the intersection of those three rings would have required a strength which not only we did not possess but which is very doubtful any of the super-powers today could possibly command.

So I come to the point—what would have been necessary to remedy this deficiency? I think what would have been necessary to remedy them are qualities which are very rare—qualities of imagination, of vision and, perhaps, above all, of courage. In the absence of these qualities we have made do with economic management and, alas—and I speak as one trained in what I regard as a very important and a very fruitful science, economics—alas, it is no substitute. I am sure that no one in this room would for one moment confuse the science of accountancy with the art of business management. Similarly, I think it was a grave error to think that economic management, however refined, however much based upon the latest advances of economic theory and econometrics, statistical techniques, and all the rest of it, can possibly be a substitute for a courageous vision of the fundamentals of our situation. I say this, I need hardly stress here, without any partisan concern whatsoever because, as I said before, the qualities that would have been necessary to see these problems soon enough are very rare on both sides of the House and in both Houses.

SOME ADVANCES AND IMPROVEMENTS

In this rather lofty view of our troubles and of the background of our present discontents, I must say that there have been some advances and some improvements in recent years. I am rather reminded of a remark which is credited to the Israeli Foreign Minister, who said recently that governments, like individuals, always behave with the utmost wisdom after all other alternatives have been exhausted. This may well be our situation. I take some comfort from the fact that during the last few years we have seen a whole procession of sacred cows being gently but firmly led to the slaughter. In regard to our ability to maintain a certain defence posture, certain things have happened which I think would have been unthinkable five or ten years ago. I think some of the recent events in regard to the reserve currency function of sterling also show a greater sense of realism of what is and what is not possible in the modern world. I think there are things now being said and debated which five years ago would have been regarded as almost approaching blasphemy. And that is all to the good.

But I think there is still a great deal which remains to be done. I think these shocks we have experienced in the last three or four years, particularly in the international monetary field, may well lead to some review of our present arrangements, perhaps on the lines originally envisaged by Keynes at Bretton Woods which, alas, he was not allowed to carry out. You know it is one of those curious things. Nations seem to be dancing a dance in which partners and positions are always changing. At Bretton Woods, the Americans would not let Keynes have his way to make the IMF a central bankers' Central Bank. If we had it today things would have been very different. Six years ago at the IMF meeting in Vienna, a system of relatively modest pooling of reserves, a multi-currency account, was recommended. Again the Americans wouldn't have it. Later on, they would have been delighted with it, but it was no longer generally acceptable. And so it is, each time someone has advocated something the others have not supported it, and then they change places again.

But perhaps there is a prospect now of people learning from their mistakes and learning from the shocks we have had. Perhaps there will be another Bretton Woods. I am not very confident that it will happen very soon, or that it will not be a very difficult struggle, when it does happen, to get some more rationality into our international affairs. But, at any rate, things seem to be on the march.

NEW ATTITUDES

I think in our country too, attitudes still require to be changed. It is so easy when you talk to a person across the table to recognize that human beings are, just to take one example, moved by all kinds of different motives. The profit motive is not by any means what moves any one individual all the time to the exclusion of other things, any more than loftier moral motives and objectives. But it is terribly hard, despite slogans about living in a mixed economy, and so on, to make some people realize that, for example, the profit motive is a perfectly normal and reasonable concern for individual material betterment— that is to say not only a normal human instinct but also a valuable instrument for regulating, to some degree spontaneously, the actions of individuals and, therefore, the actions of the economy as a whole. I am by no means an unqualified, or undiscriminating admirer of things American, but I think we would be awfully foolish not to learn from some of the things in the United States, for example, in regard to the profit motive and the ordinary human desire for material betterment.

But above all, what I think distinguishes us from the best in the United States or in North America generally is the attitude to change itself. I think the time has probably come when we should welcome change rather more readily and indeed sometimes, as the Americans do, go out and seek it. I am convinced that a perpetual posture of veneration for what is, is not as good as one of ready welcome for what might be.

IS BRITAIN PREPARED TO PAY THE PRICE OF GROWTH?

Published in The Times, *28 June 1968*

How lucky we are to have such candid friends; genuinely concerned for our well-being and their candour matched by so high a level of competence that even Canning would have welcomed them! This book[1] published in the United States yesterday and to be published in London shortly, is the most up-to-date, comprehensive and penetrating study of our economy, its problems and prospects, to appear between the covers of one volume. A distinguished group, mainly of the younger generation of American economists, under the leadership of Professor Caves, the chairman of the Economics Department at Harvard, was got together by that eminent body, the Brookings Institution, to produce his invaluable analysis. It is a striking sign of the development of Economics in the United States during the last thirty years and of the resources now available to the science in that country that this should have been accomplished in little more than a year. I wish I could feel confident that we could render a similar service to America.

The authors bring to their difficult task not only a splendid technical equipment but just the right balance between excessive familiarity and total detachment. There are stretches that are hard going for the non-expert; but generally the book can be understood by an intelligent layman: and no one concerned with making or influencing policy should miss it. It is well and simply written, with not too much jargon (the occasional Americanisms that are not yet fully acclimatized here, such as 'trade-off', deserve to be). Naturally, the British reader will here and there find some rather naïve statements about his own country and the ultra-sensitive may be irritated by an occasional lapse into a lecturing tone, particularly where it concerns non-economic matters such as foreign and defence policy. But none of this should diminish the usefulness of the book or the great debt of

---

[1] *Britain's Economic Prospects*, by Richard E. Caves and Associates, The Brookings Institution, Washington. Published in London by George Allen & Unwin Ltd.

gratitude that we must all owe to the Brookings Institution and to Professor Caves and his colleagues.

DEMAND MANAGEMENT

The ten chapters are broadly of equal length, though one, significantly perhaps, that on 'Alternatives for public expenditure', is much longer than the rest. As each is written by a different author, they differ somewhat in approach and style. That on fiscal policy, by the distinguished Harvard couple, Professor and Mrs. Musgrave, emphasizes the historical and analytical aspects and is more reticent on policy recommendation than I would have liked. On the other hand, the chapter on the highly technical, and contentious, subject of monetary policy is quite outspoken in its distribution of praise and blame to our Authorities; and the particularly interesting chapters on public expenditure and industrial efficiency are also quite explicit in their pronouncements on policy. Nevertheless, there is a remarkable sense of unity about the whole book; and, generally, it is a model of how complex and often sensitive subjects can be treated in a manner that is both down-to-earth and inoffensive. At the end the authors give us a collective epilogue. Here I felt the only lack. I wish this conclusion had been much longer—perhaps even a short second volume—which, written by one hand, would have brought together all the different strands into one coherent pattern of policy appraisal and recommendation.

The clinical findings from which the learned doctors start are familiar: a remarkable economic performance since the war, but one not adequate to the immense tasks, domestic and, above all, external, of the post-war period. Between 1950 and the early sixties Britain's national income has grown more slowly as compared with the United States and several Western European countries. Their faster growth resulted not only from a faster increase of input, but also from an increase of output per unit of input. There were some obvious causes for this deficiency: gains through transfers of labour from agriculture or self-employment open to other countries had in Britain already been secured earlier. But the main reasons must lie in relatively low rates of capital formation and of growth in what the authors call 'residual productivity', i.e. those aspects of productivity (e.g. skills and initiative of enterprise and management) that cannot be directly and separately estimated. Together with this slow growth, payments crises and 'stop-go' complete the picture.

The possible interrelation between these three is of the greatest importance for correct diagnosis and prescription. Accordingly, the authors in the three parts into which the book is divided take us in turn through the means of managing total demand, the constraints of the international nexus of trade and payments, and the more fundamental problems of the growth and efficiency of the domestic economy. Throughout the period they examine, the main emphasis in British economic policy has, more consistently than in any other country, been on the short-term management of total demand, largely in relation to balance of payments fluctuations. This gives the authors an opportunity to evaluate the effectiveness of fiscal monetary and incomes policy as the main instruments to this end. Their extremely important assessment is, at best, sceptical, at worst negative.

As one who has long since suspected that we were excessively addicted to demand management to the point of suffering from what I christened 'macro-economicosis', I am delighted to have such distinguished support.

In the authors' view, the policy of adjusting demand and employment in this country has not only had destabilizing effects, it has not avoided a heavy cost in terms of failure to sustain growth. It is impossible to do justice in a brief summary to the analysis that leads to this conclusion. The one-year time-lag between employment and aggregate demand, the reliance on taxation changes against a background of a secular rising trend of public expenditure, and the difficulties of fitting a balance-of-payments-oriented monetary policy into a domestic stabilization programme are among the many factors reviewed.

As for the balance of payments constraint itself, Professor Cooper, who deals with this subject, examines carefully the relation between our capabilities and our various commitments (full employment with fast growth, unrestricted current account transactions, an extensive diplomatic and military world role, exports of capital to the rest of the world and the maintenance of London as an international financial centre and, with it, a fixed exchange rate) which, taken as a whole, proved a very heavy—and, in the end, too heavy—load given the relatively unfavourable external circumstances in which we operated. Against this basically precarious background, it is perhaps not surprising that both restrictionist and expansionary fiscal and monetary policies should have proved so often mistimed. Given also a certain scepticism about the long-term effectiveness of incomes policy, the authors' conclusion is against reliance on demand management as the main instrument for improving Britain's economic performance.

Nevertheless, the book contains many interesting, though obviously controversial, disquisitions on individual aspects of this policy. SET for example, is criticized as is the theory of what encourages growth on which it rests. 'Verdoorn's law', which correlates total growth with growth of productivity, is seen to be borne out by Britain's experience, but the causal connection is found to run from the latter to the former factor and not, as has often been thought, the other way round. The pre-eminence of the City is not thought to be significantly dependent on the reserve currency function of sterling. Some preference is expressed for a greater use of product taxation (as opposed to income and profit taxation or credit, including hire-purchase, control), for bringing about desired changes in consumption. Despite their doubts about the efficacy of aggregate demand management, the authors welcome devaluation as a relaxation of the balance of payments constraint. They regard the 14.3 per cent reduction in sterling's external value as more than adequate to restore equilibrium, estimating its eventual favourable effect on the balance of trade at over £800 million per annum.

Much the most important, and to me welcome, conclusion of the book is that it places a strong emphasis on increase of economic efficiency as the chief encouragement of growth. This means greater managerial efficiency, less restrictive labour and management practices, more flexibility in recruitment and promotion and, in general, a more adaptable industrial structure. The views which are expressed on particular policies to this end will certainly be much debated. For example, the authors do not consider the general scale of business enterprise in Britain to be too small for optimizing efficiency; and they are, accordingly, by no means enthusiastic and undiscriminating advocates of mergers. On the other hand, they find product differentiation to be excessive; though its roots, as of so much else in this area, are to be sought in social rather than in purely economic factors.

CRUCIAL DEFICIENCY

Professor Shepherd, who writes on public expenditure, is not only dubious about the size of the road building programme or the non-selectivity of social benefits; he also casts doubt on the electricity generating programme and on the speed of run-down of the coal industry. Investment grants come in for some critical examination, as do regional policies. On the other hand, educational expenditure is thought to be too small in total and ill distributed, particularly in its emphasis on pure science (which seems to have taken, hierarchically, the position of the humanities) as against technology and engineering.

Professor Peck (now a member of the President's Council of Economic Advisers) who has worked much in this field, is convinced that this is one of the most crucial deficiencies of our whole socio-economic structure. It is a pity, in this general context, that not enough is said about the wider problem of taxation reform in relation to the need to make the industrial structure more adaptable. All this, as I say, can and will be much debated. But it is certainly highly salutary to have the emphasis thus redressed.

The authors are, in their own words, 'guardedly optimistic' about our prospects. They would, I think, say that we are at last on the right road towards remedying the basic deficiencies, though neither they, nor anyone else, could predict accurately the speed at which we shall be travelling along it. At the end, the authors' remaining doubt is summed up in the question whether the price of growth will be paid in 'a society where don and docker alike prefer tradition, leisure and stability', even though both may 'have declared for growth or at least the fruits of growth'.

Thus stated, the problem is by no means Britain's alone. But there is nothing in this country's history of the last two hundred years to lead one to fear that we are worse placed than others to find an answer. Indeed, there is much in our history to make one hope that we might be the first of the advanced industrial countries to resolve this basic dilemma of the present age.

BRITAIN AND WORLD TRADE

A paper read at the Business Economists' Group Conference, Cambridge, March 1969.

The subject on which I want to talk to you this afternoon is itself not a very cheerful one, and I feel particularly hesitant to speak about 'Britain and world trade', knowing that this is one topic which is peculiarly the business of business economists and which they follow closely. Given the kind of expert knowledge which is assembled here in this hall, I think I ought to begin by saying what I do *not* propose to talk about. I shall not produce for you any elaborate models, new or old, relating the movements of world trade with the movements of the constituents of the British balance of payments—exports or imports and their performance over the years. I shall not attempt any forecast of whether world trade will go on growing at the rate of 8 per cent per annum which, I believe, was the average over the last fifteen years or so, and therefore I am not going to produce any forecast of what the export or import performance of this country is going to be, this year or next, or how this is going to affect the total balance of payments of the United Kingdom. Nor am I going to parade before you a lot of statistics.

What I thought it might be useful to do is to offer to you for what they are worth some general reflections on the British economy as it has behaved over the last twenty years or so and more particularly on its trade performance, on the role of the balance of payments in judging the performance of the economy and perhaps, above all, on the vexed question of the relationship between economic management, both as it has actually evolved in the last twenty years and as it might theoretically be conducted with special reference to influencing the balance of payments or the visible trade balance. Finally I want to add some remarks on the role of the international corporation in trade and financial matters. If on the latter point I do to some extent poach on the subject which others will talk about tomorrow, I hope that perhaps, since they don't constitute a very polished and finished scientific paper, they will at any rate provoke enough discussion and questions in your subsequent session.

Now just let us look at a few general propositions about this much examined, much maligned, British economy in the last twenty years. I suppose there has never been in history a national economy which has been so closely examined by so many clinicians from both sides of the Atlantic as the British economy in recent years. Sometimes you feel that if it is really as sick as it is sometimes thought, one ought to ask the diagnosticians and therapists to stand aside a bit and give the patient a little air and leave him in peace for a while. We all know that the most outward and visible signs of malaise has been the performance of the British balance of payments, and since it is much the largest element in it, particularly the trade balance, this has been very much examined, and very many different diagnoses have been offered as to its weaknesses as well as prescriptions on how to cure them. At any rate since the war this has been, I suppose, the single most important element in the whole economic pattern for examination, for attention by successive governments and for action either to operate directly or indirectly on imports and exports. The popular impression, of course, not here, I need hardly say, but in the world at large, is that this problem of the relationship between imports and exports in the British balance of payments is a relatively novel problem and is a problem that is peculiar to the post-war period. Of course we all know that this is not so. I think the correct figures, in so far as the statistics are available, are that for something like 260 or 270 years, that is ever since 1700, there has been no consistent surplus of exports over imports in the British trade balance. In fact, judging by some recent investigations there have only been six occasions in the last 266 years on which there has been an annual export surplus recorded and, of these, two have been in the last ten years or so. Generally, until recent years, exports have only covered between 75 per cent to 80 per cent of British imports, and in fact before the war the normal pattern was for only two-thirds of our imports to be covered by our exports. So the notion that somehow or other the existence of a trade deficit is something new in the British economy is clearly not correct. Although it would take one very far afield, and this is certainly not our task this afternoon, to go into the historic reasons for this particular pattern of the trade balance and its place in the total balance of payments, I think it is at any rate significant that, even though the situation as it existed before the war may have concealed a fairly long-standing malaise, at least we've managed with that situation for a very long time. It must therefore suffice to say that the export/import balance by itself is not a novel feature, and thus I would have thought not by itself an adequate index of what is wrong with our position in world trade and with the balance of payments as an aspect of our total national economy. In any event it has improved if anything in recent years. As I said a few moments ago, we could assume roughly speaking that two-thirds of our imports were covered by exports before the war: today the proportion is generally nearly 90 per cent and in some years over 90 per cent.

The next point I want to make is that, despite the fact that this is a fairly long-standing pattern, it is quite clear that the behaviour of the other items in the balance of payments is such that some change in the pattern of exports/imports was required or would have been necessary to correct our balance of payment difficulties in the past and will certainly be required in future if these balance of payment difficulties are to be corrected. As you know the latest edition of the Government's thoughts on the future of the economy, in a Green Paper called 'The Task Ahead' which came out not long ago, and is not on a plan but a pattern of performance, shows by what means something like a £300 million a year surplus on visible trade might be achieved as a means of correcting the balance of payments. So we can assume that whatever the historical position might be, some change in this export/import balance will in future be needed. I leave aside the possibilities for changing the invisible items and achieving major improvements there. This is a very big subject. I don't myself believe that any very radical changes are possible within a short period of time in the invisible terms, though obviously when one gets into the more sophisticated questions of the relations between the capital account and the current account there are certain changes that might conceivably have made quite a difference. I just mention in passing that if, for example, say ten or fifteen years ago—certainly before the passing of the Interest Equalization Tax in the United States and the first voluntary and then later mandatory balance of payments programme of the United States—the British Government's attitude to long-term borrowing, not necessarily by itself but by, for example, the nationalized industries had been different from what it was at the time, then quite conceivably some very substantial changes in the long-term capital account might have been achieved, which could in turn have produced some very interesting repercussions on the balance of payments during that period and could have left us in a somewhat different position today from that in which we find ourselves.

Let us now leave the general question of the relationship between exports and imports and begin to look at each separately. If we take imports first of all, it is a fact that they have grown very substantially in recent years, and perhaps superficially this coincides with the progress of liberalization since the early fifties in world trade. Between 1956 and 1966 imports as a percentage of gross domestic product increased and now constitute, more particularly perhaps imports of manufactured products, a substantial percentage of GDP. However, the position is not dissimilar from that which we find elsewhere. The 8 per cent or so which imports of manufactured goods now constitute of GDP is not very dissimilar from that of France or Germany and other advanced industrial countries. It is generally to be expected on theoretical grounds, and I am sure it is now generally accepted that this is a common feature of the advance of world trade in the highly developed countries where liberalization is fairly progressive. Thus the primitive correlation that one might see between liberalization and the growth of imports into this country must not lead one to the wrong set of conclusions about the significance of liberalization. However, if you look at the export side the position is rather different. There is no doubt that there has been a relative stagnation of exports from this country compared with the picture to be seen in other countries, notably in the so-called, super-growth countries like Germany and Japan. Our share of exports of manufactured goods has declined within the total of the exports of the advanced industrialized countries of the world; in the period 1953 to 1967, for example it fell from 19 per cent to 12 per cent. At the same time, as I said a moment ago, roughly during that period the proportion of imports in the GDP, particularly of manufactured goods, has increased significantly.

It is, in my view, very difficult to say to what this is due. I have searched pretty hard in the theories of the subject. Those are very brief admittedly, but I think quite an authoritative and on the whole fairly objective summing-up of this subject is to be found in the Brookings Report, which no doubt most of you have read. I must confess, however, that to me it does not lead to any decisive conclusions about which relationship between growth and exports is the significant one. I think there is also a great deal in this argument which, to my mind, still has not produced anything conclusive about the various elements in British exports that are to be particularly focused upon in analysing our deficiencies in this regard: whether it is price competitiveness, delivery, design, after-sales service and all the rest of it. The fact remains, and the fact cannot be denied, that our export performance, given all the other circumstances in which we find ourselves, would have had to be a great deal better and no doubt will need to be a great deal better if there is to be a significant improvement in the balance of payments. And since I believe that the development of imports is something which is to be expected, not something to be considered as exceptional, then this reinforces the view that it is the export performance that will have to show the major change. This naturally brings one to the most difficult part of all, and that is how this is to be achieved. Again searching high and low and reading what has been written on the subject—not all of it because that would be impossible in a lifetime, but reading a certain amount of it—I still find myself extremely puzzled both about the theoretical explanations for this state of affairs and the prescriptions for remedying it. Let me just give you my own reflections on what I have read of these explanations and a few words therefore on the possibilities of, first, direct action on exports or imports (which is very quickly disposed of), secondly, indirect action through management of the domestic economy, and perhaps, thirdly, a few words about the relevance of international monetary reform or monetary action of one kind or another in this particular regard.

As far as direct action on imports is concerned, quite apart from international obligations, this cannot be regarded as anything in the nature of a long-term remedy and must simply be reserved for short-term action where inevitable. Even here of course doubt about its efficacy has always existed and has been, if anything, reinforced by our experience with the import surcharge and perhaps also now with the import deposit scheme, although it is possibly a little too early to judge that. As far as direct action on exports is concerned, that again is highly limited by international obligations, except possibly in regard to the effects of changes in the tax system and the moves towards value-added tax. I know you have already touched upon these in another context, and I therefore do not propose to say anything about it now. In any event I know that this is a highly contentious subject. I for one do not rule out the possibility of improving our export performance by an appropriate change in taxation and by the introduction of a value-added tax.

Thus, as far as direct action to improve the performance of exports or imports one way or the other is concerned, there is clearly very little scope. One is therefore driven back to the very difficult question of what domestic economic management can achieve in improving exports and restraining imports. This is, of course, a subject on which one can talk forever. Broadly speaking, I think, most people nowadays seem to me to have a fairly, shall I say, optimistic view about the possibilities of influencing relatively quickly the balance of payments via imports and exports by appropriate measures of economic policy. I am afraid that I am in a somewhat pessimistic mood, generally speaking, on this subject. As far as general measures are concerned such as appropriate domestic demand management, short- and long-term, or changes in the rate of exchange, I doubt if these are really effective at all or effective sufficiently quickly to make a significant difference. I am struck by the fact that the analysis of our own performance in imports and exports does not give one enough of a guide to encourage confidence that any one particular action will effectively change the relationship. For example, I had recently the opportunity of looking at a new study which has been made—it is not altogether novel but it produces some rather new figures and I do not believe it is public yet—a study which tries to correlate the income elasticity of demand for imports and the world's income elasticity of demand for exports of a large number of countries over the last fifteen years. Not surprisingly the United States and this country come at one end of the spectrum and Germany and Japan at the other end.

I find that if these results are reliable, and I have no reason to think they are not, then one must certainly be sceptical, about changing this pattern at all quickly either by adequate doses of domestic inflation or deflation, suitable credit terms, or even changes in exchange rates of the order of magnitude that can be regarded as reasonable in terms of practical politics. Because they seem to indicate certain fairly deep-seated structural problems in different countries, if you like, Germany and Japan at one end and Britain and the United States at the other, it is highly unlikely that the mix of what is politically tolerable and what is economically feasible can be such as to bring about a rapid change through macro-economic management. Of course, theoretically, it is possible to argue that there is a rate of exchange, or a series of movements in relative rates of exchange, which will correct the situation. Of course, it is possible to argue that there is a degree of deflation, for example, in this country, which is bound to correct the import/export balance at some stage at a certain level of employment or unemployment and with a certain pattern of changes in terms of trade. But the real question is (whatever the theoretical pattern is that emerges), is this politically at all practicable, is it practical politics to think in those terms? If it is true that our income elasticity of demand for imports is relatively low and if it is true that the world's income elasticity of demand for our exports is relatively high then the degree of deflation that would be required in the present situation by itself to bring about the required change, is I think something which is utterly and completely outside the realm of practical politics. And I think equally that any change in the exchange rate mechanism, however sophisticated and theoretically attractive, whether it is by means of wider bands or by means of more frequent changes in parities or by means of quasi-automatic changes of the parity, simply will not cope with what the statistics seem to indicate is the basic problem.

Leaving this aside altogether the question is whether (even if, as a matter of practical politics, a change in the export/import balance can be brought about by appropriate changes in the management of domestic demand) the longer-term consequences of so doing are not going to have much more serious secondary and tertiary effects as far as the longer-term balance of payments is concerned. I have rather reluctantly, as one who has for some years had perforce to be concerned with practical measures, come to have a somewhat pessimistic view of the relationship between economic management and changes in the balance of payments and in the export/import pattern, particularly of a country like ours. This may apply equally perhaps to other countries, even the United States, though of course there it is of much less significance.

If I am at all right in regarding the claims of modern economic analysis to be useful in terms of practical politics with a certain degree of scepticism in this particular realm, then does it mean that we are reduced to relative impotence in this field? I do not quite know the answer to this yet, but I will give you some of my thoughts in this regard.

It has become relatively common nowadays, certainly in this country and certainly since 1964, to recognize, however vaguely and however implicitly, that there are certain changes that are required in the British economy if the trade and payments pattern is to be altered, over and above the possible good that could be done by economic management of one kind or another.

These are usually referred to as structural changes. If it is the case that Germany and Japan are at one end of the spectrum and the United States and Britain at the other, what does this mean in terms of the structure of the economy and in terms of the nature of the changes that might be required? I should like to indicate what I think might be the directions in which answers may need to be sought. First of all, I think it is clear that both in Germany and in Japan, perhaps more particularly in the former, the last twenty-five years or so and even beyond have been characterized by a very different set of attitudes and expectations in regard to the pattern of resource allocation. The expectations of consumers both in the present and in the future compared with the expectations of investors, the expectations of management and of labour, the claims of capital as against current consumption have been very different in those two countries from what they have been in this country. I am not saying that the reasons which have brought this about are such that we ought to try and emulate them. No doubt these reasons are to be found in hyper-inflation, in Nazism, in the war, in destruction, in occupation and all the rest of it and I am not suggesting for one moment that this is the appropriate way in which these changes should be brought about. I am merely pointing to the fact that far more significant in explaining the different performance of exports and imports of those two countries are these socio-political factors which show themselves in, shall I say, the viscosity of the expectations in regard to resource allocation. If this is so, and if this accounts in part for the readiness to go in for new industries, to postpone current satisfactions, to have very low unemployment rates together with not very rapidly rising real incomes—as was the case in Germany at any rate for a very considerable period of time—if these are the things that are responsible, how can one bring this about in a country such as this or in the United States? Well, a great deal has been done since 1964, or a great deal at least has been attempted since 1964 and to some extent even before 1964, in terms of education, changes in attitude, dissemination of new knowledge in managerial techniques and in technology and all the rest of it. There have been changes even in industrial structure. But of course, these things work extremely slowly as you all know and I am not at all sure that they can work fast enough, certainly as far as Britain is concerned, to give us the necessary change quickly enough. I think what is probably necessary here is a combination of some pretty radical thinking in regard to sticks and carrots—that is to say incentives and penalties—and in so far as the tax system can bring these about, this is probably one element in a programme of reform.

Secondly, I think education has, I will not say neglected, but has perhaps not sufficiently taken into account these particular objectives in regard to the economic system, industrial structure and the trading system. As a result attitudes and expectations have not adjusted quickly enough.

Thirdly, there are probably two or three important institutional arrangements that could be identified as being critical in this regard; the trade union structure is one that might be mentioned among them. By that I mean particularly the need for the emergence of large, comprehensive industrial unions in industries such as automobiles. If it can be done, and, of course, in a democratic system this is difficult, I would submit that a programme concentrating on three reforms: fiscal, educational and institutional may be more effective, and more quickly effective, than all the remedies derived from highly sophisticated economic analyses of international trade and international finance. But on the other side there are also some obstacles that need to be removed. I think, and I have said so on a number of occasions, that if you were to list the errors of British economic policies since the war such as, for example, the excessively generous settlement of sterling balances in 1946–7, the premature return to convertibility in 1947, the excessive defence programme of 1949–50 and so on, you would find that together with the prolonged clinging to the role of having a reserve currency and being the world's banker, they have one thing in common, i.e. a failure to recognize soon enough the change in our total position in the world brought about not only by a change in ourselves, but by change in other countries too and in our relation to other countries. This is the kind of thing which I know is very hard to measure, very hard to pinpoint, very hard to express in precise types of measures. It is not surprising therefore that those—and economists are certainly in the forefront—who are anxious to mitigate evil should be hesitant to pin their faith too much on these very slow, longer-term reforms and should naturally concentrate more on specific macro-economic management possibilities which they derive readily from their own theoretical and analytical apparatus. But having seen the disappointments that have attended our attempts both of short-term and long-term economic management, including the undoubtedly disappointing results of the devaluation of November 1967, I do want to end up, Mr. Chairman, by asking even so hard-headed an audience as this one of business economists to consider for a few minutes at least whether there isn't here another area in which longer-term reforms of various kinds may in the end be more fruitful.

IV.
EUROPE

TEN YEARS OF EUROPEAN CO-OPERATION

Published in Lloyds Bank Review, *April 1958.*

Ten years ago, on 16 April 1948, representatives of sixteen European countries and the Commanders-in-Chief of the Western Zones of occupation in Germany signed the Convention for European Economic Co-operation, and the OEEC was born. It is a striking testimony to the success of this institution that one cannot think or write of the economic history of Europe during the last decade (and of a great deal of the rest of the world as well), without frequently having to refer to the activities of the OEEC, and, on many major issues putting these activities in the centre of the account.

The Organization was conceived nearly a year earlier. In the late spring of 1947, in the United States no less than in Europe, the true measure of the economic consequences of the Second World War was at last being fully realized. The improvement in industrial production which had been achieved in several European countries in the first post-war years was not maintained during the winter of 1946–7. Exceptionally severe weather, added to the underlying economic weakness, quickly created conditions of widespread food shortage, industrial stagnation and unemployment of the gravest kind. For the first time, what had been recognized by a few far-sighted men became generally accepted in Europe and the United States, namely, that the imbalance between the economic resources and potential of the western hemisphere and those of the rest of the world, symbolized in the dollar shortage, was deep-seated and persistent and had been only temporarily concealed by the final stages of Lend-Lease and by massive American loans.

With a foresight of which there are not many examples in history, a small group of officials in the US State Department analysed this situation in May 1947, and presented a clear statement of the policy issues arising from it to Mr. Marshall, the then Secretary of State. On 5 June, Mr. Marshall made his historic speech at Harvard University. In it, he made it clear that Europe's requirements were such that she had to have substantial additional help if she was not to face economic, social and political deterioration of a very grave character. At the same time he stressed that it was not for the United States to draw up unilaterally a programme to put Europe on its feet. 'The initiative must come from Europe'; and the role of the United States had to consist, first, in 'friendly aid' in the drawing-up of a European programme of recovery and, later, in supporting it. He invited Europe to prepare a joint programme which would show that the countries of Europe agreed among themselves 'as to the requirements of the situation and the part those countries themselves will take in order to give proper effect to whatever action might be undertaken by this Government'.

It was in response to this speech that Mr. Bevin and M. Bidault, after abortive negotiations for the participation of Russia and the Eastern European countries, called a conference which met in Paris on 12 July. This conference set up a Committee of European Economic Co-operation, under the Chairmanship of Sir Oliver Franks, for the purpose of producing what Secretary Marshall had asked for: a joint European recovery programme. In less than two-and-a-half months, by 22 September 1947, the Committee had completed its task and had produced a report which, as an economic analysis and statement of policy, has remained unequalled in depth and scope to this day. In two volumes, the first a general review and declaration of policy, the second a detailed report of its four technical sub-committees on food and agriculture, iron and steel, fuel and power, and transport, this report gave a complete survey of the state and prospects of the economies of the participating countries. It contained a series of commitments on broad lines of policy, and a closely reasoned case for the 'missing component' in European recovery, dollar aid.

Moreover, virtually the complete pattern of the organization of the OEEC, of its methods of work, of the principles underlying its main activities, and, above all, of the basic relationship between it (as an organization of European countries) and the US government were established in the Grand Palais in Paris during those few weeks of feverish activity in the hot summer of 1947. The Committee of European Economic Co-operation (CEEC), representing all the participating countries, was a forerunner of the Council of the OEEC, its Executive Committee of the Executive Committee of the OEEC, its four technical committees (with considerable subsequent proliferation) of the 'vertical' committees of the OEEC. Special sub-committees set up by the CEEC on such general matters as balance of payments, internal finance, etc., were the prototypes of the 'horizontal' committees of the OEEC which dealt with broad economic questions as distinct from the commodity or industrial sector scope of the 'vertical' committees. The method of the question-naire to ascertain participating countries' plans, expectations and prospects as well as their requirements, which was the basic raw material for the report of the CEEC, became from the very beginn-ing the central technique of the OEEC; and, although it no longer has the politico-economic significance that it had in the time of American aid, it remains to this day the method by which annual reports, as well as major *ad hoc* 'exercises', are carried out.

In two important respects only did the OEEC pattern differ from that of its progenitor. The CEEC did not have a secretariat other than for housekeeping purposes. However, the small 'central group' drawn from a few delegations, and the somewhat larger informal grouping of members of delegations that clustered round it (many of whom later on became associated with the OEEC's central activities), developed a collective view and a co-operative spirit which can be said to have continued to inspire the OEEC's inter-national secretariat. These attitudes helped to create the admirable relations which have always existed between the secretariat and national delegations. The main credit in this respect, as in very much else that the organization achieved, must, however, go to Robert Marjolin, the outstanding first Secretary General which the OEEC was fortunate to have.

The other point of difference was this. In the CEEC the Chair-manship of the main Committee and that of the Executive Com-mittee were held by the same country. It had originally been in-tended to follow this example in the organization of the OEEC. In fact, however, this was not done and the difference was not without some significance during the early years of the OEEC's life. Differ-ences in national policies and attitudes were at times complicated, at least when they reached the ministerial level, by the fact that the day-to-day management was in the hands of the United Kingdom (through its Chairmanship, at the official level, of the Executive Committee), while the Council's Chairman was a minister of another nationality, alternately Belgian and Dutch.

The history of the OEEC in the ten years since its creation can be roughly divided into three phases: from 1948 to the autumn of 1950, from then until the middle of 1952, and the period since then.

The successes which the OEEC has to its credit in the first phase of its life, undoubtedly the period of greatest zest and most spectacular achievement, are quickly told. The development of the Organization in its first few months was extremely rapid and affords impressive proof of the speed with which institutions and techniques can be developed and perfected, so long as there exists the stimulus of a real job to be done Notwithstanding the great scarcity of highly skilled administrative and technical manpower so keenly felt at that time in all European capitals, and in the United States as well, a remarkable assortment of talent was drawn into this work, whether in the central secretariat at the Hôtel de Tabac and, later, the Château de la Muette, in the national delegations in Paris, or in the rear-link machinery set up to deal with the problem of economic co-operation, in all national capitals. Most indicative, perhaps, of the importance attached to this work was the speedy collection and focusing of extremely able American personnel. The latter, whether in Paris, in Washington, in ECA Missions in the participating countries' capitals or peripatetically in all three, was an especially important feature of this, the 'heroic', period in European and European-American co-operation.

The first task of the OEEC (its assignment by the American Administration came as a staggering surprise), was to recommend to the US Government the division of aid to be received by Europe under the appropriation for the first fiscal year of the American Economic Co-operation Act. Within an incredibly short time a most intricate questionnaire had been despatched to participating countries and the replies received and analysed. Within a week the 'Four Wise Men'—the original of a lengthening series of post-war *dei ex machina*—managed, in the seclusion of a small hotel in the forest of Chantilly, to work out a suggested division of a sum of dollar aid substantially less than the original, unscreened, requirements of dollar assistance of the participating countries, but still amounting to nearly $5 billion. In parallel, a system of intra-European credits, so-called drawing rights, was being worked out. By 16 October, at a meeting at the ministerial level, the first annual programme of the OEEC was handed over to Mr. Harriman, the United States Special Representative, and the first intra-European Payments Agreement was signed.

Not long thereafter, on 30 December 1948, the Organization was able to present to the US Government and to publish to the world the first of what has become a regular series of annual reports. This, the Interim Report on the European Recovery Programme, as all subsequent ones, was based on memoranda and tables submitted by individual countries. But, unlike its more recent successors, it was essentially a plan of action designed to sustain the annual programmes, which were the combined European bid for continued American assistance, by providing a framework of broad policy objectives to which participating countries remained committed. Its major contribution lay in the emphasis it placed upon the need for a three-pronged attack on the problem of European viability as measured by its ability to do without dollar aid: the creation of internal financial stability as the basis for a greater production effort, measures to save imports and to stimulate exports and the development of intra-European trade.

Throughout 1949 the activities of the Organization proceeded on the pattern already set. A second division of aid which, largely because of the sudden deterioration in the United Kingdom balance of payments during 1949, gave rise to a good deal of friction and was in fact the last operation of its kind, a second intra-European Payments Agreement, and the continued and enlarged activities of the technical committees in various sectors of industry and on various commodities were the mainstay of the Organization's activity.

To these, however, was added an extremely important new activity based on a British initiative: namely, a plan for the progressive liberalization of trade within Europe. For the rest of this first phase, the programme for freeing trade within Europe from quantitative restrictions was a major feature of the activity of the OEEC. It was greatly advanced by the establishment on 19 September 1950, of the European Payments Union, which, next to the distribution of American aid, has undoubtedly been the most substantial and lasting of the strictly 'operational' achievements of the OEEC. Its creation was foreshadowed in the Second Annual Report of the Organization in February 1950. Its conception owed a great deal to American initiative; and the working out of its detailed provisions was greatly benefited by the technical competence and ingenuity of a handful of devoted American officials and economists.

No sooner had the EPU Agreement been signed than the OEEC entered upon its second and more difficult phase. The Korean war had created new problems ranging from the severe scarcity of certain raw materials, particularly metals, to the financial consequences, both internal and external, of enlarged defence programmes and adverse terms of trade. During the last few months of 1950, the OEEC was making fresh strides in intra-European economic relations by taking 75 per cent as the target for the abolition of quantitative restrictions and by agreeing to certain recommendations of the EPU to improve the balance of payments of Germany (the first and the most notable example of the OEEC's activity in relation to an individual member country). Nevertheless, it was torn by a fierce internal crisis due to the frustrating effects of a worldwide scarcity of raw materials. At once the limitations due to the regional character of the Organization became obvious and when, as a result of Anglo-American discussion, to which France later became a party, the International Materials Conference was set up in Washington, the OEEC had to content itself with no more than passive liaison with that body.

A second and even more serious crisis confronted the Organization in 1951 and the early months of 1952 as a result of the increasing impact of defence programmes upon the economies of the member countries, as well as upon the United States and Canada. This development led to an increasing preoccupation of NATO (itself undergoing a reorganization at that time) with economic matters. For some months the future of the OEEC hung in the balance. As the so-called 'burden-sharing' exercise in NATO, designed to ascertain and, if possible, equalize the relative burdens of their defence efforts upon the economies of member countries, proceeded, and as the flow of American assistance and possible intra-European credits and transfers became increasingly linked to defence measures, it seemed to some countries that NATO was the appropriate forum for all major economic questions, particularly since it had the United States and Canada as full members and could deal with these questions on the only relevant basis, an Atlantic one. Other members of the OEEC feared that if major economic work was undertaken in NATO, the OEEC would be emptied of its substance and the co-operation of the neutrals and Germany would be lost. In the end this did not happen. The report on the economic burden of defence produced by NATO's Financial and Economic Board, perhaps the sharpest post-war document of its kind, remained the high-water mark of NATO's economic work. The symbol of the decision that OEEC was not expendable and, indeed, the best guarantee that it would not be so, was the decision to establish the headquarters of the reorganized NATO in Paris. Once this was done, OEEC's primacy in economic matters remained undisputed. A *modus vivendi* was worked out between the secretariats of the two bodies so far as economic matters were concerned and the delegations of those countries which were members of both bodies could apportion their manpower for the economic work however it suited them best.

Since the middle of 1952, there has been much technical work of varying usefulness, but essentially of a marginal character. Occasionally, it is true, as at the time of the oil shortage during the Suez crisis, the existence of ready machinery has proved very helpful. The central activities, however, of the OEEC have been dominated, first, by intensive preparation for a collective approach towards the convertibility of currencies and, secondly, by the efforts of six of its member countries to form a closer economic union among themselves. Not much need be said about the first of these since, for the time being at least, it is not in the centre of discussion. It was once again a British initiative which, for over two years, provided the most active feature of the discussions and activities of the OEEC. In the spring of 1953 the United Kingdom presented to the Organization ideas for a collective approach to a wider system of trade and payments. These ideas had been thrashed out a year earlier in Commonwealth Conferences; and when the plan for a unilateral adoption of convertibility by the United Kingdom was abandoned, the problem was put before the OEEC. Much work was done during the remainder of 1953, throughout 1954, and in the summer of 1955 in working out on paper the consequences of a return to convertibility of a substantial proportion of the participating countries. This work culminated in the signature, on 29 July 1955, by the Council of the OEEC, of a Protocol which, while extending EPU for another year, also provided for the establishment of a European Monetary Agreement to come into force when a specified proportion of EPU members had made their currencies convertible and had agreed to bring this Agreement into operation. Much of this work remained theoretical. Partly through changes in the economic and financial situation of the European countries themselves, partly and, indeed, mainly owing to a lack of response on the part of the US Government, the plans for a greater degree of convertibility of currencies, as then conceived, were abandoned. Nevertheless, the discussions influenced considerably the subsequent modifications in the EPU. The historical significance for OEEC and European economic development of the fact that the United Kingdom did not return to convertibility—as that of the earlier discussions

F

concerning the relation between OEEC and NATO—must remain one of the major 'ifs' of post-war economic history.

More recently, OEEC has been under the increasing impact of the efforts of six of its member countries, those which in 1949 had subscribed to the Schuman Plan and had later created the European Coal and Steel Community, to extend economic integration among themselves. These tendencies have been in evidence for several years, but it is only recently that they have created an acute problem for OEEC. They go back to the very inception of the European Recovery Programme. Already in 1947 a certain section of Continental opinion, led usually by some French spokesmen, had pressed solutions upon the other partners which were clearly inspired by a desire for rapid progress towards political federation in Europe. Whether in connection with the exploration of a European Customs Union (left on one side in 1947) or with the more pedestrian problems of the powers to be assigned to the international secretariat, there was a basic difference of approach which sometimes led to open disagreement between the United Kingdom and the Scandinavian countries, who favoured inter-governmental methods, and some at least of the representatives of France, Belgium, the Netherlands and Italy, who advocated supra-national solutions. For a time the creation of the Coal and Steel Community seemed to threaten an open breach. In the end, however, perfectly smooth working relations were established between the two bodies and the OEEC was able to continue to devote itself, without any major diminution, to its general tasks in the field of European economic relations.

Since 1955 all discussions in the OEEC have been dominated by the problem of whether the further economic integration of the 'Six' can be reconciled in some form, such as the United Kingdom proposal for a Free Trade Area, with continued co-operation in the economic field among the larger number who form the OEEC. In July 1956, the OEEC Council set on foot the technical work relating to the Free Trade Area proposal, and in February 1957, negotiations were opened. However, before these were concluded, the signing of the Treaty of Rome, with its prospect of a European Economic Community (towards which the first step has now been taken by the establishment of the European Economic Commission and the other common institutions of the Six) has raised a serious question-mark over the future of the OEEC. In October, 1957, the decisive stage in the negotiations to find a common ground between the Six and their partners and to maintain the wider economic co-operation in Europe was reached. While the life of the OEEC as an institution may not depend upon the outcome of these prolonged negotiations, it is no exaggeration to say that its continued existence as a force in European economic affairs does. It is not inappropriate, on this tenth anniversary and while it is at this critical point in its life, to try to appraise its work to date.

Against this sketchy historical background what are to be accounted as the achievements of the OEEC? First and foremost, it must be said that the recovery of Europe from the ravages of war would have been impossible without the Marshall Plan. National policies, national effort, and American help must take the main credit for what has been achieved. But in economic matters, even more than in other aspects of human society, intention, however good, and policy, however wise, have to be canalized through institutions; and if the OEEC had not existed, something very like it would have had to be created sooner or later to give substance as well as moral impetus to the recovery programme. Looking back upon the often fierce discussions between the Europeans and the small group of American representatives giving 'friendly aid' in 1947 and in the early days of the OEEC, one European at least is prepared to admit the wisdom of the continual American pressure for greater institutionalization and for more explicit and detailed undertakings concerning co-operation as against the 'co-opération larvée', the reliance on the invisible hand, which, in international matters at least, appeared at the time to be the European guiding principle. Without the dollars and the goods which they represented, neither production nor trade could have been restored so quickly to their pre-war level and so quickly developed far beyond it. Without them, the European standard of living could certainly not have been raised to its present levels. But without an institution—that is to say, without a constitution and, over and beyond it, a network of people and particular methods of work—the beneficial effects of American assistance would have taken far longer to be felt. In addition to its major role in making American aid more speedily fruitful and multiplying its effect by intra-European payments arrangements, the OEEC has many other achievements to its credit. Most direct and voluminous evidence of its work can be found in the large quantity of literature that it has produced on a variety of technical subjects. Admittedly these are of unequal value. Many are of no great moment, and some, as in all international organizations, may represent a wastage of energy. But in a large number of technical fields, ranging from surveys of oil refining capacity in Europe to technical handbooks on the advantages of hybrid maize, from studies of retial distribution in the United States to those covering tourism in Europe, the OEEC has produced useful additions to economic literature. These studies are partly the work of the secretariat, partly, and perhaps mainly, of experts, government officials, as well as those drawn from industry and trade, brought together in Paris in the technical committees or in *ad hoc* working parties. Much of this work may not be of a kind that it would be worth while to undertake or maintain for its own sake; and if the OEEC were to lose its main role in economic affairs, it is not certain whether many of these ancillary activities could long continue. But, while they do, they undoubtedly provide a valuable supplement to what is being done elsewhere.

Of perhaps more lasting and more fundamental value is the work of the OEEC in the general field of economic and financial analysis. Its annual reports have justly achieved an assured place in the economic literature of Europe. As the second report, perhaps the most pregnant that it has issued, said of itself, it 'is not a mere exercise in research and analysis . . . it is a statement agreed by the Governments of 18 participating countries outlining their problems and the manner in which they propose to deal with them'. Other bodies may have produced more highly skilled, more subtle, and perhaps more profound, economic analyses; but these lack something which the 'negotiated' and, therefore, diluted documents produced by the OEEC have: the agreement of the governments concerned.

However, the importance of these documents has tended to change. In the early years they were vital, partly as a basis for continuing American aid, partly as a framework for the future activities of the Organization, partly as a declaration of intentions of which the conscience of participating governments could always be reminded when policies were embarked upon which were thought to be harmful to the collective interest. As time has gone on and as, significantly, more of the work involved in writing the annual reports has been undertaken by the professional technicians of the OEEC secretariat, the reports have tended to approximate more to the research products of other organizations.

Besides its annual reports, the OEEC has been responsible for a large number of documents on particular aspects of general economic policy, produced sometimes by its own committees, sometimes by a group of distinguished outside experts, and sometimes by the secretariat. To mention only a few, it has published reports on internal financial stability, on foreign investment, on national income comparisons, many of which have become minor classics in economic literature.

In the outcome, however, it is for its contribution to European, and, therefore, world, economic recovery and advance that the work of the OEEC must be assessed. Here, three solid achievements will remain for ever to its credit. First, it initiated and promoted the freeing of trade from wartime and, indeed, many pre-war restrictions. Secondly, it created a payments mechanism in Europe without which all the efforts for freeing trade would have been in vain. This provided a source of much needed mutual credits and enabled continual progress to be made towards greater transferability of currencies within Europe and (through the membership of the United Kingdom) between Europe and the whole of the sterling area. It also provided a shield between European currencies and the dollar and by this very fact made it possible for greater progress towards convertibility to be made. Thirdly, it created, through the programming technique of its early division-of-aid days, a powerful machinery for what has since come to be known as the harmonization of economic policies.

It is true that the OEEC was never seriously tempted to embark upon any grandiose scheme of central planning for all its members. Some of its members have even complained from time to time about the Organization's lack of enterprise in these matters, for example, when suggestions for the co-ordination of investment in participating countries or for the creation of an investment bank linked to trade liberalization proposals were under discussion. The screening of dollar import programmes for the purpose of the division of Marshall Aid was never pushed to the point of becoming an attempt to impose rigid common criteria. Fortunately, the leaders in the OEEC, whether in the secretariat or in the national delegations, were only too well aware of the narrow limits within which paper plans elaborated in Paris could have any effective reality in national capitals.

Nevertheless, the technique of questionnaire and the mutual analysis of replies, the cross-examination of one's expectations and plans by one's peers, have had a powerful effect in moulding national policies. At the very least, they have created a general readiness to 'look over one's shoulder' before taking any major step in economic policy, of asking what consequences it might have for one's partners and how any adverse results might be mitigated. Subtler in its working, often as powerful, and sometimes even more so, than more rigorous constitutional obligations, this habit of consultation and co-operation has resulted in a real limitation of national sovereignty in economic matters. Pressure through the OEEC has on a number of occasions stopped 'backsliders'; and ministers and officials have often testified to the support which they have derived from the work of OEEC when advocating policies of international co-operation in their own countries.

Whatever the future may hold, these are lasting achievements. That they are not greater than they are is due to the limitations to which the Organization is necessarily subject owing to its restricted membership (notwithstanding the undoubted value of Canadian and American association), even more than to the fact that it had its origins in a specific, emergency, operation. The OEEC has always been conscious of the wider economic problems of the world. Controversy has raged from time to time over the part that it might play, for example, in relation to tariffs or worldwide monetary matters; but in the end it has had to content itself with its own pre-occupations, even when wider institutions, upon which the world's hopes of major post-war reorganization have rested, were relatively inactive. This is not to say that the OEEC has not played some part: it has never hesitated to emphasize, for example, the effect upon European recovery of US policy in the field of tariffs, and one cannot deny that it has often raised its voice in these matters to good purpose. In the end, however, in the measure that the urgency of strictly European problems has grown less, the intractable problems of the wider world have obtruded more and the limits of OEEC's scope have been more keenly realized.

Perhaps more lasting, if less tangible, an achievement has been the training in the practice of the new techniques of co-operation developed by the OEEC which has been afforded to a very large number of people through their work in the Organization. An ever increasing number of Civil Servants, permanent or temporary, diplomats, economists, and businessmen in all the participating European countries, in Canada and in the United States, have been drawn into this machinery. However short their contact with it, they have been changed by it.

For those who have had the privilege to be associated with the central machine of OEEC, this experience has for ever profoundly affected the manner in which they view and tackle the processes of international relations. They now hold in common an expertise in certain techniques with large numbers of fellow workers in many countries. But more important than that, however fierce the negotiations and the controversies in which they were engaged, they will have carried away from their work in the OEEC a common attitude. For they have learned that it is not impossible zealously to defend a particular national interest and yet to look upon the problems to be solved as common problems. No doubt this attitude is born of a basic political will; and no doubt, if that will is absent, the attitude cannot long survive. But so far, at least, it has survived and has had a most beneficial influence in many fields other than the OEEC itself. It may not be out of place in writing from London about this decade to mention especially the contribution which the European Recovery Programme has made to increasing the intimacy of Anglo-American relations.

For the European countries themselves, it can, at any rate, be said that Ernest Bevin's hope, expressed in 1947, that this work would be acclaimed 'as a unifying effort never equalled in Europe's long and troubled past', has not been disappointed.

Finally, an even wider reflection may be permitted on an occasion like this. It is, alas, not often in international relations, and particularly in economic matters, that the recognition of what needs to be done, and the power and readiness to do it, go together. In those days of the late spring of 1947 when the Marshall Plan was conceived in Washington they did; and the effects of this combination have been beneficial beyond the most sanguine expectations of the Plan's authors. If the more fundamental economic imbalances in the world have not yet been removed, it is certainly not their fault. Much remains to be done; and one may perhaps take hope from this retrospect that, once again, wisdom, power and will may be united and find as effective an expression.

BRITAIN AND THE COMMON AGRICULTURAL POLICY

(In the months preceding the announcement on 31 July 1961 that we were to enter into negotiation with the European Economic Community, one of the subjects to which a great deal of thought was given in Whitehall was the effect on Britain of having to apply the Common Agricultural Policy. That policy had not yet been fully developed by the Six, which made the task of assessing its effects particularly difficult. I have among my papers some notes which I prepared at the time (May 1961) setting down, in summary form, some of the considerations as I saw them.)

ECONOMIC EFFECTS

The UK farmer. The picture here is reasonably satisfactory. There is no reason to think that, taking UK agriculture as a whole, the support provided by the methods likely to be evolved by a community of which we were a part would be less than that which we are now giving our farmers. The incidence of the change will vary from one section to another. Thus, in the short run, the bacon factories and the specialist bacon-pig producer may be under somewhat greater strain; and so may be the less efficient egg producer. But given an adequate transition period, even the short-run consequences could be greatly mitigated. In the longer run, the widening of the market should provide both greater opportunities and the stimulus to profit from these by improved efficiency. Even horticulture need not be gravely affected.

It is, moreover, most important not to compare the existing situation with that under the Common Market, especially for some of the producers who are likely to come under particular pressure as a result of entering the Community, e.g. pigs, eggs and horticulture. For them the strains are bound to increase even under our present system, unless we were prepared either to see the Exchequer bill rise to intolerable levels or to restrict, if not abolish, the free market régime, i.e. to move towards a managed market of our own. A managed market of our own would probably give us the worst of all possible worlds.

The consumer. Here again, the outlook is not as threatening as is sometimes believed. There will undoubtedly be a tendency for food prices to go up but the rise will be gradual and, in the aggregate, not in-tolerable.

The Exchequer and the balance of payments. There will be considerable savings plus some additional revenue to the Exchequer which could be used to mitigate the rise in the cost of living. The impact on the cost of food imports should not be serious and, in any event, will need to be set against other factors that would influence the balance of payments as a whole.

The Commonwealth. Provided that we can (a) successfully reinforce French and Dutch efforts to keep the producer price levels in the Community reasonable, (b) have an adequate transitional period and (c) negotiate suitable arrangements on two or three commodities of special concern to the Commonwealth, there is no reason to think that Commonwealth agricultural interests would be gravely affected by our entry into the Common Market. We may need to be prepared to see certain minor (or theoretical) Commonwealth interests, e.g. pigmeat, left without any special safeguards, if we are to secure the essential safeguards on the things that really matter most, e.g. hard wheat from Canada, butter and lamb from New Zealand and soft wheat from Australia.

THE POLITICAL PROBLEM

The assessment above is concerned with the substantive economic effects of the arrangements we might make. These might raise political difficulties. Further, and more general, political difficulty will have to be faced if we adopt agricultural support and food import arrange-ments in the form which they are to take in the Community.

The UK farmer. It will not be possible to negotiate arrangements which in sum total amount to a preservation of our existing system of support with the particular legislation and machinery that we have designed to give it effect. In other words, no negotiation is possible that does not begin by our acceptance that there shall be a common agricultural policy. (This, of course, leaves a great deal of scope for negotiation both on the provisions of the Treaty—see Article 237[1]—as well as on the precise content of the Common Agricultural Policy.) The problem *vis-à-vis* the farmers is, therefore,

[1] Which allows any European state to apply for membership.

not only that of convincing them that broadly acceptable economic arrangements can be negotiated, but that they must accept a different way of looking at agricultural support and at the Government's responsibility for it. This would require not only negotiation with the NFUs, but a carefully orchestrated campaign directed at farming and general public opinion.

The consumer. Some adverse comment must be expected on the broad ground that food will be made dear. This, however, should be much less difficult to deal with. There is already considerable acceptance of this point in quarters where hostility might have been most expected.

The food trades. Some will be very vocal in criticizing restrictions on their freedom, particularly the cereals trades. But with careful treatment it should be possible to get their co-operation; especially as the more knowledgeable ones will appreciate that restrictions may have to come anyway.

The Commonwealth. Given a modicum of goodwill on the other side and skill and tenacity in negotiation on ours, the substance of the major Commonwealth economic interests can be secured. But it will not be possible to secure the principle of free and duty-free entry (some of it contractual, some of it traditional) which now governs our food import policy *vis-à-vis* the Commonwealth. The French will certainly resist it and there will be no support elsewhere for a principle which would effectively nullify our acceptance of the Common Agricultural Policy as such. If this is so, then there is, quite apart from detailed economic consultation and negotiation with the Commonwealth, a major political point to be coped with. It may be that in some cases Commonwealth Governments will be content to wait and see what kind of economic arrangements can be secured and assess their total effect before they decide whether to make an uncompromising stand on the principle. But this may not hold for all of them.

CONCLUSION

We must not suppose that we can square the circle. A solution which pleases everyone is out of the question. But our best chance of making the best of it lies in influencing the Common Agricultural Policy before it is completely settled. 'If it were done when 'tis done, 'twere well it were done quickly.'

COMMONWEALTH AND COMMON MARKET

A study of the Treaty of Rome. Published—anonymously—in The Round Table, *December 1961.*

The British Government has always emphasized that the future relationship of the United Kingdom with the European Economic Community raised three main problems: the Commonwealth, British agriculture and the European Free Trade Association. In the debate that preceded the summer recess last year these were regarded as the three main difficulties that stood in the way of a closer association. In the debate just before the summer recess this year, which preceded the Government's application to enter into negotiations for membership under Article 237 of the Rome Treaty, adequate safeguards for these three interests were described as the essential conditions of British membership.

In the public discussion in and out of Parliament during the last few months it has become increasingly clear that the last two problems are of a different order of complexity and gravity from the first. The problem of EFTA is narrowing. Denmark has followed Britain in applying for full membership of the EEC; Norway is expected to do so within a few weeks. The three neutral countries, Sweden, Switzerland and Austria, are likely before the end of this year to have applied for an association under Article 238 of the Rome Treaty, leaving Portugal as the only EFTA member for which even a beginning of a negotiation has still to be made. This is not to say that this is not a most difficult problem, caused on the one hand by the great difference in economic development between Portugal and the rest of western Europe and aggravated on the other by the political anxieties created by Portugal's relations with her African colonies. Nor is a solution of the problem of the neutral countries likely to be achieved without a good deal of further negotiation in which many doctrinal prejudices to be found on both sides of the Atlantic will need to be removed. But the problems created by clashes of economic interests or the difficulty of devising suitable trading arrangements between the three neutral countries and an enlarged European Economic Community should clearly be manageable.

The early fears about the fate of British agriculture in the Common Market seem also to have given way to a more sober assessment. The spread of knowledge of the conditions of farming on the Continent, of the objectives of the Rome Treaty, and, not least, of the difficulties the Six themselves are encountering in their efforts to make progress with a common agricultural policy, have all contributed to making the view more widely held that it is not inherently impossible for the British farmer to be gradually integrated into a single European agricultural market.

The Commonwealth problem, however, remains almost completely intact. It is no exaggeration to say that it forms the core of the hesitation or out-and-out opposition to the Government's present policy both on the part of many of its own supporters and of a substantial section of the Labour Party. There are, of course, other grounds of opposition extending from the pure milk of the doctrine of sovereignty on the one side to the fear that a liberal, capitalist (if not reactionary) Europe will make Socialist planning in Britain impossible on the other. But if a solution for the problem of Commonwealth trade could be shown to be possible and could then be advocated as reasonable and fair in all the existing circumstances, opposition to Britain's entry into the European Community would, one may confidently predict, dwindle to negligible proportions.

The Government clearly believe that there is a chance that this state of affairs can be brought about, or they would not have embarked on negotiations. In this, they are in advance of a good deal of political opinion at home and abroad. The reactions, so far, of Commonwealth countries have in general been, at the very least, discouraging. The consultations which British Ministers had in the summer led to reactions which ranged from reluctant acquiescence to relative indifference. By the time the Commonwealth Finance Ministers met at Accra in September, the British Government had made its application and the range of Commonwealth views had changed, stretching from the cautionary to the almost plainly hostile. No doubt, a heavy discount needs to be applied to these views. In Australia the economic situation is difficult, an election is pending and the two strongest Ministers belong to different parties. Canada, too, has been faced with serious economic problems; the Government has passed through a number of difficult internal embarrassments, notably the Coyne affair; the latent psychosis caused by the conflicting US–Commonwealth pull is always ready to break out into the open; and an election may not be far off. In Asia and Africa the political overtones, real or imagined, of western European integration have been tending to create suspicions, which have also been exploited by extreme left-wing groups. Above all, a collective occasion like Accra must lead to the striking of more emphatic attitudes than real feelings might justify.

But even when all the allowances have been made, there remains, at best, doubt and confusion. This is well illustrated in a recent issue[1] of the Bombay *Economic Weekly*, in which one writer speaks of the Commonwealth attitude as not being very helpful and criticizes the Indian Finance Minister Morarji Desai for having categorically refused to accept associate membership, while another writer, speaking for Africa, expresses the most extreme hostility to what is described as an attempt to establish a collective imperialism of the west European countries.

UNFOUNDED FEARS

These attitudes have their reflection here. The purely economic risks to Britain from any readjustment of Commonwealth trading arrangements do not appear to be a major cause for concern. Admittedly, certain interests have shown some anxiety over the effect of any reduction or disappearance of the preferences which Britain enjoys in the Commonwealth, but it is unlikely that this factor by itself could create a major political difficulty for the Government. It is the economic effect on the other Commonwealth countries that is uppermost in people's minds. It results in the fear that harm to the trading interests of our fellow members will weaken the political links that tie them to the Commonwealth, whose cohesion may in any event be threatened by the increasing political intimacy of our relation with Europe, which membership of the Community must bring about.

The grounds from which these fears are derived are often inadequately examined; and ill-assorted attitudes are often found together. Some of the most vociferous opponents of negotiation with the Community, let alone entry into it, have shown scant appreciation of the position of the newly independent, or shortly to be independent, members of the Commonwealth. They are primarily concerned with the old, white Dominions and their concern for the Commonwealth is little more than a projection of a 'Little-England' attitude. The more thoughtful critics, keenly aware of the inner

[1] 16 September 1961.

tensions already existing within this loosely knit institution, the Commonwealth, and of the difficulty of maintaining it as an effective force in the world, are fearful that the changes likely to be brought about by British membership in the EEC may be altogether too violent to be absorbed.

The question then is whether a reasonable and fair solution is intellectually conceivable and whether it is likely to emerge as a practical proposition from the present negotiation. The first part of this question resolves itself primarily into an analysis of the economic problems posed by an attempt to reconcile the Commonwealth trading system with a European Common Market. The second turns on the political prospects of negotiating such a reconciliation with the Six (with the added complication of making it acceptable to other countries, notably the United States), and, at the same time, with the other Commonwealth countries, to a point where British political opinion, at least, will be prepared to accept it.

WIDE RANGE OF THE TREATY

The provisions of the Treaty of Rome cover a vast range of the activities of the Community's members. Most, if not all, of these affect Britain's present relations with the other members of the Commonwealth, whether these derive from tradition and accepted practice or are embodied in treaties or other agreements. They cover not only economic matters in the strict sense, but many social arrangements, such as social security or labour migration as well as fiscal and financial institutions and practices. Some of these may give rise to special difficulties where Commonwealth countries are concerned. However, these are not likely to be so great as to make the Commonwealth aspect the decisive feature of the negotiation: if they are, in the end, found acceptable by Britain on domestic grounds, they will be capable of being fitted in with the Commonwealth relationship. Moreover, progress on most of these questions among the Six themselves has so far been slow and it should be possible to do much to ease the transition from existing practice to the new communal arrangements.

The core of the Treaty, however, relates to trade within the Community and with the outside world, and to those factors which directly and immediately affect the conditions of trading. The Community aims at the complete abolition of all tariff or other barriers to trade within itself, and at a common external commercial policy, including a common tariff, towards the outside world. A common agricultural policy is an integral part of the common trade policy, and agriculture is to be a part of the future single internal market. It is in this field that the really serious problems affecting the Commonwealth arise, for at first sight at least it is hard to see how one regional trading system can be reconciled with another. It is this obvious difficulty that led the British Government originally to seek a solution through an industrial free trade area. This would have left the two systems intact while providing for a more liberal trading régime, over a part of the field at least, between Britain and the Six. Under such an arrangement the ultimate reconciliation of trading policies over the whole field and between the Six, the Commonwealth and the rest of the world would have been left to be done on a worldwide basis through GATT and other worldwide institutions.

Such an 'easy' solution is now hardly ever mentioned again, even by the most nostalgic. The lesson of 1958 has at last sunk in, and it is now generally accepted that a solution for the Commonwealth problem must be found within the framework of the Common Market. There are few who would quarrel with the way in which the British Government has now presented the different aspects of the Commonwealth problem—as regards both Commonwealth countries and sectors of Commonwealth trade—when it expounded its approach to the negotiations at a meeting with the Six on 10 October. It is becoming increasingly clear that this problem must be taken apart into its main constituents and that each one must be made to yield to its own separate and appropriate solution. Nevertheless, to give such an approach a genuine prospect of success will require a basic recognition by the Six (the British Government may be assumed to have it in full measure!) that there is a total Commonwealth problem to be solved, that a collective Commonwealth interest must, therefore, be acknowledged. The sectional approach will not succeed unless it proceeds from this initial acknowledgement.

Some of the problems faced by the Six when they negotiated the Treaty of Rome were not unlike those now presented by the British application. They also had 'associated oversea territories', dependent, independent, or soon to be independent. In Part Four of the Treaty, in a Protocol 'relating to goods originating in and coming from certain countries' (the so-called 'Morocco protocol') and in the continued availability of Part Four treatment to associated territories that had become independent, the special trading relations between European metropolitan countries and their colonies or ex-colonies were, to a considerable extent, carried into the Community. Existing preferences for associated countries' exports were preserved and extended from the metropolitan country to all the members of the Community. The associated country's participation in the tariff reduction incumbent upon members of the Community was limited by its own need for revenue, or infant industry, duties. Independent associated countries, like Morocco and Tunisia, continued to benefit from 'their' metropolitan country's import régime. No radical departure from special arrangements by which the metropolitan country helped the associated country, such as bulk purchase of tropical products at special prices or other form of subsidy, was imposed.

It is tempting to say that what the Six could do should be available to Britain and the Commonwealth. But there are several reasons why such a wholesale solution of the Commonwealth problem is highly unlikely. The associated countries and territories of the Six were all underdeveloped areas, very largely in Africa. The competition of their main exports between each other in the markets of the Six was relatively unimportant; nor was there any competition of any great consequence between those exports and the products of the metropolitan countries. Moreover, since the signing of the Treaty of Rome a number of the associated countries have become independent, and, although the terms provided in the Treaty of Rome have continued to be available to them, the political penumbra around the original concept of associated territory has become increasingly awkward and has led to a re-examination within the Community of the future link between members and those underdeveloped countries with whom they had special relations.

COMMONWEALTH COMPLICATIONS

The Commonwealth problem is much greater in volume of trade involved, in the scope of countries concerned (both geographical and in regard to the stage of development reached) and in the complexity of constitutional and political relationships with the 'metropolitan' country than that of the associated territories of the Six. Above all, the impact of the competition of their exports on the trade of members of the Six (particularly in temperate foodstuffs) or on the trade of third countries (e.g. of tropical products on the exports of Latin America) is so considerable that an across-the-board solution by means of 'associated territory' status for all members of the Commonwealth will not be acceptable to the Six. More-over, even though the precise nature of that status is now in the melting-pot and may be purged of any colonialist flavour, it is not likely to commend itself even to all the Commonwealth countries who might, in theory, qualify by reason of the degree of economic development they have reached.

But this is not to say that 'AOT' status may not offer a valid and acceptable solution for a number of Commonwealth countries. It is certainly *prima facie* the solution for remaining British colonies, or countries which are on, or have only just passed, the threshold of independence. The problem here will be, fundamentally, not very different from that with which the Six are already faced in any event. It is, in the first place, to take account of political susceptibilities, by moving from the arrangements laid down in Part Four of the Rome Treaty more nearly towards association agreements as contemplated in Article 238 of the Treaty. The replacement of arrangements derived automatically from a past constitutional link by contractual obligations on both sides should enable the underdeveloped countries concerned to drop any remaining scruples against benefiting from arrangements which, Communist or extreme nationalist criticism notwithstanding, are plainly to their advantage.

The other problem will be to fashion trading arrangements which are not intolerable to other interested parties. In some tropical products, for example, a straightforward exchange of preferences, that is to say, an extension of the area in which they are enjoyed (the enlarged European Community) and of the countries which enjoy them (the associated territories of old members and those of the new), might create intolerable conditions for certain outside pro-ducers, particularly in South America. They (and the United States), either directly or through GATT, can be relied upon to put this point most forcibly; and it would be very unwise for Europe, with Britain, not to be mindful of these wider considerations. Fortunately, this problem already exists: Britain's application may enlarge it, but it does not create it. Britain herself has always insisted on the need to ensure that the Community is liberal and outward-looking, and her influence can be expected to be beneficent. Whether through the gradual elimination of preferences and reduction of the external tariff (where this can be done without grave harm to the economy of the associated country) or their replacement by other devices, such as special subsidies or higher buying prices (where this does not lead to permanent economic distortions), the interests of third countries can be taken into account. Embryonic worldwide commodity agreements already exist for some tropical products, such as coffee and cocoa. These too can help both the associated territories and the third countries. And where the liberalizing effects of arrangements designed with a view to preventing vital interests of third countries from being damaged are too severe for the economies of associated countries, development aid from the Community can be brought into play. In short, while there are some highly intractable problems, such as bananas or citrus fruit, a painstaking negotiation, taking different countries and tropical products in turn and based on an imaginative use of the association formula, can provide a solution for an important group of Commonwealth countries and sectors of trade.

The approach to the Commonwealth problem through the provisions for association in one form or another provides the possibility of a solution for the whole trade of the Commonwealth countries that can be covered by it. Subject to the points made above, it would also solve in large measure the problem of trade in tropical products, since most of the countries that are most likely to fall under the association solution are primarily producers of tropical products. Where the association formula proves impossible, the approach will necessarily have to be commodity by commodity. Here, three groups may be distinguished: materials, manufactured goods and foodstuffs (other than tropical). Fortunately, the problem for materials is limited. For most of them the common external tariff is zero or very low; and the acceptance of it by Britain should not cause great difficulty to Commonwealth exporters. There are, however, a handful of materials, such as aluminium, or lead and zinc, for which the common tariff is still too high and where it will be necessary to negotiate reductions, preferably to zero, or at least some tariff-free quotas (as provided for in Article 25 of the Treaty), for Commonwealth suppliers. It is not possible to be positive about the prospects of achieving this. But, having regard to the small number of products involved and to the Community's own desire, manifested in their actions up to now, to keep the tariff on materials for industry low, one can be reasonably confident that an acceptable solution will be found. If it is, a further important sector of Commonwealth trade, affecting in this case not only underdeveloped countries, but also the old Dominions, such as Canada and Australia, will have been safeguarded.

Manufactured goods present a much more difficult problem. In this instance the economic interest of the existing members of the

Community, as well as the interest of third countries who are watching on the sidelines, and, finally, the pure doctrine of the Common Market, all combine to make special treatment for Commonwealth goods a most difficult negotiating objective. These difficulties arise with special force in the case of the developed Commonwealth countries, Canada and Australia. The trade concerned is, of course, very small: only about 7 per cent of Britain's imports from the Commonwealth consists of industrial products; and the proportion of Canada's or Australia's exports of manufactures that come to Britain is even less. These exports, moreover, have grown up under the shelter of a Commonwealth preferential system, which was based upon, even if it was not explicitly intended to preserve, a complementary economic relationship. The essential counterpart for the preferences which British manufacturers enjoy in Commonwealth markets is the unrestricted duty-free or preferential entry which Commonwealth foodstuffs and materials enjoy in the British market.

Nevertheless, the exports of manufactures to Britain from the economically developed members of the Commonwealth is a valuable trade to them and one, moreover, to which considerable political importance attaches. When processed foodstuffs are added (ranging from canned fruits through cocktail sausages to pickles), the trade is so important, both in total and in its relation to employment in particular localities, that neither Britain nor the Commonwealth countries concerned could view with indifference the rapid disappearance of preferences, let alone the imposition of 'reverse preferences' which the application of the common external tariff and the disappearance of the intra-community tariff would involve.

A SCALE OF PRIORITIES

It must, however, be clear that, in the end, some scale of priorities, as regards both commodities and time, will have to be adopted if the negotiations are to be successful. The Six cannot reasonably expect the application to this trade of the full rigour of third-country treatment. This would be against their own actions—the coming into force of the Treaty of Rome did not involve the imposition of a single tariff against an associated country where one did not exist before; and it would be contrary to their professed desire not to deal a damaging blow to the Commonwealth relationship. On the other hand, Canada and Australia cannot reasonably expect Britain to insist on the preservation, for all time and for all the commodities involved, of a preferential relationship which has grown up as part of a system designed for a different purpose and which economic development, including changing competitive conditions in the British market itself, would in any event be likely to call in question. The smallness of the trade serves as an argument on both sides; and a reasonable compromise will need to be worked out.

The export of manufactured goods from the less developed countries of the Commonwealth presents a rather different problem. There is, first, the need to avoid giving substance to the political arguments against linking these countries with Europe. The writer in the *Economic Weekly* already quoted says that 'the effect of the Common Market on industrial development in African countries is likely to be disastrous' because 'the Western powers are biased in favour of agricultural development in Africa'. This is, of course, a travesty of the facts. But if Communist propaganda is not to be given unnecessary nourishment, it is most important that existing or developing industries in the economically less advanced countries should not be harmed by any new European trading arrangements.

Association would, of course, solve most of these problems. It is, however, at least doubtful whether it will in the end prove possible for some of the countries most concerned, such as India. Furthermore, even where it might be, as in the case of a 'dependent' overseas territory such as Hong Kong, the most acute aspect of the problem is that of so-called 'low-cost' competition, for example in textiles; and this would have to be solved by negotiation, whether there is association or not. In a way it is fortunate that this problem has already arisen in Britain's own relations with Commonwealth countries and has, as for example in the case of Hong Kong, led to *ad hoc*, albeit temporary, solutions. Moreover, other countries are also directly and heavily involved, both exporters, such as Japan, and importers, such as the United States. The recent textile conference under the auspices of GATT may not have done more than patch up a temporary easement, and one which is not much to the liking of some countries. But it has perhaps shown the way in which this problem of low-cost competition might be tackled.

Finally, and most complex of all, is the problem of Commonwealth trade in the foodstuffs grown in temperate zones, cereals, dairy and livestock products, some horticultural products and sugar (which is also grown as a tropical product). The difficulties here spring from Britain's traditional free import policy for food, the specialization of the old Dominions to supply the British market, a common agricultural policy in the Community with potentially strongly protectionist features, and the existence or threat of large surpluses of these commodities in the developed countries of the Western world. These surpluses, given continued progress of technique, amounting in places to an agricultural revolution, are likely to grow rather than to diminish. The British Government has indicated that its methods of support for home agriculture could be changed to fit in with a common policy to support the European farmer. Can British food import policy with its traditional (or contractual) unrestricted and duty-free entry (accompanied in some instances by a tariff preference) for Commonwealth products also be fitted in?

This problem, too, must be taken apart before it can be fully appraised. What is at stake here is Australian soft wheat, beef, mutton and lamb, butter and cheese, and sugar; New Zealand lamb, butter and cheese; and Canadian hard wheat. The other major interests are feed grains, mainly barley and maize from Canada, Australia and Rhodesia; and there is also an important interest in certain fruits, notably apples from Australia, New Zealand and Canada. This list is by no means exhaustive; but it contains the items of greatest difficulty, partly because they matter greatly to the exporting country, partly because they raise in the acutest form the issue of outside supplies versus the Community's own production under the Common Agricultural Policy.

The British Government has stated that its aim in the present negotiations is to secure for Commonwealth countries opportunities for outlets comparable to those they now enjoy. There is no inherently insuperable technical difficulty in devising arrangements which will achieve this aim. What is at issue is whether in the long run the Community's agriculture is to aim at a degree of self-sufficiency which will mean the eventual elimination of supplies from the large, efficient producers overseas. In the short run, it is whether the import arrangements under the Common Agricultural Policy for the so-called transitional period, that is before a full common market is in being, are made so restrictive that trading conditions are significantly tilted against Commonwealth suppliers compared with what they might reasonably have expected.

There are, thus, two aspects of this problem and each must be adequately taken into account in whatever solution is negotiated. If the formula of 'comparable outlets' is accepted it will mean that the Community has accepted certain principles that will guide it in the elaboration of its Common Agricultural Policy into the final Common Market stage. These principles will determine the ultimate level of prices for the main products within the Community and any other features of agricultural policy that may significantly affect production or consumption. This, in turn, must set certain limits to the amount of protection against outside supplies: in short, the policy must be so devised as to leave room for products from outside, not only in theory but also as a matter of practical access to the market. The negotiations between the Six and Britain are not the occasion for determining in detail how this is to be achieved in the long run. But if the principles are agreed, there will be the opportunity of giving them practical expression as the Common Agricultural Policy evolves.

MAJOR AGRICULTURAL PRODUCTS

But for the short run precise arrangements will be necessary. These do not present insuperable difficulties. Canadian hard wheat is virtually not grown in Europe and it would be fantastic if the import levy arrangements proposed by the European Commission for regulating grain imports were deliberately devised for the purpose of preventing the British (and some Continental) consumers from having the sort of bread they like and are used to. Australian soft wheat is more difficult, being directly competitive with Continental (and, indeed, British) wheat. But this is a traditional trade and, provided that the French, British and Australian farmers do not display inordinate appetites for the European market, there is no reason why it should not continue on much the same scale as in recent years. French producers can legitimately expect to find some new outlets in Germany (and to some extent Italy) which has the highest-cost production in Europe, and there is no reason why Australian wheat should be put at a deliberate disadvantage compared with French wheat as far as the British market is concerned.

  Butter is already a serious problem. The British market, the only free market in the world, has recently been seriously glutted and returns to even the most efficient producers, the New Zealanders, have fallen below a remunerative level. An embryonic—and short-term—market-sharing arrangement is to be instituted; and this perhaps shows the way for the future. But, in any event, something will need to be done to cope with the mounting flood of dairy production, of which the butter surplus is at the moment the most acute expression. It is clearly nonsensical for the price of butter in many countries of the Six to be twice that in Britain, thus encouraging further production and stifling any possible increase in consumption. Fortunately, the European Commission has not yet produced proposals for dairy products and it is to be expected that the prospect of British membership together with the Commonwealth aspects will significantly influence what ultimately emerges. As for sugar, there is a long-standing Commonwealth Sugar Agreement which is an integral part of an equally long-standing International Sugar Agreement. There is no reason why these forms of international arrangement should not continue.

It is not necessary to go through the whole list of commodities in detail. These examples illustrate what can be done if there is a will to succeed. Lamb might, however, also be mentioned, not only because it is extremely important to New Zealand, but also because it illustrates the problems in agricultural trade that exist quite apart from the complications arising from Britain's prospective membership. The Six produce little, and eat little, lamb. There is hardly any trade in it among them or between them and the outside world. Yet lamb must clearly be included in the Common Agricultural Policy because its price and therefore its supply, must be related to the price of other meat. The problem of what this price is to be is almost wholly one for solution between New Zealand and Britain, the only two important trading partners in this commodity. But it is a problem that would have to be solved whether Britain enters the Community or not. The increasing supplies of New Zealand lamb on the British market have already caused a serious fall in price which, apart from its repercussions on other meats, is pushing up the subsidy the British Government has to pay to its own producers to very high, and perhaps intolerable, levels. New Zealand has been warned that the British market is limited. Here then is an example of the need to find a solution irrespective of the impact of the Common Market.

Indeed, many of the problems in the field of temperate agriculture are problems of evolving or increasing surpluses, affecting many countries. It is tempting to think that Britain's Commonwealth problem in relation to these products could, therefore, find a solution within the framework of worldwide arrangements—be they in the nature of commodity stabilization schemes like the International Wheat, or Sugar, Agreement, or be they new devices for linking the disposal of food surpluses with programmes of aid to underdeveloped countries. It is true that the attention which will have to be devoted to finding a solution to Britain's food imports from the Commonwealth within an enlarged European Community may sharpen awareness of the wider issues and perhaps provide a new impetus towards the evolution of wider and longer-term solutions. But it would be hazardous in the extreme to divert, as it were, the particular problem of Britain's accession to the EEC on terms tolerable to the Commonwealth into the wider arena of world problems. These two sets of considerations, much though they may be expected to converge in the long run, belong to two different universes of discourse and, indeed, use different institutional channels for discussion and resolution. A premature attempt to seek the solution of specific Commonwealth problems in these wider arrangements might prove destructive of any prospect of British membership of the EEC.

Nor is this necessary. As already stated, given the acceptance for the short- and long-term of the principle of comparable outlets and given an awareness by both the Commonwealth and the Continental exporters of the limits of the British market, there is no doubt that suitable arrangements can be made. Above all, both must recognize that it is by no means certain that, in the absence of such arrangements, glittering prizes can be won on the British market; just as the British farmer is beginning to recognize that for him, too, the choice is between two different forms of change, not between change and standing still.

POLITICAL HESITATIONS

But even if suitable arrangements can be made for a transitional period and some general assurance obtained for the longer term, the Commonwealth countries may well ask whether this is enough. Does it mean some temporary alleviations, on temperate foodstuffs, tropical products, some materials, perhaps even some manufactured goods, but inevitably in the end the disappearance of the total Commonwealth trading system? Alternatively, the Six may ask whether these arrangements do not add up to such a dilution of the concept of a European Common Market, that it will cease to have practical meaning. It is from this sort of doubt that the political hesitations on both sides spring. Certainly, on the Commonwealth side, the direct political consequences of Britain's joining the Community cannot, without a good deal of special pleading, be made to look very serious. The Treaty of Rome itself contains no political provisions. And such closer political institutions as may yet come about can hardly be regarded as derogating more severely from British sovereignty, or to be more likely to be inimical to the intimacy of Commonwealth consultation, than WEU, NATO, SEATO, or ANZUS. European federation would, of course, make a difference. But federation cannot be forced upon members of the EEC and it is hardly good sense to speculate on the conditions that may obtain if and when it were to be on the agenda as a practical proposition, any more than it would have been useful to speculate in 1939 on Sir Winston Churchill's offer to France, a year later, of joint citizenship; or than it would be to speculate on the precise changes that may occur over the next few years in the political circumstances within the Commonwealth itself.

The only political fears which it is worth while arguing about as a practical matter are those which spring from concern over the indirect political consequences of disturbances to the pattern of economic relations. For the existing European Community, the safeguard lies in Britain's wholehearted acceptance of the basic objectives of the Rome Treaty. To find an accommodation for Commonwealth trade should not be fundamentally more difficult than was the negotiation of arrangements which the Six made for their own associated territories or those which they will have to make either through GATT or otherwise in respect of their trade with others of their trading partners. They have acknowledged the value of the Commonwealth politically: the consequence of this is that they must have due regard to the Commonwealth's economic well-being. They have professed a desire to be outward-looking: the Commonwealth could well be the touchstone by which their sincerity can be tested.

For the Commonwealth countries, the essential is to recognize the inevitability of change. There is no field of Commonwealth trade—from lamb to motor cars, from grey cotton cloth to cocoa—in which the conditions of trade have not changed radically in recent years and in which the one thing that it is safe to forecast is further change. Mr. Duncan Sandys, the Commonwealth Secretary, speaking of its political content, has described the Commonwealth as the child of change. This is no less true of its economic content. It is a hard thing, particularly for politicians, to compare not what is with what is proposed, but what is proposed with what might otherwise be. Commonwealth trade with Britain and with the rest of the world is at this moment undergoing rapid changes. Only this year the wheat situation has been dramatically transformed by Australia's large sales to China and by Canada's poor crop. The British market for food is becoming more and more hazardous to Commonwealth exporters; and if the EEC is not enlarged by Britain's entry there is no guarantee that it will become less, rather than more so. Of course, the Commonwealth exporter likes to think that whatever happens it will be the British Government he will have to deal with rather than 'the Community'. But what matters in the end is what Britain inside or outside the Community can do for and with the Commonwealth. A Britain with a faster rate of economic growth, with wider trading possibilities, with a stronger voice in Europe, must be a more useful member of the Commonwealth, even if, say, free entry for meat or wheat has to give way to some other arrangement. But it takes statesmen to see this; and in this respect, too, the present negotiations will be a test for all the members of the Commonwealth.

For Britain, too, the inevitability of change must be the guiding thought. Cheap food is already threatened by the need to prevent Exchequer subsidies from rising while still supporting the farmer. Market sharing can no longer be regarded as anathema when it is the only way of reconciling the interests of domestic, Commonwealth and European producers. Preferences are poor guarantees of a market when not only price but competitiveness in delivery, design and service determine sales. In short, it is not a clinging to what is that can bring salvation. 'Our stability is but balance, and conduct lies in masterful administration of the unforeseen.'

AGRICULTURE AND INTERNATIONAL TRADE

The eighth Heath Memorial Lecture, delivered at the University of Nottingham on 21 May 1962.

INTRODUCTION

I am much honoured by your invitation to give the Heath Memorial Lecture this year and to join so distinguished a list of lecturers. I am bound to say at once that I am awed by their eminence in the field of agriculture and agricultural economics, in both of which such knowledge as I have has been acquired along the administrative route. The only basic equipment I can bring to my task lies in the field of general economics. Moreover, those who have preceded me have been able to lecture on their subject without any inhibition; indeed, it was their job to speak freely. Either because of their academic position, or because they were known to be associated with particular interests, it was possible for them to express their points of view with clarity and directness. My position is rather different. When Professor Britton invited me to give the lecture this year I had to point out to him the restraints under which I, as a public servant, would be in regard to matters with which I am concerned, or with which I have been concerned, in the course of official business. Thus, not for me the fearless path of pure reason or the open espousal of sectional interest.

I am nevertheless delighted to make this brief return to a university audience and to be enjoying at least some of the latitude appropriate in an academic environment. I hope, however, that you will understand it if I walk somewhat warily around those parts of the field which, however interesting they might be, are full of land-mines since they are the object of current Governmental activities. I would like, therefore, to take refuge in the now time-honoured phrase of the cinema that any resemblance between what I am saying and current preoccupations, whether in Whitehall or in Brussels, is purely 'coincidental'.

The subject I have chosen is, of course, a very large one; and I propose, therefore, to pick out some of the major features to concentrate on. One selection which I will make for the sake of compression is to deal with foodstuffs only and to leave out agricultural raw materials such as cotton, which raise somewhat different problems. Finally, you will, of course, understand that my treatment of the problems with which I shall be dealing will be that of an administrator rather than that of a pure economist.

SOME BASIC ECONOMIC CONSIDERATIONS

May I, however, begin by recalling certain basic economic considerations. Up to the period of classical political economy, land had occupied a very special position in thinking about economic matters. Indeed, the immediate forerunners of the classical economists, the Physiocrats, built the whole of their theory round land, which they regarded as the ultimate source of all wealth. It was not until the time of Ricardo that the great emancipation from all the fetters of pre-classical thought, physiocratic or mercantilist, finally took place. The remnants of pre-scientific thought were discarded, and the broad general principles of economics made their appearance. Among these general scientific laws of classical political economy the doctrine of comparative costs and, with it, the belief in the wealth-creating effects of the international division of labour acquired a central and highly important place. It became one of the most solidly based and widely accepted parts of the general body of economic doctrine. From the extreme liberal, on the one hand, to Marx on the other— though I must at once point out that he had quite special reasons for wanting 'wage goods' to be low—the principle of free trade, including free trade in foodstuffs, was accepted as part of that régime in economic matters most likely to contribute to the optimum use of resources, and, therefore, to the highest development of material wealth.

I do not wish to suggest that this principle was immediately accepted. It took some time to assert itself even in its home, England. It was not until the abolition of the Corn Laws under Peel that England finally broke with the protectionist traditions and installed a free trade régime which remained virtually intact until the Great Depression of the thirties. On the Continent, progress was perhaps even slower. Free trade in food—like other blessings of classical political economy—was not so readily accepted as it had been in England and, if world trade in food expanded during the nineteenth century and in the first few decades of the twentieth century, this was more often in spite of remaining restraints rather than because of their removal. Even after the liberalizing influences of the second quarter of the nineteenth century, free trade was, by the middle of that century, still European rather than worldwide.

THE DEVELOPMENT OF INTERNATIONAL TRADE IN FOOD

It was not until the second half of the nineteenth century that an amazing upsurge took place and trade in general and in foodstuffs in particular became worldwide. This development was both accompanied by, and, in part at least, reinforced by the opening up of great areas of cultivation such as the United States Midwest, the Canadian West, Argentina and Australia. Taking 1913 as 100, the quantum of exports of food and of all other exports, according to the very interesting studies of Mr. Lamartine Yates, developed as follows:

	1876	*1929*
Food exports	33	136
All exports	30	135

The causes for these tremendous increases, apart from technological development and the opening up of new areas of production, to which I just referred, as well as to the gradual spread of more liberal policies, are to be found in the rapid fall throughout that period of the death-rate, resulting in a rising population as well as in rising real incomes. This produced a marked shift in diets to fats, sugar, animal products, fruit and tropical beverages. At the same time, technical advances, for example in the field of refrigeration, made transport from distant lands easier. European settlers in the temperate zones were responsible for large-scale increases in agricultural production in those areas, while European and, later, North American capital, through plantations cultivated by native labour, greatly expanded production of tropical products in the tropical areas of the world.

This great upsurge of world trade in foodstuffs masked the extent to which special and protectionist policies in regard to agriculture continued to exist and, therefore, diminished the attention given to the special problems which were latent.

The trend to which I refer was not an uninterrupted one, wars being the most important causes of a temporary halt in the trend. Taking, for example, the quantum of exports as 100 in 1913, we find that in the forty years to 1913 world food exports trebled, while in the forty years after 1913 they rose by only 54 per cent. The momentum was getting less all the time. In the twenties and thirties food exports ran at about one-third above the 1913 figure, while in the fifties they ran at about only 15 per cent above 1937. Food prices also have lagged, possibly due to a more rapid lowering of costs in the field of agriculture in recent decades as a result of intensified technological progress. Taking 1913 as the base year, we find the following position of the price of food compared with all exports:

	1929	*1953*
Food exports	113	225
All exports	125	259

These figures, both of volume and of prices, mirror, I think, the cycle of wars and depressions. The former have always given a powerful stimulus to greater production, to more intensive efforts to achieve efficiency as well as self-sufficiency in food production. The Napoleonic Wars were, as everyone knows, an important watershed in this respect, exemplified particularly by the tremendous increase of sugar production on the Continent and the consequent difficulties created for tropical countries. It is interesting to observe the rhythm of world sugar production during the present century and how closely correlated that is with the cycle of war and post-war, as the following figures show:

Percentage of total world production

	beet	cane
1901/02	54	45
1913/14	49	51
1919/20	29	71
1938/39	37	63
1945/46	28	72
1953/54	40	60

The strategic argument in favour of self-sufficiency in food production has always been powerful. In Britain it has asserted itself particularly during the Second World War, leading to considerable increases in food production, so that today almost two-thirds of all the 'temperate' foodstuffs consumed in Britain are home-produced.

THE PRESENT POSITION

What is the present position? Most countries exhibit, I think, a similar pattern. First of all, there has been a relative decline in the importance of agricultural production in the economy as a whole, which shows itself particularly in a diminution in the percentage of the population engaged in agriculture and in the percentage of the gross national product contributed by agriculture. Of course, this movement has been more rapid in some countries than in others, but the trend is, I believe, the same in all the advanced countries of the world. At the same time, there has been rapid, and, indeed, rapidly increasing technical progress, so that the absolute increases in output have been enough, and often more than enough, to meet the increasing demand of a rising and more opulent population. We have also witnessed recurrent government action, primarily for social reasons, to delay the adjustment which would otherwise have taken place, by means which certainly very often and perhaps inevitably have led to restrictions on international trade and to recurrent surplus problems.

Perhaps I should interpolate here that what I have just said requires some qualification in that a distinction has to be drawn between the products of the temperate zone and those of tropical areas. In the former, the development of the last few decades has shown a combination of international and domestic aspects, whereas, as far as the tropical products are concerned, recent events have been wholly related to international trade. There has been no decline in the relative importance of tropical agriculture in the countries concerned. The move away from monoculture, or reliance on a few crops, is very difficult and the rigidities of supply are very great. The latter aspect is particularly powerful in those tropical tree products which have a long production cycle. Coffee is an extreme example of this feature.

WHY IS AGRICULTURE PROTECTED?

It is an interesting study to explain why the attempts to insulate agriculture, or at any rate to protect it from the effects of the cold winds of economic change, should have been so persistent and so widespread. Some of the reasons are obvious: they lie in the technical, as well as in the social conditions of agricultural production. Agriculture is tied to the soil. The mobility of capital is low and that of labour low or often completely non-existent. But on top of these technical reasons there can be found what one modern economist, Professor Boulding, has called an 'agricultural fundamentalism', reaching back to Biblical history, which helps to account for the unique position of the agricultural way of life in many societies. This agricultural fundamentalism has its political expression also; that is to say, the strength of the rural influence in the political life of a country is often not in proportion to the numerical or economic significance of those engaged in agriculture. Some of us, for example, will have noticed that in the United Kingdom there is, regardless of party, a strong and persistent influence of the 'rural vote' which cannot be measured at all by the four per cent or so of the working population which is engaged in agriculture or by the roughly similar percentage which is the agricultural contribution to the Gross National Product.

It is not easy to find a single unifying explanation for the peculiar position which the agricultural sector has always occupied in the economy; for example the degree of subsidization of agriculture is by no means related to the importance of agriculture in the economy. Indeed, it is very tempting to see a converse relation. I have already drawn attention to the position in this country. On the other hand, you find in some countries in which agriculture is predominant, as in Denmark or New Zealand, that there is no, or hardly any subsidization, while at the same time the agricultural community is highly prosperous. This is a fascinating subject for study, but I think it would take us too far afield tonight to go much further into it. My own feeling is that the explanation and evaluation of this agricultural phenomenon must be eclectic. In Europe, notably, national and military history have played an important part, as I have already indicated when I mentioned sugar. In the old German Empire agricultural protection was undoubtedly undertaken both as a political counterbalance to what was then the heavy industry of Austria as well as to provide a readily available supply of manpower, which was equated with military strength. A Europe free from war might well have developed differently in regard to the balance of agriculture and the urban economy. Another striking contrast is offered by the Soviet Union, which has shown persistently recurring examples of the systematic exploitation of the rural areas by the urban population without the least concern for 'agricultural fundamentalism'.

THE METHODS AND CONSEQUENCES OF AGRICULTURAL PROTECTION

Whatever may be the scientific explanation for the place which agriculture occupies, there is very little doubt about the arguments by which agricultural protectionism has over the centuries been justified. These have been, broadly speaking, in three classes: social, strategic, or economic (related in recent years in particular to the balance of payments). I do not propose to analyse these arguments or to say how valid they are. This I must leave to the professional economist. As an administrator, I can only ascertain the facts of the situation, examine their consequences and see what means are available for solving, or mitigating, the problems to which they give rise.

The first and most important consequence to which the concern for the welfare of agriculture gives rise is that of the restriction of international trade. The Biblical saying about the camel and the rich man and the eye of the needle can very often be adapted to the ease with which agricultural produce can move across national boundaries. There are many commodities that I can think of, but will refrain from mentioning here, which it is almost impossible to import into one country from another. I hasten to add, still using a Biblical saying, that I think we can none of us afford to throw stones. All countries sin in this respect, though some sin more than others.

From an economic point of view the methods adopted are relatively secondary. The important thing is that the object and result are generally similar, namely to achieve a higher level of domestic agricultural output than would otherwise be the case, thus interfering with the results of the international division of labour which the textbook would stipulate.

From a political and administrative point of view, however, the methods can be of considerable importance. It is now generally appeciated that while both in Britain, and in most Continental countries, notably the countries of the European Economic Community, agriculture is supported by the State, the methods that have been in force to this end for many years are basically very different. Broadly speaking, in the countries of the European Economic Community such support as the State has wished to give to agriculture has taken the form of managing the market, either by means of direct intervention or by means of control of imports through tariffs, levies and quotas, or by a combination of these measures, so as to raise the return which the farmer gets to whatever is considered the adequate level. In Great Britain, on the other hand, the system in operation since the immediate post-war period has, broadly speaking, been one in which the market return is allowed to find its own level, interventions whether at the frontier or internally being virtually absent, while the desired income of the farmer has been achieved by giving him a direct supplement in the form of subsidies, the so-called deficiency payments. Having stated this fundamental difference, I think it is only right to add that there are, nevertheless, some similarities between Britain and the countries of the Community. For example, direct subsidies are not entirely absent on the Continent, especially in Germany, while the British system is not exclusively one of deficiency payments (for example, milk).

It is very difficult to say which combination of methods produces a higher degree of protection. Indeed, measuring the level of protection itself is an almost impossible task as the recurrent attempts to do so, for example in the framework of the GATT, have shown. One advantage that is sometimes claimed for the British system is that it is one which makes the cost of supporting agriculture plain and obvious to every member of the electorate. An educated electorate in a democratic system, it is argued, would rather take the cost of supporting a particular section of the community on the taxes so as to be able to see exactly what it is spending and to have a direct control over it. I would not venture to pronounce on whether there is really a substantial difference, from this broad political point of view, in the two systems, one which supports agriculture by placing the cost squarely on the consumer or one which does so by making the taxpayer foot the bill. I think it can be argued that such difference as there may be between these two approaches is becoming less and will progressively disappear as society becomes more affluent, on the ground that it could be said that there is a tendency in more affluent societies for the supposed advantages, from the point of view of equity, of direct taxation as compared with indirect taxation, to fade away.

By the same token, the advantage that is sometimes claimed for one's own economy from having something like the British system is, at best, not easy to measure. It might even be doubted whether it exists at all. This advantage is said to consist in the fact that the availability of cheap food produces a better competitive position in regard to industrial costs. It is also said that it provides a better yardstick for measuring the true economic cost of agricultural support because it allows for the continued existence of a 'free' world market price.

As I have already said, the first of these two arguments must assume a different significance according to the degree of development and affluence of the society which we are considering. Similarly, the more direct effect of low food prices may be no indication whatever of the significance, in terms of industrial costs, not only because there is a compensating additional burden of taxation to be taken into account, but also because the unit price of a particular article of food (as the unit cost of any other consumption item) is not an indication of the significance which this occupies in the family budget, the level of wages, the level of earnings, the level of labour costs, and all the other items that enter into industrial costs of production. I am sure I need not belabour this particular point to an audience of economists.

Again, as far as having the yardstick of a free world price is concerned, the extent to which agriculture is subsidized, both directly and indirectly, domestically as well as directly for the purposes of export, the effect of differential freight rates and all the other means for 'distorting competition', are factors which do not make it easy to claim that world prices are necessarily indicators of economic cost.

From the point of view of the countries that export food it may be argued that free access to an importing country, even though that country supports its own agriculture by means of Exchequer payments, is an important advantage and makes direct subsidies preferable to any other system of agricultural support. This view is sometimes expressed by saying that the Chancellor of the Exchequer is the exporting countries' best ally. There are, however, at least some off-setting disadvantages. As I have already said, in times in which price formation in a free world market is apt to be distorted by export subsidies, by dumping, by artificial freight rates, etc., free access will often be regarded by the primary producing countries as a mixed blessing, since it does not provide a guarantee against unduly depressed prices and consequent low returns to the producers.

I have made these points not in order to make a case for or against one system or another, but rather to show that from the point of view—perhaps the somewhat cynical point of view—of an administrator, the different forms of agricultural protection cannot be painted in black and white.

THE POSITION OF THE FARMER

But what about the farmer? Is there a distinct advantage for him of one system as against another? I suppose an ideal system for the farmer might be the one that existed in Britain during, and immediately after the war, namely that of fixed prices at which the whole of his annual output was purchased. Of course, this system operated in a period of shortage when all, and literally all, that the farmer could produce was wanted by the community and was bought, allocated and rationed by the Government; when, moreover, the whole of the economy was carefully regulated so that the prices which were negotiated for the output of the 'national farm' were carefully geared into the pattern of prices and incomes determined by the overall economic strategy of the war.

I remember still vividly from my own experience the doubts and uncertainties, sometimes the resistance, of our own farmers when the system of fixed prices and bulk government purchase had to give way at the end of the war to the freer system that we now have of deficiency payments and 'standard prices', i.e. prices which are not necessarily attained for every unit of output by every farmer. But now that the farming community has become used to this system it sees clearly its advantages, and equally clearly the disadvantages of any alternative system. Some farmers at least see also some of the difficulties to which the present system gives rise, notably the high margin of uncertainty of what the total cost to the Exchequer will turn out to be and the unwelcome attention of the taxpayer when that cost rises too much. There are also sometimes actual difficulties of disposal of what is produced, which the system by itself cannot overcome. I suppose a mixed system, providing assurance against all possible contingencies, would be ideal as far as the producer is concerned. To some extent a mixture does now exist or, perhaps I should say, has been forced upon us, by the exigencies of an expanding farm output. In Britain we have tried through a Barley Working Party, to guide (I am glad to say usually successfully) the market rather than to leave it entirely to itself; and we know that in the case of butter, the disorganization of the market has forced us to have recourse to a system of quantitative restriction of imports. Nor is this kind of development confined to Britain. On the Continent, too, no one single system has been found to cope with all contingencies; and new features have had to be added from time to time. It is perhaps worth emphasizing again what I said a few moments ago, that our system is not a single uniform one. We have different arrangements for milk, eggs and potatoes, for example, from those which obtain for cereals or fatstock, which show the method of deficiency payments probably in its purest form. For pigs, again, the flexible guarantee system introduced not along ago is an attempt to introduce some element of long-term planning of production of a quantitative character into an otherwise free price system, supplemented by deficiency payments.

THE FUTURE

Can we discern any clear tendencies for the future? Or, better still, can we establish certain guidelines for the future development of agricultural protection, taking it as a basic fact of the situation that in all countries there will be continued agricultural support and that, whatever the pure economist may say, the politician and the administrator will have to wrestle with the problem of how best to organize it? To make the question more precise, is there any means of so adapting the method of agricultural support as to avoid aggravating the problems of international trade, better still, so as to alleviate them, while at the same time absorbing the technical progress which we may be sure will continue, and even accelerate? If this task can be accomplished, this would clearly mark a tremendous advance from the point of view of bettering international economic relations, and, beyond that, avoiding political frictions at a time when the consolidation of the Western world must be an over-riding objective.

Perhaps the problem can be looked at under three separate headings. The first is that of the problem posed for all of us in Europe by the creation of the European Economic Community and, in particular, by its Common Agricultural Policy, and by the prospect of the enlargement of that Community through the accession of the United Kingdom and of other European countries. The second aspect is that of the wider, perhaps I might say worldwide, problem of agricultural trade, and the third is the problem of tropical agriculture.

On the first of these, in many ways perhaps the most pressing and the most interesting, I am unfortunately in a position in which I am able to say the least. What I can do is to point to the fact that opinions differ very widely on what effects the gradual approximation of the United Kingdom system to that of the common agricultural policy—which is what would be involved in our membership— would have. For example, one distinguished economist, Professor Meade, who has taken at best a doubtful view of the consequence of our membership in the European Economic Community, has said in an article that 'unification of United Kingdom agricultural arrangements with the agricultural arrangements of the Six would involve a wholly undesirable increase in the amount of protection afforded to the British farmer. This danger is especially real for those who, like myself, would like on the contrary to see a substantial reduction in the degree of protection given to the United Kingdom farmers.'

Here is a liberal economist speaking, and his fears contrast strangely with those which one hears from some, though probably not all, of the representatives of the farming community who, on the contrary, fear that the degree of protection available to them under the Continental system will be less, or at least less certain and in a less satisfactory form than the one that they have enjoyed hitherto. You will forgive me if I don't go any further into this particular argument, but rather turn to another aspect of it which is this. As a highly industrialized country with vital interests in the ability to export our industrial products, while at the same time committed to continuing to maintain a healthy agriculture, we have in recent years had a most difficult and delicate balancing act to perform. We have had to strike a balance between the needs of our own farmers and the needs imposed by our worldwide trade interests, in which must be included more particularly those of our fellow members of the Commonwealth, many of whom are especially interested in their continuing market in Britain for the same sort of foodstuffs that our own farmers produce. This problem is, of course, not peculiar to us. It is one which faces many industrialized countries of the world and many of the countries in Europe who would be our partners in an enlarged European Economic Community. They, too, in varying degrees, perhaps most notably Germany, have had to achieve this balance. They have done so by different means, and it may be argued that the system we have had in the last nine or ten years in Britain provides a simpler mechanism for achieving a balance of the kind I have described. Relatively free imports, relatively low or non-existent tariffs for the bulk of our agricultural imports other than horticulture, and a virtually automatic means of supplementing farmers' returns through the system of guarantees which we have with its annual reviews and so on, provides, so it may be thought, a smooth mechanism for reconciling the interests of our home producers with those of our overseas trade partners.

I think myself that this is much too simple a view. In the first place, as I have already said before, our system is not as uniform as the description of it devised for the purpose of simplifying the exposition.

In the second place, the interests that have to be reconciled are often so varied that a highly complicated, not to say agonizing, appraisal is usually involved in trying to achieve the right balance.

It is, of course, true that a switch to a different system of support, such as that provided by the Common Agricultural Policy, while not altering in any way the basic need to achieve a balance of interests, would present us with new problems of methods and mechanics, and this is something which the great supplying countries, and particularly our fellow members in the Commonwealth, are bound to view with a measure of doubt and uncertainty.

Again, this is a point on which I cannot elaborate. I must leave it at what has been said publicly by those who can speak for the Government on these matters. What I would rather wish to emphasize to an audience of fellow economists is the simple point that the problem of this reconciliation between the needs of trade and the needs of domestic agriculture is with us already, would still be with us in the new circumstances created by an enlarged Community, and is continually getting more difficult. I think it is not overstepping the bounds of propriety to say that any objective observer must have realized already that this problem will become increasingly difficult to solve, whether we become members of the European Economic Community or not, and that it can by no means be clear that the solution would be more easily achieved in the one hypothesis than in the other. From a broad, long-term, economic point of view, this is a problem that requires a wider international solution if it is to be a durable one.

One may, of course, hope that on the positive side one could count upon increases in consumption following upon rising standards of living; but can that in itself cope with the problem? We all know Adam Smith's remark about the limited capacity of the human stomach, although perhaps since the days of Adam Smith we have learned something of the wider limits set for the capacity of the human palate and of the possibilities, through improved presentation, to find increasing outlets for food. But I would certainly not dissent from those who doubt whether such possibilities will be enough to provide solutions to the problems I have described.

How are patterns of trade to be adjusted in a way that minimizes harmful consequences? I think myself that this can only be done by a recognition of the mutual responsibilities of the countries involved, including the European Economic Community, and the Commonwealth countries, and by a readiness, through wider international arrangements and agreements, to stabilize prices, allow production and consumption patterns, as well as patterns of trade, to be continuously adjusted to changes of technology of agriculture in a manner least harmful to the interests of the individual countries concerned. I have no great illusions about the complete efficacy of worldwide agreements which are really attempts to manage agricultural markets on a wider international basis. I am not sure that they will necessarily achieve what the unaided classical price mechanism (were it realistic to expect that it would ever function perfectly), or that half-hearted price mechanism which has operated in spite of national policies designed to frustrate it, has failed to achieve, namely, to balance supply and demand. In short, I have little doubt that we shall be faced, even with the best devised and managed international schemes, with the alternative of either seeing price stabilization frustrated or surpluses emerging which cannot be disposed of in the normal commercial way. It is likely, therefore, that no international commodity agreement will be wholly satisfactory unless it also includes some provisions for dealing with any surpluses that may emerge.

THE PROBLEM OF SURPLUSES

In this connection, I would merely wish to draw your attention to three problems that arise, and which are usually overlooked, in often well-meant statements about the need to find new surplus disposal methods. First of all, there is the question of how these surpluses are to be financed. Clearly, a fair distribution is essential, both as far as the donors and the recipients are concerned. In the second place, if these surpluses are to be disposed of in a non-commercial way to help, for example, the developing countries, it is important to be clear first as to the form in which the surpluses are to be made available, and secondly, as to the effect they will have on the economy of the donor country. Disposal in kind of food surpluses must be carefully integrated with other forms of aid to developing countries, both from their point of view and from the point of view of the donors. What can be said with certainty, I believe, is that it would do neither the donor nor the recipient much good if the system of surplus disposal was such as to result in the deliberate and continuous creation of surpluses, however much that may be regarded as an easy way of solving the problem of adjusting agricultural production to a new situation, both in the donor and in the recipient country.

Lastly, a word about tropical products, for which I have now left myself very little time. I would, however, like to stress that this problem has rather special features different from those that apply to temperate foodstuffs. Generally, these are products on which the economy of certain developing countries is highly dependent. Also, very often, if not always, they are produced in countries which have a special relationship, for historical reasons, with some advanced industrial country; and even where that relationship has ceased to be a political one, certain economic features such as preferences or special price arrangements continue to exist. Ideally, one could argue that the best thing to do for developing countries who are dependent for their income on one or two or, at any rate, very few tropical products, is to free the trade in these products entirely. I think one can discern that there is a trend to this effect in the world; and this is one which any economist must welcome. At the same time, one has to recognize that the pace of this advance will have to take account of the needs of some countries which will continue to require some kind of preferential treatment and which cannot be immediately exposed to the full force of competition from all other producers.

There are other means which must be employed for helping these countries. One is to expand consumption by appropriate price and fiscal policies, notably by the reduction or the abolition of revenue duties, for example, on tropical beverages. The other is by means of price stabilization schemes, for example, for sugar, cocoa, and coffee, for all of which schemes either exist or are in prospect, even though some of them, notably the Sugar Agreement, are not fully effective at the moment.

CONCLUSION

I fear that I have done little more than to present you with a vast array of problems which I have tried to group in some sort of order without, however, being able to indicate very clearly what the solutions might be. For the economist to devise solutions may not be too difficult. I remember my own lack of inhibition in this regard some twenty-five years or so ago. But for the politician and the administrator the problem is different. They are constantly exposed to many and conflicting pressures which bring home to them that they are dealing with real problems of real people, whose real livelihood has to be safeguarded, and who, in a democracy, have the means of

making it abundantly clear when they feel that their interests are
threatened! What the statesman, therefore, must strive for and what
the administrator can help him to achieve, is a continuous compromise between conflicting interests. I am persuaded by my own experience that this is possible even in this very difficult field, provided that the appetites of those directly concerned are not excessive.
It is for the economist to seek the truth and to pronounce it fearlessly
as he sees it. The aim of the statesman, though less exalted, is not an
ignoble one; the prize to be won is that of strengthening rather than
of weakening the bonds that unite the comity of nations.

EUROPE—THE ONLY WAY

A review of After the Common Market *by Douglas Jay. Published in* The Times *25 April 1968.*

Since his liberation from the fetters of office, Douglas Jay, once an accomplished journalist, has again become a publicist, mainly to campaign in magazine and newspaper articles against Britain's entry into the Common Market. In a new Penguin Special, *After the Common Market*, out today, he returns to this task with unabated zeal. I shall have to say some rather critical things about it. Let me therefore emphasize at once that this is a serious contribution to an important subject. As one would expect from a distinguished writer and experienced politician, Douglas Jay provides a most vigorous presentation of the 'anti' case. He does not fall into the error of thinking that the 1961–3 negotiations were (or could have been) about kangaroo meat: he knows that extremely important issues were, and are, at stake, political no less than economic. Nevertheless, this is not a coldly objective book. The sort of 'on the one hand—on the other hand' type of analysis is not Douglas Jay's forte. Sam Goldwyn would have found him a splendid one-armed lawyer, who goes in for hard-hitting polemical stuff with no nonsense about motes and beams. Indeed, by the time one has finished reading Douglas Jay one is amazed that anyone in his senses could ever have conceived the idea of Britain joining a movement for an integrated Europe; let alone that both a Conservative and a Labour Government should have actively tried to do so—to say nothing of the support for it of the Liberal Party, the CBI and the frequent majorities of those who answer public opinion polls.

The case he makes so vividly is already well known: it rests on the twin horrors of the Common Agricultural Policy with its effect on Britain's balance of payments and cost of living, and of the Treaty of Rome with its reliance on an un-democratic machine run by an irresponsible bureaucracy in Brussels. Many of his points are well argued. The Common Agricultural Policy, one can readily admit, is not the most sensible form of agricultural support that human ingenuity can devise. It is, of course, admirably designed to give the

French a privileged position, as the Italians are finding out this year, when an increase in the French GNP is largely due to agricultural exports subsidized out of community funds. The 1961–3 negotiations, which started before the CAP had got to the present point of elaboration, were precisely designed not only to secure special easements for Britain (Douglas Jay does not, for example, mention the objective of isolating the liquid milk market) and for Commonwealth trade, including an adequate transition period, but also to make the system—in regard to the level of prices and to the provisions relating to finance—one which would be less onerous for Britain in the longer term and much more sensible for the world as a whole.

It is, therefore, permissible to ask where Douglas Jay stood at that time, or, earlier, before the CAP was even a gleam in Dr. Mansholt's eye, or, indeed at the very beginning of it all when the coal and steel industries were the sole objects of European integration. The answer is not far to seek. As he makes it clear in later parts of his pamphlet, the economic argument and particularly that relating to the CAP is really only subsidiary. Even as far as agriculture is concerned, he objects almost as much to the emphasis on indirect taxation which the CAP involves (as does, explicitly, the Community's tax system as a whole) as he does to its other aspects. (As he finished writing before 19 March, one does not know what Douglas Jay would say to the remarkable statement of doctrine on this point—though so far doctrine only—of his former colleague, the present Chancellor!)

As for the machinery of decision-making of the Treaty of Rome and the developments since, Douglas Jay, as may be expected, minimizes the changes that have taken place and that have greatly redressed the balance as between the Commission and the Council of Ministers and Permanent Representatives. More important, he does not acknowledge the emphasis which the founders have always placed on the need to build up and strengthen the instruments of democratic control over the Community's institutions.

It is, however, in the passages dealing with the more political aspects that Douglas Jay writes with real passion. It is here that one realizes that he would have been opposed to our joining the Common Market regardless of its agricultural policy. His view of history is simple to the point of sometimes being reminiscent of *1066 and All That*. There are goodies and there are baddies, though sometimes he gets a bit confused over what it is all about. For example, we must give up 'disputing fruitlessly with France the control of this particular corner of one continent'; but later we are warned against joining the Community because it is sure to be dominated by Germany; and for him, as for many others of us, the political consequences if such a development really happened are only too obvious. But, one may ask, if this is a reasonable fear, is it really sensible for Britain to stand apart from a movement one of the main purposes of which has always been to prevent just such a development? As Jean Monnet has argued again and again, to avoid both discrimination and isolation as far as Germany is concerned is one of the main aims of European integration. Again we are told in one place that there is no such thing as Europe, though in another it re-emerges as an entity, 'from the Atlantic to the Urals'. One cannot escape the impression that Douglas Jay does not really like foreigners at all, but will tolerate some if they speak English or, at least, are Scandinavians! Here again, reality is sometimes too strong even for his simple schema: one feels that, with a little effort, one might persuade him to admit the Swiss and the Dutch to honorary membership of the Commonwealth, while, on the other hand, South Africa is hardly mentioned at all. This way of looking at things may be a very good antidote to the views of those 'gastronomic' Europeans who want to join the Community because they like foreign food; but it is hardly a better approach to policy-making.

Douglas Jay's positive alternative is, first, free trade area arrangements (without an agricultural content) between the EEC and EFTA. Later on this could lead to a wider free trade area in industrial products, though this might have to be formed at first between EFTA, the USA, Canada, Australia and New Zealand, if the EEC could not be persuaded to make a reality of General de Gaulle's various obscure suggestions. If the EEC then wanted to join, so much the better. But if not, it would still be possible for Britain to have the best of all possible economic worlds by joining up with the USA and the white Commonwealth: it would have cheap food imports, a wider industrial market, and continued political independence. In describing the implications of such arrangements, Douglas Jay makes use of a recent work by the Atlantic Study Group which has produced many interesting analyses on a number of aspects of these proposals. They all deserve very serious study, though it is for consideration whether the suggestion of further progress in tariff-cutting as far as industrial products are concerned (combined with a more liberal attitude to the trade needs of the developing countries) has to be clothed in this 'regional' garb at all and could not be just as well or even better pursued through GATT and UNCTAD. In any event, I doubt whether Douglas Jay's hard sell for these views combined with his hardly veiled anti-Europeanism is the best way of making recruits for this idea on either side of the Atlantic. He reminds me of some pro-Europeans whose undiscriminating support of integration has often threatened to prove the kiss of death for the idea!

The real trouble is precisely that Douglas Jay wants to have the best of all possible worlds. In arguing for cheap food imports, he does not seem to have heard of the difficulties our own support system gets into from time to time when it has to be buttressed with minimum import price agreements, or voluntary quota arrangements. He seems unconcerned about the nexus between taxation systems and growth rates and is content to rely on the good old (-fashioned) argument that direct taxation is good and indirect taxation bad. He wants more, and freer, trade, but shows a disturbing penchant for freedom to impose import quotas. He rightly says that overseas investment is one of the conditions of our future prosperity, but dislikes the Common Market because membership would prevent us from imposing restrictions on capital exports (and, indeed, exchange control generally); while the (Atlantic) Free Trade Area would preserve this freedom (how long, one wonders?) In the process of scattering his grapeshot so indiscriminately, he tends to overlook some real targets, such as the French Government's ideas on the proper organization of the world monetary system—now happily (touch wood) in retreat.

Still, I admit that these are all things that reasonable people may reasonably disagree about. Ultimately, therefore, what really worries me about this pamphlet is Douglas Jay's basic approach. For example, when it comes to distinguishing between 'good' countries and 'bad' countries, not in terms of their current policies, but on some sort of permanent basis of national character, I would have thought it wise to remember that glass houses abound, and that stone-throwing should be severely discouraged. We all have our prejudices, but we should not let them become the basis of national policy. And when it comes to assessing Britain's national interest, we must surely regretfully conclude that Douglas Jay's triumphant ending about 'not burning boats and keeping all the options open' is about the most hazardous advice he could have given because it would make events the sole master of our destiny. Is not the reluctance to make strategic choices precisely what has bedevilled British policy for the last twenty-three years?

INTERNATIONAL MONETARY DEVELOPMENTS AND THE EUROPEAN COMMON MARKET

An address to the Bank of England–University of Bradford Conference, 6 June 1972.

It is only future historians possessing an adequate perspective who will be able to discern and evaluate which are the critical ones among the fissures that have appeared in the course of the evolution of the present international financial system. To the contemporary observer—and many of us are old enough to have been that over the whole post-war period—that evolution appears as a seamless garment where different patterns succeed one another in apparent inevitability. It is not possible to assess the current situation, let alone speculate about the future, without some reference to, at any rate, the recent past. I hope, therefore, that you will bear with me while I first try to outline what seem to me to be the most significant aspects of the background against which the post-war system was set up, what were the principles on which it was founded, what hopes and expectations were placed in it, and how it has performed in the twenty-five years since it came into being.

The first thing to remember—particularly so at a time when everyone talks of the breakdown of the present system and of the need to devise a new one to take its place for the longer term—is that it was precisely because of the experience of breakdown of the international financial and trading system in the years preceding the Second World War that the Bretton Woods system was constructed.

The memory of the total disorder of the late twenties and thirties was still most vivid in the minds of those who set about the task—be it remembered to their lasting credit, in the darkest days of the war— to lay the foundation for a new and better system. The legacy of the world depression had been the disruption of world trade by restrictive and protectionist practices, the spread of bilateral trade and barter arrangements, the luxuriant growth of exchange restrictions of all kinds both for current and capital transactions. These were designed to sustain a structure of parities among currencies which had become largely artificial and which included both multiple and floating rates. Thanks to the fact that the financial strength of

Britain, though greatly diminished compared with what it had been in the early years of the century, was still an important factor and that American experience and willingness to shoulder international responsibilities, though still rudimentary and quite out of proportion to the country's real strength, were beginning to emerge, co-operation between the new and the old financial centres, New York and London, developed rapidly. This alone prevented the complete collapse of the system even before the war totally changed the scene. But the need for co-operation between the major financial powers had been sufficiently established to form one of the basic elements in the construction of the post-war system.

Another was the much better appreciation of the connection, in modern economic conditions, between domestic economic policy—its desiderata and its results—and the international commercial and financial nexus. The builders of the post-war system were no longer inspired by the simple principles of the nineteenth-century gold standard: the classic 'mechanism' linking inflows and outflows of reserves via monetary policy with expansion and contraction of domestic economic activity. They had to take into account the duty of the State, newly acknowledged in all the major countries of the world, to ensure the maintenance of high and stable levels of economic activity. They also knew that the relation between monetary and other instruments of economic policy, or between international money flows and trade patterns, was much more complex than was recognized in the economic theory prevalent in the twenties and early thirties. The 'New Economics', largely associated with the name of Keynes, accepted that the 'gearing', if I may so call it, of domestic and international policy had to be much more complex, given the powerful economic and political pressures for a higher degree of autonomy for domestic policy than could have been achieved by a return to the gold-exchange standard of the inter-war years.

Thus, the system constructed at Bretton Woods must be viewed not simply as a financial one, which found its sole expression in the articles of the International Monetary Fund, but as a composite one in which there were two other equal essential elements. The first was a code of conduct in trade matters, and an institution to administer it; the second, one to deal with the twin problems of post-war reconstruction and development of the less developed parts of the world so as to make them better able to become members of the international financial and trading community and faithfully to observe its rules.

This is not the place to rehearse in detail the directly monetary objectives of the system. Essentially they were the maintenance of a degree of international discipline in domestic policy and at the same time to attenuate its severity by the provision of credit facilities. It was also hoped that this would ensure an adequate supply of liquidity for the system as a whole. But it is worth recalling that the ambitious total post-war construction did not immediately come alive. The International Trade Organization was stillborn and its work in trade liberalization carried on at first in practice mainly by the OECC, later by the GATT (though not as fully as was originally envisaged). Owing to the tremendous disparity in economic strength between the USA and Western Europe, an 'auxiliary engine', the Marshall Plan, had to be applied before any significant degree of economic co-operation through the Bretton Woods machinery itself could become possible. All this, however, should not blind us to the essential connection between these different parts whose joint operation was really a basic assumption for the full functioning of the monetary system itself.

That monetary system was constitutionally meant to be a Dollar/Gold-Exchange Standard. In effect, as that distinguished central Banker, Dr. Stopper has recently pointed out, it was a dollar-exchange standard with gold playing a fluctuating but generally only residual role. Its functioning, undisputedly for fifteen years, was conditioned by the economic preponderance of the United States, by the concentration after the war of the vast bulk of the world's monetary gold reserves in the United States, by the willingness of the United States to accept the consequences of her position, namely to indulge in large-scale aid and to tolerate for a long time trade discrimination against herself, and by the close involvement of sterling as a subsidiary reserve currency most intimately linked in terms of balance of payments and, therefore, largely domestic economic policy, with the dollar.

After the first fifteen years of its existence, that is, since the early sixties, the system came increasingly under pressure. As more countries improved their international trading position and strengthened their reserves, including the building-up of the gold component, thereby diminishing the American gold reserves, both these countries and the United States herself became conscious of the difficulty of continuing to sustain American balance of payments deficits of the magnitude then experienced. Various measures were tried to remedy the situation. Attempts to enlarge the area of trade liberalization by rounds of negotiated tariff cuts, like the Kennedy Round, American restrictions on capital movements, central bank operations, including a number of devices to diminish the convertibility of growing dollar balances in central reserves, were tried. These however, proved unavailing, particularly in the face of continuing substantial outflows from the United States on account of defence expenditures and the persistent strengths of the balance of payments of some countries, notably Japan and Germany. The crisis finally came last year when dollar convertibility was formally suspended, and certain emergency trade measures instituted by the United States.

It was widely held that on 15 August 1971, the post-war monetary system had definitely broken down. It would be an idle semantic exercise to debate whether this is the correct description of what happened, though more and more people are now inclined to the view that what happened was not a sudden breakdown. It was more that some of the underlying facts and some of the accepted practices which alone had made the system workable had been eroded to the point where the mechanism required a complete overhaul notwithstanding that some of its working parts were still serviceable. Its basic purposes, however, continued to be still valid. At any rate a temporary realignment of parities, including a semi-theoretical depreciation of the dollar in terms of gold, together with the institution of wider bands of permitted fluctuations, was achieved in December; and the international monetary system has since functioned on the basis of this 'Smithsonian' agreement.

It is recognized on all sides that this can only be a temporary arrangement and that pending a more thoroughgoing reform of the system which would promise to be at least as long-lasting as the previous régime, a number of important problems remain which such a reform must resolve. I would list these problems as follows, taking first those that fall within the strict framework of monetary arrangements. The first of these is the adequacy of the existing parities (allowing for the wider bands of fluctuations) and the future régime by which changes in parities are to be brought about. The second is what the future role of gold, the dollar and of special drawing rights should be in relation to each other, or in other words, what should constitute ultimate reserve assets. Within this problem are impounded both a short-term problem, namely the functioning of the IMF mechanism under a régime of dollar inconvertibility, as well as the longer-term problem of dollar convertibility *per se*. Third, there is the question of the régime, if any, to be applied to dollar balances already held by central banks as well as the methods by which future balances are to be dealt with, since these may well continue to arise at least for some little time ahead until there is a major reversal of current US balance of payments trends. The fourth question is how the long-run needs for increased liquidity in the world as a whole are to be met on the assumption that a continuous replenishment through American deficits and dollar accumulations is in the long term not acceptable on either side of the Atlantic or Pacific. Finally, there is the problem whether the maintenance of the present régime, until a more lasting system is put in place, requires special measures in regard to money flows, both short- and long-term; and indeed whether the long-term solution needs to make provision for such controls to be applied in certain circumstances.

No doubt, this list could be enlarged, but these seem to me to be the main categories into which these and related problems can be grouped. Over and beyond there are problems which the crisis of the last few years has brought to the fore, and which many people, including some of those responsible for fashioning their countries' policies, are tending to link with the purely monetary ones. There is, for example, the problem of how trade liberalization can not only be maintained at the level so far achieved but can be rapidly and significantly extended. Then there are the problems connected with international investment. These have not only a monetary aspect, that is through the direct effects of long-term capital movements on balances of payments and international equilibrium; they raise the even more complex long-term economic problem—with its social and political overtones—of the effects of direct international investment, particularly as practised by the large multi-national corporations, on the location of production and employment as well as on the long-run currents of trade.

Even if all these, shall we say more transcendental, problems are left out of account (though they are unlikely to be wholly absent from the minds of the negotiators), it is clear that to bring a negotiation for a long-term reform of the financial system to a successful conclusion, be it in a group of twenty or in a group of ten, will take a considerable time. Meanwhile, we have to make the present régime work without undue disturbance. Meanwhile also, the world does not stand still, in particular, despite the recent turbulence (which at

present, happily, is not too intense) the Europe of the Economic
Community has been trying, is trying, and will assuredly go on trying to evolve for itself a suitable monetary system to serve the needs
of a customs union which is anxious to move rapidly towards a closer
economic union of wider scope not only between its six original
members, but within the wider framework of an enlarged membership of ten.

Let me first say a word about 'the story so far'. I do not mean by
this that I want to give you a stage-by-stage account of the detailed
negotiations that have taken place in the last few years, of the twists
and turns of debate which are inevitable in an enterprise of this
magnitude. I want rather to highlight what seem to me to be the
significant trends and to set the effort towards a monetary union in
the general context of the evolving Community.

The first thing to remember is that the objectives of the founding
fathers of the Community have always been political. That is not to
say that the aim was always and has consistently been to work towards a European Federation, let alone one that would come into
being in the foreseeable future; but the greater political cohesion of
Europe was always the openly avowed goal, whatever the form this
might in due course take. It followed that economic unification was
a means to an end, and moreover that each step in the direction of
closer economic union was conceived of as a means of achieving the
next and bigger step. Thus, the Coal and Steel Community was an
example of the 'sector' approach, the essential precondition for
moving towards the attempt to set up an Economic Community.
Within the Economic Community itself, each step was designed to
help establish a Community identity and to consolidate it by attempt-
ing successively more difficult tasks of economic unification. The first
was to create the common external tariff, the second to move towards a full customs union with a common commercial policy, the
third to produce a common agricultural policy, the fourth, via the
agricultural fund, and the communalization of customs receipts, to
make major progress in the creation of a really significant Community
budget. These steps, I should add, being taken not necessarily in
chronological order but being generally pursued simultaneously.
Simultaneously, too, progress has been attempted and in a measure
achieved, in creating generally similar conditions affecting competition, harmonizing taxation, social provisions and regulations of
various kinds—all of which fall under the general heading of
'economic union'.

It was always recognized that monetary unification would have to play a major part in this process. But it was also accepted that this was a particularly difficult area in which to make rapid progress. In the first place, monetary policy, domestic and international, goes directly to the heart of the question of the abandonment of national sovereignty, though I should add at once that this is often a more apparent than real problem owing to the inescapable necessity for any advanced country of accepting the constraints of membership of some international system. In the second place, the international system includes as vitally important members many more countries not only than the six original members of the Community, but many more than were ever likely to become members.

Despite these difficulties, co-operation was begun some years ago, by the setting up of the Monetary Committee, thus bringing together leading officials of the member countries, and by regular meetings of Ministers of Finance and of Central Bank Governors. These meetings were designed to provide opportunities for exchanges of view on common problems, more particularly to attempt to harmonize the views of the members in advance of important wider international meetings, such as those of the Group of Ten, of Working Party Three of the OECD or of the International Monetary Fund. It is no disparagement of all these efforts of the Six to say that for a number of years they had only achieved a very limited success. They were brought up short by successive alternations of crises in the major member countries, France, Germany, Italy, partly generated by domestic developments, partly as reflections of international disturbances, which required emergency measures of a unilateral character, including the imposition of controls and/or changes of currency parities. Not surprisingly also, when one surveys the monetary history of the last few years, the attempt to forge a common attitude in wider international negotiations rarely got very far. Given the disturbed conditions of the last decade, it was perhaps to be expected that the most ambitious plan for a step-by-step attempt at creating a complete European Monetary Union, the Werner Plan, evolved under the leadership of the Luxembourg Prime Minister, remained for some time only a blueprint. For its emergence coincided, on the one hand with a sharp intensification of the dollar crisis, and on the other, with the sudden resolution, in a positive sense, of the long drawn-out debate on the enlargement of the Community. This was particularly important in the monetary sphere since it would lead to the inclusion of Britain, the country with the strongest European financial centre, and with a currency which still had important trading and, to some extent, reserve functions to fulfil.

Perhaps paradoxically, though not altogether unprecedented in history, the crisis of August 1971 produced a greater coalescence, rather than an intensified divergence of views among the members of the Community and between them and the principal candidates for membership. Despite the fact that the first indications of crisis earlier in 1971 had evoked quite different reactions from the principal European countries affected, the resolutions adopted by the Six at the beginning of that year recording their determination to introduce within ten years an economic and monetary union was made into something of a living reality by the recent adoption, and implementation, of the first steps towards that end. From 15 April, and, in the case of the British from only about two weeks later, the countries of the Community and the most important candidates have agreed to ensure that their exchange rates do not fluctuate beyond a range which is only half as wide as that adopted as part of the currency realignment of last year, namely $2\frac{1}{4}$ per cent as against $4\frac{1}{2}$ per cent. This agreement is being operated for a period of about three months, but this must not be thought of as a trial period, but rather as a running-in phase: the intention is to continue this practice, indeed, as conditions make possible, to go further in narrowing the band as far as Community currencies are concerned.

Happily for all concerned, this major step in European unification was taken at a time when there has been relative calm on the currency front: though the positions of European currencies in relation to the Smithsonian parities differ, none has been outside the narrower European band. That is to say that none seems to have required any intervention to 'nudge' it into the new European range. The girth of the so-called European snake in the dollar tunnel was fortunately not outside the new permitted limits. One would, however, have to be very bold indeed to be quite confident that the maintenance of this dual range system can be counted upon to continue for any considerable time without some definite action on the part of the monetary authorities. Not only is there the possibility that the fluctuating fortunes of the dollar may affect European currencies in different ways, but a glance at the disparities in economic and, indeed, social and political circumstances within the about-to-be-enlarged Community should suffice to show that pressures may arise which would tend to push this or that currency outside the new limits.

Nevertheless, the fact is that this is the system now in force, and that the authorities are committed to making it work. While no one would deny that to operate this dual system is a novel task and therefore that those operating the technique must be necessarily somewhat inexperienced, there can be no doubt that it will be pursued energetically. Failure to make it succeed, let alone failure to make every effort to this end, would gravely impair the credibility of this important attempt to make a great leap forward in European unification. This judgement must, I am sure apply to Britain, not only as a new member whose practical commitment to the new Union will be carefully watched, but also as the member most experienced in international monetary management and, therefore, having both a special power and a special responsibility as far as success in this operation is concerned.

We thus find ourselves in a situation in which three important tendencies are at work at the same time. First of all there is the undoubted and universally acknowledged need to keep the world's monetary system as it has been patched up by the Smithsonian agreement in reasonable working shape and to avoid disturbances of the magnitude that shook the international order to its foundations last year or, even in some earlier phases in recent years. In the second place, it is necessary to move with 'all deliberate speed' towards a reformed international system whose long-term viability can be demonstrated not only intellectually but which will command a high degree of credibility in the world's markets. In the third place it is extremely desirable that these two objectives should be pursued in a manner which will not impede, but, on the contrary, will encourage progress on the European monetary front, or, conversely, that European monetary unification should proceed in a manner which will not militate against the achievement of a wider long-term solution.

It must be said that at first sight there are no solid grounds for expecting these three desiderata to be necessarily or even easily compatible with one another. As with so many important economic policy objectives, in this area too, those things that are desirable are rarely obtainable at the same time. In this field of finance there are special difficulties. The needs of the longer term may militate against the best short-term solution and vice versa. Let me take an example: in the short term it may well be that the problems of the proper function of the repurchase provisions of the International Monetary Fund may be solved, as they seem to have been solved in the case of the repayment of the British debt, without raising in an excessively acute form the question of the ultimate convertibility of the dollar or of the role that gold should play in the system. In the longer term, of course, these problems cannot be avoided, and it is easy to see that if very strong positions are adopted by different countries on these issues in so far as they concern a permanent solution, they would colour the attitude of the parties concerned in the shorter term, and may, therefore, contribute to aggravating current difficulties and increasing the general uncertainty.

Similarly, views on longer-term solutions and views on the validity of existing currency parities—which are already subject to divergent tendencies in different countries—may tend to get mixed up, thereby making more difficult the maintenance of that relative calm and stability in the short term without which agreement on the longer term is not possible or at least much more difficult.

In this connection, I would draw attention to another factor which is of importance. The debate on currency problems, whether long or short term, is now carried on in an environment which is completely unlike that which existed even forty years ago, let alone at the beginning of this century. Then, monetary problems, while freely discussed in academic circles and specialist publications, were negotiated between governments and central banks very much in an atmosphere of secret diplomacy. Today, they are debated virtually in an open forum. We are all familiar with the reasons that have led to this state of affairs. Whatever one may think of the fundamental value of 'open government' or at least open discussions—and I am certainly in favour of it—the fact remains that in currency matters, at any rate, public semi-academic discussions and Government negotiations combined with continuous public comments thereon, inevitably have an effect on markets. And the effect which they have is not necessarily always that which is desirable in itself, that which the Authorities wish, or above all, that which is consistent with the smooth functioning of the system over the longer term. Thus a situation in which three major issues of the kind I have described have simultaneously to be dealt with in an atmosphere of continual public comment and debate is wrought with considerable difficulties.

As regards the first two of these three problems, this is not the place to pursue them in any detail. The needs, however, are clear enough. We must aim at stabilizing the present *modus vivendi*, or, if modifications in the existing arrangements prove necessary or desirable, we must ensure that these take place in an atmosphere of calm and without exacerbating the conflicts, economic, political, and perhaps even personal that often tend to lurk not far behind the openly debated issues. Clearly also, there is a pressing need to arrive at a long-term solution and to achieve as speedy and as wide as possible an agreement on what reforms the international monetary system requires. The broad outlines of what is required are sufficiently well known and have recently been stated with great clarity and precision by Dr. Arthur Burns. I have already said that the maintenance of the existing system is reasonable stability, and the simultaneous active search for long-term reform may generate some friction and conflict. I have no ready prescription of how this can be avoided. I note that there is already some evidence that conflicting views—and apparently strongly conflicting views—are held on the speed with which progress towards long-term reform should be made. But it should not be impossible, given the necessary political will, to devote adequate energies to the search for agreement on the reform of Bretton Woods, while at the same time making the existing interim system work smoothly. I have put the emphasis on the political will: I can only hope that this will be present in adequate measure.

Whatever may be the right view on all this, there is still the question of what room there is for progress on European monetary unification, the third in my list of items on the current agenda.

The first thing I would say is that it is important to distinguish between principles and practical problems. There is no doubt whatsoever in my mind that once the principle of the need for European economic union is acknowledged, monetary unification has to be accepted as an integral part of it; and every effort towards its practical achievement has to be made.

I would further say that one should not conceal from oneself the fact that monetary union cannot be sustained, even if it could be achieved, without a very high degree of unification in all the main aspects of economic policy. A narrow band of exchange fluctuations, *a fortiori* fixed parities, and, in the limit, a single currency, means one of two things. It could mean automatic responses of monetary policy in the different countries belonging to the monetary union to balance of payments disequilibrium, i.e. something equivalent to the classical 'mechanism' in which outflows of funds lead to deflationary measures and inflows to expansionary ones. If, on the other hand, this is not acceptable, as it clearly would not be in the light of present-day requirements of economic management, then it must imply that the balance of payments problem of individual countries with other countries of the Community must be virtually eliminated. This means, in fact, automatic balance of payments support or, if one wishes to put it in more extreme terms, the pooling of reserves. As this is difficult to visualize without a high degree of unification not only of monetary policy but also of fiscal, and, indeed, economic policy generally (since it is unlikely that a country would be given a blank cheque by its fellow members unless it accepted close surveillance of its policies), it is easy to see why, in the limit, monetary unification is virtually equivalent to total economic union.

I deliberately put the emphasis in the way I have, although in recent discussions the emphasis has been placed rather on the methods to bring about monetary unification than on its implications. While I cannot go into the detail of that debate here, I think it is fair to say that the point I have made about the relation of monetary unification to economic unification generally has a great relevance to it. In fact, the different methods that have been advocated essentially rest on different views as to what should precede what: pooling of reserves or a high degree of co-ordination of all monetary policies (involving that strong infusion of central authority which is a characteristic element in Community thinking) or an agreement to narrow exchange fluctuations. As long as one is clear about the intimate relationship between these various aspects of the financial nexus between the member countries, it is probably unnecessary to waste a great deal of time and heat on debating the precise sequence in which one should progress, for it is at least theoretically possible to make limited progress in each of these areas in turn: as I said earlier, each step leading to the next and making that next step easier to take. The fact that the emphasis has now been placed on the narrowing of exchange fluctuations is not surprising since it follows somewhat the pattern, adopted in connection with the successive stages of the agricultural policy, and thus corresponds to the philosophy that seems to underly much of Community thinking, namely that once a mechanism has been put in place, the acceptance of certain policies which alone can make that mechanism work effectively will be virtually forced upon the participants.

I repeat, however, that one should be under no illusion that narrow exchange fluctuations or fixed parities can be anything more than a mechanism. The central banks will, I am sure, do all they can to make it function in a technically perfect manner, but they will be powerless to ensure its continued viability unless there is an assurance that there will be the necessary political will to implement the degree of economic policy unification that will be required. It is a platitude to say that this will not be easy, but it is, nevertheless, worth saying. It will not be easy, not only because co-ordination of national economic policies will have to overcome powerful obstacles of national policy interests—whether rightly or wrongly conceived—but the requirements of economic policy in the various countries of the Community will be affected, and sometimes vitally affected, by their relations with non-member countries, and particularly with the United States.

This brings me finally to the equally important, and in the short term, more pressing problem, namely the relationship between progressive monetary unification within Europe and the international monetary order.

Narrow exchange rate fluctuations in European currencies and even full monetary unification in Europe can, in theory, co-exist with more orthodox payment relationships with the outside world. If one visualizes Europe as a single economic unit with a single currency, the problem becomes simple, namely that of the relation of one country with the rest of the world, and of its method of adjusting its payments terms within whatever the international monetary system is. But for some considerable time at least it must be supposed that this will not be the relationship and that we shall have to deal with a régime in which, while Europe is progressing towards monetary union, there is still considerable scope for individual payments relationships between each of its members and the outside world, or, to put it in another way, for the 'collective' relationship between 'Europe' and the rest of the world to be only a partial one.

If these individual balance of payments relationships are allowed full scope in terms of their possible effect on exchange rates, yet another form of disturbance of the narrow range of exchange fluctuations within the Community that is aimed at will be present, additional to that which may directly arise from divergences in 'autonomous' national economic policies. In the end, such a situation cannot be allowed to exist, since it would be disruptive of the whole idea of moving towards monetary union along the road of progressive narrowing of exchange fluctuations between the members. As Professor Cooper has recently shown, there are a number of ways in which this problem can be met. The first would be to have virtually all exchange markets concentrated in official dealings at announced buying and selling rates. This would, of course, destroy the competitive foreign exchange market; and if, in order to avoid this, official intervention were to be limited to keep exchange fluctuations within the margins permitted in the international system, this would not only fail to achieve the narrowing of the Community range, but would involve continued use of the dollar as the intervention currency. The solution might be to use one of the Community currencies as the general intervention currency within the system, and that currency as the sole and 'final' intervention currency *vis-à-vis* the dollar. Alternatively an attempt can be made by all member central banks to intervene in a closely co-ordinated fashion both in respect to each other's currencies and in respect to the dollar with the object of ultimately reaching the stage when there are fixed parities in Europe which move together against all outside currencies, and particularly against the dollar.

Merely to state this proposition is enough to highlight the very great technical difficulty of achieving this objective in practice, particularly during the interim period before European parities are entirely fixed. A distinguished French expert, M. Guindey, has recently drawn attention to this point by calling for an early separation between intervention in European currencies for the purpose of maintaining the width of the 'snake' and those in dollars designed to keep the whole European system within the required margins of fluctuations in relation to the dollar.

One may entertain the hope that despite the enormous practical difficulties that these problems pose, European monetary authorities would be able in a reasonable time to perfect their technical methods, including what I believe would be essential: the forms of technical co-operation with the American monetary authorities.

But while the problem appears in a technical guise, it will be clear from what I said earlier that I consider it basically as a political problem, namely of the degree of willingness to progress in the co-ordination of economic policies to whatever level the successful accomplishment of monetary unification may require. Thus one must come back to the question of whether this collective European willingness will be forthcoming, and whether it can at the same time be made sufficiently conscious of the needs of monetary co-operation in the wider setting of the future international monetary order. It is no use shutting one's eyes to the fact that there is a potential conflict here, moreover, one at two levels: between the pressure for autonomy in domestic economic policy and European unification; and between the need to make a reality of that unification without losing the benefits of an international system, a requirement which is probably more vital in monetary matters than in perhaps any other area of economic activity.

The danger that I see in this situation is that the will to accept the need for closer economic co-ordination may falter when put to a serious test, and that in order not to abandon what successes monetary unification may by then appear to have achieved, recourse may be had to measures of exchange control, particularly as regards capital flows, either directly by setting up a two-tier exchange system or through attempts at control of intermediaries such as those operating in the Euro-currency markets. It is not surprising that those of us with the experience and trading of London behind us should be sceptical, to put it mildly, about such possibilities; and I for one fully share the doubts in this regard which have recently been again expressed by the Governor of the Bank of England.

My own conclusions would, therefore, be that whenever the needs of monetary unification, be it in the more rigorous sense of a European community or in the more general context of reforming and reconstructing Bretton Woods, come up against the obstacle of real or imagined national interest, no effort must be spared to overcome this by an even higher degree of co-operation and co-ordination of policy and by the strengthening of the appropriate institutions to this end. I hope that in this process, the European Community will assume an enlightened leadership, both in its own interest and in that of the world.

BRITAIN IN THE COMMUNITY

Published in The Banker, *January 1973*.

The editor has asked me for some personal reflections on the occasion of our entry into the European Economic Community. So much has been talked and written about this, so many hopes—and not a few fears—expressed that it would be understandable if boredom were now to be the general reaction to the whole subject. If boredom there is, 1 January is not likely to have dispelled it. Nothing dramatic happened; nothing seemed to have changed; we did not suddenly all have to speak French, or have to adopt a republican form of government or see *Carabinieri* patrolling the streets of London.

Yet this New Year's day was the culmination of a long process which has taken over a quarter of a century and which has passed through many critical phases. Looking back over this period, we tend to view the major events which we have witnessed ourselves more dramatically and climactically than will the future historian. He will see a slow accretion of influences, eventually producing a major effect, a change of degree into one of kind. But, I think he, too, will see this 1 January as a momentous one, and the year 1972, in which the British Parliament passed the legislation for our membership, as the most important since the end of the Second World War.

The momentous nature of this change is first and foremost more subtle than something arising from new legal and institutional arrangements. It is, above all, the end of a long period of uncertainty and consequent vacillation in our international affairs. For a quarter of a century our efforts in different fields in their international setting have lacked a main theme. They have, therefore, tended to alternate according to different strains and stresses: the needs of European recovery, reconstruction and security; our dependence on United States strategic power and, often, financial support; the economic, political and sentimental ties of the Commonwealth; and so on. It would, I think, be relatively easy to write our post-war history entirely in terms of alternating pulls and pressures of these various aspects of national interest, or, at any rate, national interest as conceived by successive governments.

A THEME

So the first thing to stress is that we now do have a main theme, one around which many, perhaps most, of our international preoccupations can be grouped. Of course, it would have been better if this had happened ten years ago when the government of the day, to its lasting credit, first made the effort to secure membership in the EEC. It would have been better still if, in the second half of the 1950s, when we had the opportunity of being in on the creation of the EEC from the beginning, we had grasped it; and even better still if we had accepted the invitation more than twenty years ago to join in the creation of the Coal and Steel Community.

Still, better now than not at all.

However, it may be argued, that while 'main themes' are, no doubt, a great comfort to philosophers and historians, they do not butter any parsnips for the ordinary citizen. What is this Community, what will it be and do; above all, what will it mean to us? Here the first thing to realize is that we are latecomers. The bus of history does not travel on a regular route. If you miss it at a certain time and place, you cannot expect to catch it again later, at the same place. This particular bus has certainly travelled a circuitous route, marked by twists and turns, and one on which there have been many, many stops. But it has gone a long way, nevertheless, since it set out and we catch it, not where it was in 1963 or 1956 or 1951, but where it is now, in 1973.

The desire of many of our Continental neighbours to have us with them on this journey has been strong; but we must not suppose that we shall be able to alter greatly or quickly the direction and speed. The Community has been in the making for nearly fifteen years. The Six have had to accept change, sometimes difficult change. We, too, must now be prepared for change. We may comfort ourselves with the thought that it will not come suddenly, but come it will.

HOW EUROPE ADVANCES

First, then, what about the Community? While it would surely be a travesty of the truth to say that so far it has developed merely into a customs union with a somewhat costly and cumbersome agricultural support system, it is nevertheless the case that the many other advances in the direction of a common budget, a high degree of common economic policy or of progress towards a monetary union —to say nothing of political integration—are still in a very embryonic stage. It is in these directions that the next items on the Community's agenda will lie. But before we look at them, there is one thing that we must be clear about. We may take a more or less generous view of the Community's progress to date, we may joke about, or positively dislike, some of the bureaucratic excrescences to which it has given rise. We may smile at the faltering steps towards supra-nationalism and point with satisfaction—or distress, as the case may be—at the undiminished ability of member countries, in some areas at least, to go on doing what they please. What we in Britain must, however, recognize is that to its members the Community has brought a radical change in attitudes and, above all, that despite all the difficulties since the signing of the Treaty of Rome in 1958, the process of creating the Community has proved to be irreversible. Progress has been uneven during this period: sometimes, as in the periodic fits of intransigence of de Gaulle, it has been imperceptible, but the trend has been one way only: greater cohesion among the members, involving a genuine hesitation to risk a major break. As we look ahead we can confidently expect it to continue in the same direction.

More particularly, we can see the next stages, not in detail on a time-map, but in general outline. The recent summit of the Nine in Paris has established some new machinery and certain later targets: another step—beyond the narrow bands and the support fund—in monetary union on 1 January 1974, and completion of it by 1980, as well as a regional policy, to mention only two of the most important. The technique of these decisions, which closely follows that adopted at earlier stages, is a most interesting innovation in the machinery of international political action. On the one hand, where really difficult problems touching intimately national interests and sovereignty are concerned, agreement is sought and reached on very broad objectives to which in the nature of things any member wishing to remain in good standing will necessarily have to subscribe; and to fix a date by which flesh is to be put on the bones of this agreement. On the other hand, a mechanism is sometimes set up—and it is often easier to reach agreement on a mechanism than on the underlying policies— and reliance is then placed on the fact that the effort to maintain the mechanism will tend to make countries more ready to adopt the policies themselves.

Naturally, one cannot be confident that all this will work out exactly as planned. In the case of monetary union, without doubt the most important next phase in the Community's evolution, there are many hazards on the road. Intra-Community tensions have perhaps diminished—partly because enlargement of the Community itself disposes towards a more co-operative spirit, partly because, unhappily in a larger sense, all the members are suffering from broadly similar degrees of inflation and inadequacy of growth of productivity as compared with the United States and Japan; and the chances of maintaining the mechanism (narrower bands and rules for settlement)—whatever one may think of its virtues in the abstract—are not bad. On the other hand, general monetary reform on an international basis is now firmly on the agenda, and this may complicate at any rate the timetable of Community progress. Consultative machinery at all levels and for all areas of economic policy has become very elaborate; and, although that sort of machinery alone is not a substitute for political will, it can certainly help to foster an ever greater readiness to concert action. It certainly is a powerful antidote to abstract sovereignty-worship.

WHAT RESPONSE TO STRESS?

The real problem for the Community, in my view, over the next few years, lies not so much in the specific details of this or that area of greater harmonization; it is rather in the response that it will make to the appearance of severe strains and stresses originating either from within or from without. The monetary area is a good example. Putting it in a highly simplified way, I would say that the responses to great strain can apply to three areas: exchange rates, degrees of economic policy harmonization and the level of liberalization of trade and payments. The question, put crudely, is which is likely to 'give' when strains become severe enough. I cannot forecast, even if I wished to, what is most likely to happen in any given circumstance. All I can say is that since I do not believe that extreme exchange rate flexibility is that panacea that some people consider it to be, and since I would greatly regret a reversion to highly restrictive practices when strains occur, I would hope for bold progress in the area of monetary and economic policy harmonization, the *fuite en avant* as our French friends call it, when it becomes difficult to maintain what has already been achieved. I am not unduly impressed by the 'sovereignty' argument, in a fast-shrinking economic world in which

H

the export of inflation or unemployment, even if it were desirable, is becoming increasingly difficult, without provoking cumulative internecine policies.

What about our own affairs in this perspective? I am convinced that although some of the constraints of membership may be irksome —such as the 'snake'—and others really burdensome, such as the Common Agricultural Policy, the opportunities opened up by membership greatly outweigh these drawbacks. This is largely the case, because many, if not all, the disadvantages are not greatly different in their weight from those which we are under in any event, either by virtue of our inevitable membership in any kind of international trading and payments system or because of special difficulties of our own—due to structural, sociological, or plain historical circumstances—which it would be essential for us to overcome in any event. Take, for example, the Common Agricultural Policy. In the years since our failure to obtain membership in 1963, we have, because of world trading conditions and increasing Exchequer cost of agricultural support, been driven to modify our support system by increasingly introducing managed market elements; and we might easily be forced to go further along this road. But a managed market of our own would surely give us the worst of all possible worlds.

THE CITY IN EUROPE

Or take the fate of the 'Square Mile'. We have, I think rightly, maintained an open-door policy and been especially liberal and welcoming to foreign financial institutions which have wished to establish themselves in the City and do business 'out of London'. As a result, London is certainly the most important financial centre in Europe and one of the two leading ones in the world. Membership of the Community will not, as some believe, automatically consolidate or enhance that position. Indeed, the further measures of liberalization in capital movements to which we are committed, now that we are members, will not be sustainable except at some further cost in the way of unfettered freedom of action in economic policy. But without assuming these extra obligations—which not only membership in the Community, but our own aspiration to continue to accept a leading financial position require—we can only look forward to, at best, the rise in relative importance of other centres, at worst, a steady erosion of the City's absolute position.

Of course, a successful fight against inflation—now a common problem for all of us in the Community—is a *sine qua non* for any advance; but readiness to adapt our attitudes and our institutions to changing requirements is essential, and membership will provide a continuous stimulus to that end. It will expose us, no doubt, to even more competition than hitherto: competition from financial institutions with a different historical background, different functions and different attitudes. But this we shall suffer anyway, even outside the Community—unless we are prepared to build a strong insulating wall around ourselves whose cost is eventual atrophy of what is inside—while membership gives us the compensating advantage of greater opportunity in a vastly enlarged market.

It is this positive aspect that we must be mindful of and we must not carp at this or that deficiency in the existing Community and either retreat—literally—into a shell or indulge in the vain hope that we can shatter what we dislike and quickly 'rebuild it nearer to the heart's desire'. Beyond all the detailed, and sometimes parochial, issues that we shall need to worry and argue and negotiate about, it is as well to remember that it is not often given to a generation to be able to take part in an enterprise of such historic importance.

TOWARDS ECONOMIC AND MONETARY UNION

Published in The Financial Times, *3 January 1973.*

The first thing that I would like to stress on this day on which, after so many false starts, we are at last a member of the European Community is that the objectives of the Community's founding fathers and of their most active disciples have always been political. This does not mean that they all aimed at a European federation or that such a federation is to be confidently expected to be created in the foreseeable future. It rather meant sustained progress towards greater political cohesion by means of economic arrangements in which each step would sooner or later, but ineluctably, lead to a further one.

The 'sector' approach of coal and steel, the establishment of a customs union (liberal trade inside, a common external tariff outside, together with progressively more uniform commercial policy), a common method of supporting agriculture, and the creation of a significant community budget through the Agricultural Fund and the pooling of customs receipts—these are the landmarks on the road which the Community has so far travelled. Alongside them, many others, more or less successful or far-reaching measures, more directly though less acutely, bearing on economic union have been attempted; among them: harmonizing taxation and rules affecting competition, laying down directives concerning establishment, and a variety of social provisions.

MORE EASILY

Often the technique has been to aim at the—more easily reached—agreement on a mechanism rather than on the fundamental policies that determine its operation (the CAP is an example) in the hope that governments will eventually be forced, in order to ensure the continued working of the mechanism to which they have committed themselves, to make progress on the policies that in the long run can alone sustain that mechanism.

The second thing we must have in mind as we join is that it has long been clear to the Six that further progress depended on a major advance into the heart of economy policy-making, involving an inroad into sovereignty perhaps no greater than already follows in practice from membership in any form of international monetary system, but more explicit and at the same time more pregnant with the possibility of major progress. A further direct attack on those areas which immediately and visibly affect the life of the average citizen was ruled out, not only for political reasons but because it was clear that what was needed was something which would influence the total economic climate in member countries.

At the summit meeting at The Hague in December 1969, the monetary route was chosen. Not that the difficulties were underrated: for quite apart from the central role which the monetary system plays in economic policy and, therefore, in sovereignty, it also involves not only vitally important countries outside the Six, but many more than were ever likely to become members, particularly the United States.

I, among many others, have always taken the view that money is, par excellence, a subject of worldwide concern; therefore one in which partial, regional, solutions must be approached with special caution. For nearly a quarter of a century the countries of the Community had been tied together with the rest of the capitalist, industrialized world (above all, the US), with the developing countries, and even, indirectly, yet to a considerable degree, with the Soviet Union and the countries of Eastern Europe in an international monetary system, dominated by the arrangements made at Bretton Woods.

While the aim of progress towards closer European monetary union was not only understandable and proper, but also for anyone who wished the Community well and wanted to see Britain a member of it, a highly desirable one, it was extremely important that it should be achieved by means which did not prejudice, but, indeed, helped towards worldwide reform. And just at the time when the Six were thinking of closer monetary union, the Bretton Woods system had come under severe strain. In assessing what has been accomplished so far and what lies immediately ahead, it is, therefore, impossible to separate some aspects of the European problem from those of the international system as a whole.

Close co-operation inside the Community was begun some years ago by the setting-up of the Monetary Committee, bringing together leading officials, and by frequent, regular meetings of Finance

Ministers and Central Bank Governors. But, owing to the disturbed international monetary conditions at the time, the most ambitious plan for the eventual creation of a European Monetary Union, the Werner Plan, had to remain a blueprint for some time before it could begin to be implemented.

After the Smithsonian agreement of December 1971, which re-aligned parities, widened the permissible margin of fluctuations around them, and brought acceptance of the need to proceed to a general reform of the international monetary system, the time appeared ripe for a further move on the European front. It should be added that the agreement which had meanwhile been reached to enlarge the Community, particularly by the inclusion of Britain, undoubtedly played a major part in creating the conditions in which further progress towards European monetary union could be attempted.

Accordingly, in the spring of 1972, the Six decided to narrow the 'band' of fluctuation of their parities to half the width permitted under the Smithsonian agreement (while preserving countries' freedom to change the parities) and agreed on certain rules concerning intervention in markets to maintain the new bands as well as on rules for the settlements of balances resulting from swaps occasioned by these interventions. This was and is the first and most specific step taken by the Community towards monetary union, and one which Britain also adopted in anticipation of her membership, a decision which, however, did not last long, for the pressures on sterling in June 1972 made it necessary for us to float.

The introduction of these measures as, indeed, the earlier adoption of the Werner Plan, were accompanied by much argument on the parallelism of measures for economic and for monetary union. On this, two opposite views can be, and were, held.

One is that monetary union is to be looked upon as the final crowning of an already achieved economic union, and that it would therefore be ineffective without economic union; the other that monetary union is in the first place an indispensable step towards the further strengthening of a Community identity and one which must be regarded as a mechanism that will provide a powerful impulse towards further economic harmonization and, eventually, union. The adoption by different countries of one or the other of these lines of argument was no doubt influenced not only by ideological beliefs but also by their own immediate situation and their national interests as they perceived them.

The agreement that was finally reached, while it fully acknowledged the need to progress as simultaneously as possible, did mean
a victory for the mechanism school. But even apart from the major
question of balance between economic and monetary aspects, it must
remain doubtful whether the choice of narrower bands and of rules
for the settlement of balances according to the composition of
national reserves was the best mechanism to have chosen.

VARYING WAYS

Certainly, the fate of the 'snake' since it came into being, with
Britain, Italy and Denmark being obliged in varying ways and
degrees, as it were, to shed its skin, seems to raise some doubts about
the virtues of this mechanism. On the settlement question the
difficulties that have arisen in regard to gold—involving an acute
dilemma of either settling at an official price little more than half
the market price or prejudicing the whole question of the future role
of gold in the international system (a question which is very much in
the melting-pot of the Group of Twenty which is considering long-
term worldwide reform)—have strengthened these doubts.

Be this as it may, whether in order to get to monetary union one
would have started out from where the Six started, is now an
academic question. The fact that we have to accept is that this is how
they did start. There can, therefore, be no question that now that we
are members we shall have to conform to the rules, modified as they
might be by common agreement in the light of experience. That
means in the first place, that we shall have to peg the pound; and
there is no point in speculating here on the precise time and level at
which this will be done. To those, like myself, who remain highly
dubious about the advantages of floating, except for brief periods
and in special circumstances and where the alternative would be a
steady regression to greater restrictions, this is certainly no sacrifice.

We shall also have to intervene to keep the resulting rate within
the agreed bands (while, like others, being free to change the parity
according to IMF rules); and we shall have to operate the settlement rules with such revisions as may emerge from current consultations.

In this connection it must be remembered that one further
monetary step has been taken as the result of the recent Summit of
the Nine, namely the institution, as from 1 April 1973, of a European
Monetary Support Fund. This fund is to my mind of very modest

size and, therefore, not such that it can be looked upon as a major start in the direction of pooled reserves and semi-automatic balance of payments support. Nevertheless, it is a beginning; and it must be borne in mind that, as has become the practice of the Community, it has been agreed that a further step, as yet unspecified, is to be taken on 1 January 1974. Personally, I very much hope that this will include a substantial enlargement of the Support Fund.

In any event, even the present modest beginning will have a beneficial influence. Intra-Community consultation on monetary matters has already been highly developed not only among Treasuries but also among central banks, which have also long had the experience of practical co-operation in exchange markets. The Support Fund will add a very valuable new piece of machinery, and the collective operation of it will, I am sure, powerfully reinforce the habits of consultation and foster readiness for further concerted action.

FURTHER STEP

It must, however, be recognized that the further we travel along the road of monetary union, involving, as I said, increasing readiness to prevent wide exchange fluctuations (and in the limit to maintain their absolute fixity in terms of each other) the more will there be need for automatic balance of payments support and, in the limit, a pooling of reserves. The question of parallelism will therefore once again become acute. For no country will be prepared to give another a blank cheque without exacting in return the right to have a considerable say in its economic policy.

In laying down that a further step must be taken in twelve months' time, and in setting up the ultimate goal of complete economic and monetary union by the end of the decade, the heads of government of the enlarged Community, have, in effect, prescribed a programme that must embrace, even in the earlier stages, concerted monetary policy, including interest rates, as well as volume and direction of credit, and concerted fiscal policy both for long-term macro-economic purposes as well as for short-term conjunctural ones.

In the immediate future, these efforts at closer co-operation will need to be focused particularly on the most urgent problem that confronts all the members of the Community, namely the fight against the excesses of inflation, something from which—and this is cold comfort indeed—our partners are suffering to a degree no longer so very different from ours. But more specific policies, regional, industrial and social, to cope with the adjustment problems that monetary and economic union will bring, will also be necessary.

This brings me to a final word of warning. The process of making a Community is not easy. Virgil's 'Tantae molis erat . . .' applies to this effort as much as it did to the founding of Rome. However, despite all hesitations and difficulties on particular aspects, the process as such has so far proved irreversible. This we must not only accept but welcome. It imposes an obligation, particularly in the monetary field, to make every contribution we can to ensure that when the system comes under strain, the Community will not choose the line of least resistance and revert to restrictionist measures, but, on the contrary, will overcome the problem by an even more vigorous forward move in co-operation.

In the end—and this may not be so far off—a central banking system for the Community as a whole is inevitable, as I believe it also to be the eventual (though more distant) goal of international reform. If Europe can achieve this for itself, it will also have shown the way for the rest of the world.

V.
GOVERNMENT

BRITISH EXPERIENCE AND A POINT OF VIEW

A paper read at a symposium on 'Better management of the public's business', arranged by the Committee for Economic Development in Chicago on 14 May 1964. Published by the CED, July 1964.

Why should one be worried about this subject of management in government? I ask this question, although it has already been effectively answered here several times. But just to give one more answer—without entering into any emotionally charged controversy about 'big' government—I think it is quite clear that, rightly or wrongly, the sphere of government activity from now on is going to be larger than it has been in the last hundred years, both in the United States and Great Britain.

The chairman of this meeting referred to the Employment Act of 1946—that remarkable, nay revolutionary, piece of legislation. The British have something similar on their statute book as a result of the last war. It places certain duties on the central government, which the people in their wisdom have imposed upon it, and from which they cannot escape.

Whatever view one may take of, say, the proportion of the gross national product that the central government will in the future take out of the economy; whatever view one may take about the size of the central government establishment in the future; whatever one might think is right or wrong in this regard, I think we can all agree upon one thing: that the function of central government is bound to be considerably larger than it was at the time when the present structure and framework of the machinery of government were established in your country and in mine.

The functions of government, in any event, are going to be larger than the basic framework of governmental machinery that we have. Therefore, adaptations will continue to be necessary in the years to come.

Now, very briefly, what I want to do here is three things. First of all, to say something about the basic facts of the machinery of government in the United Kingdom.

Secondly, I want to try and draw attention to what seem to me to be the most significant differences between your situation and ours.

And thirdly, I want to say a word about the problems which we face, and how we are trying to cope with them.

A CENTURY OF SERVICE

The present Civil Service structure in the United Kingdom is exactly one hundred and ten years old. It stems from the 1854 reforms of Northcote and Trevelyan although, in fact, the initiation of these reforms goes back to the attacks by Burke and others on the mismanagement of central government in the eighteenth century. These attacks were due to the excesses of royal power, to sinecure, to gross inefficiency, to corruption in government, and to waste.

Reform began with changes in the pay and pensions arrangement for the public service, and went on to the tremendous reform of the central government service in 1854, and finally to the establishment of what are known as 'treasury classes' in the United Kingdom, that is to say, classifications of the Civil Service which apply regardless of the departments to which individuals are assigned.

We finally emerged in the present century with the Civil Service as we know it today. It has been, of course, a continuous process of adaptation and improvement and reform, of which the latest phase starts with an Order in Council in 1920 and ends with that of 1956, which has given us today's Civil Service.

We now have in the United Kingdom a highly organized service of 630,000 Civil Servants, excluding what are known as the industrial classes. These are people who work for the Government essentially in industrial employment, where they are classified according to the ordinary classifications of industry.

Of those 630,000 people, about 2,500—which is just 4 per cent—are what we call administrative class Civil Servants, to which Mr. Price has referred.

The proportions into which the different types of Civil Servants are divided among the different departments vary a great deal. In some departments there may be something even less than this average of administrators with a large base of executive and clerical grade Civil Servants. These are, for example, the departments dealing with the social services, administration of pensions, National Health Insurance, and so on.

THE PLACE OF THE TREASURY

At the other end of the pyramid, in the Treasury, for example, the very remarkable department to which I have the honour to belong, out of the total of some 1,400 Civil Servants something over 10 per cent are administrators. The rest are messengers, typists, clerical grades, and so on. This relatively small central department has, thus, an entirely different structure from, say, the Ministry of Aviation or the Ministry of Defence, or the Post Office, or the Social Service Ministries.

The second striking fact about this Civil Service is the extraordinary place which the Treasury occupies in it. I do not believe that there is an analogy anywhere in the world. I think it is true to say that nowhere else in this world, certainly not in the United States, where the functions of the Treasury are divided among a number of departments and where the closest analogy with our system is to be found in the Bureau of the Budget, do you have that centralized control of the whole machine that the United Kingdom has in the Treasury.

The Treasury's powers of control are best described in the last Order in Council, that of 1956, although much of it was taken over from earlier orders. I might cite one sentence which will show the extent of that power. It says, 'The Treasury may from time to time make regulations or give instructions for controlling the conduct of Her Majesty's Home Civil Service, and providing for the classification, remuneration and other conditions of all persons employed therein whether permanently or temporarily'—you can't ask for more than that!

That order gives us all we need; but it is only part of the basis of control. There is perhaps an even more powerful weapon in the hands of the Treasury in the Exchequer and Audit Act of 1866, under which no expenditure not approved by the Treasury may properly be charged against money voted by Parliament by any department of State. Expenditures of any department of State include, of course, expenditures on staff. Therefore, in the last resort, no department can properly charge against the money voted to it by Parliament any expenditure for its Civil Service establishment unless the Treasury has given prior approval.

Furthermore, it has become the practice in Britain that whenever a new department is set up to fulfil new functions, the Act of

Parliament setting up that department and laying down the powers of the Minister almost invariably includes a clause to the effect that the numbers, classification, and remuneration of the members of that department shall be with the approval of the Treasury. And that gives the Treasury still more power.

QUALIFICATIONS AND REGULATIONS

Finally, although the recruitment and selection of people for appointment to the Civil Service are in the hands of the Civil Service Commission, as in the United States, the qualifications and the regulations are laid down by the Civil Service Commission with the approval of the Treasury. The Treasury, thus, has to approve the general framework of these regulations; it is then up to the Civil Service Commission to select the individuals fitting these regulations. The Treasury also has considerable powers, going back one hundred years or more, in regard to pension rights of Civil Servants.

The Treasury is sometimes considered to be a very conservative department. In fact, however, the Treasury has, in recent years, buttressed these statutory powers by taking the lead in developing training facilities for Civil Servants. It has set up quite recently for example, a new Administrative Civil Service centre to which all new entrants to the administrative grade have to go for, I believe, at least five months before they take up their posts within their departments. It has fostered the development of what we call 'organization and methods divisions' in all departments. These are sometimes independent, but sometimes run directly from the Treasury and they are designed to foster efficient management.

Our picture may look to you a rather happy one because we have strong central leadership and central organization, uniform standards for the different grades of Civil Servants, and all the rest of it. Let us, therefore, now try to see the differences between that situation and yours. I can only give you a personal assessment, with which you may not agree.

CONTRASTS BETWEEN SYSTEMS

First there is, of course, the constitutional difference. Nothing sensible to my mind can be said about the difference in this area of government between the United States and the United Kingdom without first recognizing the tremendous importance of the constitutional difference between your system of government and the Parliamentary system which we have. The Founding Fathers perhaps read a little too deeply into Montesquieu who, I fear, rather misunderstood the British system of government. The separation of powers, which he described as being characteristic of ours, and which led to the checks and balances of the United States Constitution and machinery of government, is really virtually absent in our system.

Parliamentary government does not rest on the strict separation of powers. All powers—judiciary, legislative, and executive—reside in Parliament. That is the first thing. Because there is no strict separation of powers, there is also a much closer relationship between policy and programme on the one side and execution on the other. I don't say for one moment that the British Government always gets its way. Of course, it does not. But it is more likely to be able to execute what it sets out to do than, if I may be permitted to say so, is always the case in this country—because of the separation of powers.

This has a very important influence, I think, on the character and attitude of the public service. The public service in Britain recognizes that it is serving an executive which, generally speaking and unless something very extraordinary happens, is able to carry its policy through Parliament. And that, I think, also accounts for the second great difference that we have compared with you.

In Britain a gulf is fixed between the political and the official strata of government. Mr. Price has emphasized particularly the existence of a third stratum in the United States. These are the political-officials, sometimes hundreds in number, who change with the Administration, who are loyal to the individual Cabinet officers and, of course, above all loyal to the Chief Executive who has picked them. They are not, however, party politicians in the ordinary sense of the word. Unlike the career officials below them they change with the Administration but they are not really party politicians, like the Cabinet officers above them. Britain does not have that at all. We have about forty Junior Ministers, most of them being Parliamentary Secretaries. But they are entirely different from Civil Servants and they are party politicians.

It is the Permanent Secretary who is directly responsible to Parliament, to the Public Accounts Committee, for the expenditure of money of his department. In that respect he is individually independent of the Minister, and there have been a few occasions, when the Permanent Secretary has felt obliged to record that he has disagreed with the decision of the Minister, if that decision has related to the expenditure of money voted by Parliament.

ANONYMITY AND INSULATION

This system has certain important consequences. In the first place, it accounts for the anonymity of the British Civil Service. In the second place, it accounts for its insulation from political attack. And in the third place, it is also the cause of the rather special status, under-privileged, perhaps, in some respects, though highly regarded in others, of the British Civil Servant.

In recent years, the tradition of strict anonymity of the British Civil Service has tended to break down a little bit. This is mostly because the press has become more imaginative and more aggressive in its ways of securing news stories, and the names of Civil Servants in Britain have tended to appear in newspapers, I may say, often much to the distress of the persons concerned. I am not speaking so much for those serving abroad, because the Foreign Service, including career ambassadors, has always tended to appear in the public eye rather more than the Home Civil Servants. But what remains true is that the Civil Servant is completely isolated from Parliament. He cannot be summoned, as your officials can be, by committees of Parliament to appear and answer questions about policy. He is entirely immune to attack. It may be only two or three times in every generation that a Civil Servant is attacked in the House. Then the whole House will rise in protest and the Minister will have to object and will have to take the responsibility and the blame.

It also means that the Civil Service in Great Britain has grown up in a way that has tempted some people to liken it to a monastic order. Often it is said that it is subject to the same vows of chastity, poverty, and obedience as are the members of the monastic orders.

I cannot say much about the first of these vows, but as regards the other two, it is the case that until recently poverty has been a reasonably adequate description of the position of the British Civil Servant. Obedience there always has been, because the counter-part of the complete immunity to political attack is a complete obedience to the wishes of the Minister. It is the principal duty of the British Civil Servant to protect the Minister. That is his prime duty, regardless of his personal views of the Minister or of his policy.

The third difference that I would emphasize between the two systems is the general attitude towards government. After listening to what has been said here today, I am beginning to wonder whether the traditional assumption is really correct; namely that there is a deep-seated mistrust or doubt about government in the American mind. In Europe, and certainly in Britain, it is the common assumption that historically and traditionally government is not regarded by Americans as being, shall we say, among the most worthy of occupations.

I have myself believed this to be historically true, although it is rapidly changing today. One has only to look at the Committee for Economic Development, at the conditions which gave rise to it, and at what it is doing today to accept as a fact that, if indeed this mistrust of government as such has been true in the past, it certainly is not true today.

ACCEPTANCE AND STATUS

But be that as it may, there is certainly no question that in Britain the Government, and a devotion to the tasks of government at all levels, carries with it a degree of social acceptance and status that is still considerably higher than I believe to be the case in this country.

Perhaps one reason is that we still have in the United Kingdom a much more stratified, and perhaps rigidly stratified, society than you have here. How far your society is changing I don't know. I think it would be naïve to suppose that American society is completely free from stratification, but I think it certainly is much less rigidly so than ours, even despite the sharp changes you have undergone in the last hundred years.

The net result of all these differences—the constitutional machinery of the Government, the status of the Civil Servant, the attitude of the Civil Servant towards Government, and the general nature of the society—I think is one which gives us in Britain the advantages that are claimed for our system, but which also causes it to have certain weaknesses.

We have one problem in common—and that is the question of pay. I think that as a result of recent reforms and pay increases in the United Kingdom, the differences between what can be earned in the upper-middle branches of the British Civil Service and in comparable outside occupations, has been greatly diminished. And I think it is true to say today that, for the bulk of Civil Servants in Britain who are not likely to rise above the middle Civil Service grades, the pure monetary attractions of moving outside are not considerable.

At the bottom and at the top, however, the difference may still be rather great. The remuneration on entrance, or at least, after the first few years, is small compared with what can be earned in comparable employment outside by the type of person who is accepted into the Civil Service.

Similarly, at the top there is no doubt that a Permanent Secretary who today earns something like £8,000 a year could in the majority of cases earn a multiple of that amount in outside employment.

How far this is likely to continue to be a factor impelling people to move out of the Civil Service is very hard to determine because, as Adam Smith taught us in 1776, it is not remuneration alone but the total net advantages of an occupation that count.

The pension rights in the British Civil Service are, salary for salary, fairly good. What is, of course, lacking, and inevitably so, and what may be increasingly important in an affluent society which we hope will demonstrate the capacity for considerable economic growth, is that it is quite impossible for a Civil Servant, however high up he may rise purely as a result of his working life, to accumulate something substantial over and above his pension rights. In other words, it is difficult for him to accumulate the capital which is becoming increasingly the basis for a satisfactory economic position after retirement. And that may, I think, continue to account in the future for an exodus of people when they first reach top positions in the Civil Service and have perhaps ten or fifteen years of working life ahead of them. If I am right about this, we shall, I think, continue to have a problem here.

Fortunately, for the Higher Civil Service, Britain now has an Independent Advisory Committee under Lord Franks, who has been an academic, a high Civil Servant, an ambassador, and a banker. This committee advises the Government every few years on the pay of the Higher Civil Service. This includes, of course, not only the upper reaches of the administrative class, but also those of the scientists, engineers and other professional classes.

One has to consider these so-called other advantages of the Civil Service career, however, before one can judge the ability to retain and use most effectively those people with talent who have been recruited into the public service.

With us, the Civil Service still remains an honourable career. It is similar to what Mr. Price has described as existing in this country in the Armed Forces or the Foreign Service, but not yet, I understand, applicable here to the Home Civil Service. With us, there is still a certain family tradition of service. With many Civil Servants a public service career has been something that has gone on for some generations. Of course, how far one can live on that sort of capital is a moot question.

It is even more difficult to judge whether reliance on tradition, on the degree of social status and prestige, and on general reverence augurs well for the future. What is most difficult is to judge whether these things promote the right talents and the right attitudes in relation to the needs of the problems of today.

EDUCATION FOR CIVIL SERVICE

Most of our Civil Servants are, quite wrongly, supposed to be the products of our public schools—your *private* schools. Of the top civil servants in Britain probably not more than a third have been to a British public school. All the rest have been to the ordinary 'public' schools in the American sense of the word.

On the other hand, some 80 per cent, I think, have been to Oxford and Cambridge, and of the remainder about 10 per cent to London and Scottish universities, and only about 2 per cent, in which I have the honor to be included, to what we call 'Redbrick,' i.e., the provincial universities.

This is a striking situation, and with it goes another factor, namely, that the present basic training of our top Civil Servants tends still to be either in classics or in history. I believe that about three-fifths of all the entrants into the Civil Service are graduates in classics or history, with classics leading the list. Only about 2 to 3 per cent have been trained in the sciences and mathematics, and only about 12 per cent have been trained in the social sciences, including government, political science, or economics.

I am glad to say that this is a situation which has given rise to a certain amount of concern. The Treasury has been going all-out to diversify the intake as regards education and background and type of training. I was very interested to hear Mr. Price say that perhaps the United States Civil Service suffers from an excessive background of professionalism in the sense that the most powerful elements in American departments tend to be in the bureaux where special training, special knowledge, and special experience are to the fore. This is precisely the opposite situation from Britain's, where it is the 'generalist' who brings, perhaps, a lay but, one hopes, reasonably intelligent attitude to the problems with which he is confronted. It may be that this is one feature where both countries could profitably move towards each other in their future development.

In this connection I just want to say a word about the so-called 'brain drain', from which Britain is supposed to be suffering. Some excitement has been engendered by a few rather spectacular cases in the last year or two of distinguished scientists leaving the United Kingdom to come to the United States. Now, this has been somewhat exaggerated and distorted in the press, so much so that it has almost become an issue of political controversy.

I believe that the United States imports only about 4 per cent of its annual intake of new scientists and engineers; I believe that only one-half of one per cent of that total comes from the United Kingdom. A much bigger proportion, some 26 per cent, comes from Canada; about the same percentage comes from Western Germany, Switzerland, and Holland.

Thus, in so far as this is a phenomenon of some significance, it applies not only to the United Kingdom but to other countries, too. In fact, we are devoting to research and development somewhat about the same proportion of our gross national product that the United States does. Of course, the US Gross National Product is eight times Britain's with a population three times as large. These proportions are, therefore, somewhat misleading.

PROBLEMS OF STRUCTURE

I think I have shown you enough to indicate that we, too, are faced with serious problems in adapting our structure to the needs of the times. We start almost, as it were, at the opposite end from you. Your problems, as I have seen them described, appear to be problems of excessive professionalism, of the absence of an adequate *esprit de corps* in the career field. At the other extreme we have perhaps the problem of an excessive career feeling, of some rigidity and lack of mobility, of a certain amount of amateurishness, and a lack of scientific and professional training.

I would say that you have in your five hundred political officers, who at the same time are not ordinary party politicians, an interesting and valuable piece of machinery. I have been interested to hear others, and particularly Mr. Price, say how important it is to insure adequate remuneration for that particular class of public officials. Britain does not have that class at all, though there are some people in my country who take the view that the next great step forward in our constantly changing, and we hope improving, public service is to create just such a class. They would be officials who would change with the administration, who would be directly tied, in a political sense, to the administration of the day, who would not be career officials, but who also would not be party politicians.

Now, whether this will come about or not, I don't know. We have an election coming in October and it has been suggested—I don't know with what truth—that if the Labour Party were to find itself in power after the election it intends to import a few people (not very many, just a few people) of this kind: scientists, professors, what have you, who would be brought in not as career officials, nor yet as ordinary party politicians.

Personally I would not be unduly disturbed by such an experiment provided that it was kept within bounds and not allowed to disrupt the machinery of the Civil Service as such. After all, it would not be altogether unprecedented.

The second thing that strikes me particularly about the way you do things here, and which again comes out in Mr. Price's paper, is the extent to which the Federal Government works through and relies upon institutions and corporations outside the machinery of government altogether. This is something which Britain does not do. Of course, it does in defence contracts and that kind of thing, but I am now talking about the actual machinery of government. I am constantly struck by the extent to which outside research organizations or universities are used by the United States Government for advice and for farming out bits of work in all kinds of spheres. This is something which is virtually unknown in my country.

I was very much struck the other day when I had the privilege of being asked by a member of the Cabinet in Washington to be present at a meeting which he holds, with his sub-Cabinet officials and some thirty outside experts from universities, two or three times a year. I was given, as I say, this very unique opportunity of sitting in at this whole day's meeting, one in which intimate questions of one aspect of government were being discussed very freely. And it was quite clear that these university experts were being put in much the same position as regards the access to certain facts and statistics as the officials of government themselves, and that there was a wonderfully free interchange between them. That is something we do not do.

LEARNING FROM EACH OTHER

The United States has its problems, and so does Great Britain. One thing that I think can comfort us is that we both possess two very precious assets in this whole realm of problems which will stand us in good stead. We may both be slow to move, particularly in the sphere of government; but neither of us lacks public-spirited men and women who can diagnose what is needed, who are prepared to do their bit to bring this diagnosis home, and to bring pressure to bear for change. And, therefore, in the end your system, like ours, has a great deal of adaptability and flexibility within it.

And secondly, and this is perhaps even more important, we share one thing which I think is relatively rare in the Western world, and I suspect is completely absent on the 'other side', and that is that we are able to make things work in practice almost regardless of what the blueprint of the machinery shows. We have in Britain what we call the 'Old Boy' network—sometimes referred to as the Establishment. I don't know what you call it here; but that it exists here I haven't the slightest doubt.

You can't be in the office of a Cabinet Officer, president of a corporation, or a university professor for long without hearing the telephone buzz and overhearing a conversation which shows that whatever the organization chart and the blueprint may be, there are ways and means of making things hum which the textbooks on political science have rarely heard of. So long as we can have these auxiliary mechanisms which we can bring into play I do not think we need despair.

THE DEPARTMENT OF ECONOMIC AFFAIRS

A lecture given in a series on 'The machinery of economic planning' arranged by the Royal Institute of Public Administration. Published in Public Administration, spring 1966.

The Department of Economic Affairs has now been in existence for a little over a year, and has grown from nothing to an establishment of about 550. The very organization of a Department from scratch, its housing, staffing, the provision of office facilities in this short time represents a considerable achievement, the credit for which must go to the Whitehall machine which was able to cope with an order of this magnitude in a manner worthy of our most efficient industries. But much more significant is the fact that it has in this year established for itself an important place both in the government machine and in the development of national policy. The purpose of this lecture is to show how this has come about.

I do not think that I need dwell on the great increase in the last thirty years or so in the concern of government with economic matters, beyond its traditional regulatory activities. Long before the last war the idea of what nineteenth-century German economists called the 'night watchman State' had already disappeared. Nevertheless, it is only in the last few decades that the full significance of the State's function in, and influence on, the economy has come to be widely appreciated. For example, excluding debt interest, but including so-called transfer payments, public expenditure accounts in this country for about 40 per cent of the gross national product. In addition, all the other activities of government in the field of monetary and fiscal policy, regional development and labour market policy, to mention only a few, profoundly affect the behaviour of the private sector. Above all the acceptance by the Government of a major responsibility for employment and growth is now virtually beyond political dispute. Economic management by government, that is the rational organization and conduct of all the activities that affect the course of the economy is, therefore, inevitable. Its form and implementation have changed from time to time since the end of the war. Indeed, the attempt to provide a comprehensive and systematic framework so that the various functions of government in the economic field are carried out in a related way with the objective of keeping the economy on an even keel, its resources fully employed, yet with inflationary pressures held in check, is a development of the last twenty-five years only. It would be an interesting study—though one which would deserve at least a whole lecture, if not a series of Ph.D. theses, to itself—to trace this development, both in the progress of economic theory—including the techniques of economic analysis and policy—as well as in the actual changes of organization of the machinery of government in this country. In particular, the period during which we had a central economic staff, first in the Cabinet Office, later in the Treasury, would deserve much closer examination than it has yet received in public. Broadly speaking, until last year the Treasury had carried the central responsibility for economic management. From the days of the transfer of the central economic staff to the Treasury under the Chancellorship of Sir Stafford Cripps, to the reorganization of 1962, about which Sir Richard Clarke lectured in a similar programme at the time,[1] runs a fairly clear line of development—though one of varying degrees of thickness if I may so express it, reflecting different views of successive governments on the need for a high degree of central economic management.

THE NEW RATIONALE OF PLANNING

What then has changed; how and why has the form which central management took after 1962, that is with the Treasury in the lead, been reformed in the last twelve months? This question, like all apparently organizational questions cannot be answered in our system of government, without some reference to the substance of policy. This is, therefore, delicate ground for a civil servant to tread in public; but this lecture would be pointless unless an answer is attempted. What seems to have been at the back of the change was a belief that fiscal and monetary weapons—the traditional instruments operating over the whole area of the economy—needed to be supplemented by others. This view may, in turn, have been associated with the fact that while mass unemployment had disappeared, and had even given way from time to time to excessive in-

[1] R. W. B. Clarke, 'The Formulation of Economic Policy', *Public Administration*, spring 1963, Vol. 41, pp. 17-24.

flationary pressures, there were wide disparities between economic conditions in different parts of the country. Furthermore, the growth of industrial productivity was in general very significantly slower than that of our industrial competitors. Above all, the recurring balance of payment crises were increasingly thought to have their origin in structural deficiencies of the economy. Future historians of economic thought, as well as of public administration, may well see in the prominence given to the factors I have mentioned an interesting line of development, stemming from the final acceptance of the doctrines of Keynes. It is almost as if we had completed a cycle; and having become used to the notion that governmental economic management had to rely on the macro-economic analysis to which Keynes had introduced us, we began to realize its limitations and the need to add to it a more selective approach. It may be that as so often happened in the history of thought, the most radical new ideas tend after a few decades to become a new orthodoxy. It may have been a barely conscious realization that we were in danger of suffering from 'macro-economicosis'—to which I am sure Keynes himself would have been immune—which led to the search for new, more selective, economic tools. It was a recognition of these wider problems, and of the possible techniques for dealing with them which had already led to the reorganization of the Treasury on functional lines carried out in 1962. It had also led to the setting up of the National Economic Development Council with its own office of economists and statisticians to draw together government, management and unions in a joint effort to secure faster and more steady economic growth.

The central theme, then, which I discern in these changes is the recognition of the need to make rational choices about the development of various sectors of the economy, and to devise policies which would operate on individual parts of the economy, in addition to the more traditional means for influencing the level of economic activity as a whole. This means deliberately and carefully working out priorities in the development of the economy within the resources likely to be available; endeavouring to ensure, for example, that productive investment in certain sectors will grow faster than in others. It also means reducing regional imbalances so that more resources are called into employment without giving rise to undue inflationary pressures.

THE DEPARTMENT OF ECONOMIC AFFAIRS

The work of the Department of Economic Affairs is the elaboration of this central theme. Our task, as I see it, is to co-ordinate the activities of the economic departments of government so that their decisions are consistent with the achievement of a faster rate of growth while avoiding inflationary pressures; and through our relations with both sides of industry to secure a wide acceptance of the need to change our approach towards those factors in our economic life which impede economic growth.

So defined, the purpose of the Department may be thought to be virtually co-terminous with government economic policy as a whole. What then is its specific role, as an institution in the Whitehall scheme of things?

Before answering this question, it may be as well to pause again to consider the position as it was before the DEA was set up. A little over a year ago some of the Department's work was carried out by the National Economic Development Office, some by the Treasury, some by the Board of Trade, and some was not done at all. But NEDO was not responsible to Ministers, nor was the Government committed to carrying out its proposals (even when these had been approved by the National Economic Development Council) for allocating resources and devising policies so as to produce faster growth. Indeed it may be doubted whether in the nature of things a system operating largely outside the government machine could ever have produced so comprehensive a statement of government policies contained in one document, including public expenditure programmes, as the National Plan. The present Government has taken the view that these are subjects on which the Government itself ought to formulate views to which it would then be committed. Thus, given that the Government is determined to undertake this responsibility, it remained to decide how it could best be discharged.

The Department of Economic Affairs can be said to have, in close collaboration with the other economic departments, notably the Treasury:

> . . . responsibility for the management of the national economy as a whole. It must formulate the general objectives of economic policy in its totality and act as the co-ordinator of the policies of individual departments towards the achievement of these objectives. It, therefore, must be able:

1. to relate each department's activities and requirements to the general objective of national economic policy, to the prospective availability of economic resources, and to the total of claims upon them;

2. to provide informed advice to departments, as partners in a joint enterprise, on all aspects of economic policy, and to help them to fulfil their departmental responsibilities efficiently and economically.[1]

The words I have just used are, substantially, a quotation from Sir Richard Clarke's lecture here some three years ago on the functions of the reorganized Treasury. Let me say at once that in using these same words, I am not making a 'takeover bid'! They happen to be extremely well chosen to define the function of overall economic management in so far as it is carried out by the Whitehall machine. Of course, neither the DEA today, nor the Treasury three years ago could do this job by itself. All departments and particularly all economic departments, particularly the Treasury, the Board of Trade, the Ministry of Labour, the Ministry of Technology, the Ministry of Power, the Ministry of Transport, the Ministry of Housing and Local Government, the Ministry of Public Building and Works, and the Ministry of Agriculture[2] are also involved.

THE DEPARTMENT OF ECONOMIC AFFAIRS AND THE REST OF WHITEHALL

The most important distinguishing feature of the Department of Economic Affairs is that unlike others, for example the Board of Trade or the Ministry of Labour, it has no executive responsibilities towards those involved in practical terms in the problems with which it deals. The fact that the Department stands for the interest of the economy as a whole, that it has no executive functions, and that it has no narrow 'departmental' interest to defend has stood it in good stead. It has in particular enabled it to develop very close relations with both sides of industry both in the progress towards an agreed policy for productivity, prices and incomes, and in its work to improve industrial efficiency and productivity.

In terms of the Whitehall machine the Department of Economic

---

[1] Ibid., pp. 20-21.
[2] These titles have changed a number of times in the last ten years or so, but their presentday analogues can be readily identified.

Affairs tends to put the emphasis on questions concerning the use and development of physical resources, and hence to a great extent on longer-term problems. The Treasury on the other hand is mainly, though again not exclusively, concerned with public expenditure, taxation and finance and, therefore, with shorter-term problems. But having said this, I must emphasize that both departments accept that economic policy is, and must always be maintained, as a unity; a rigid separation of the physical from the financial or of the short-term from the long is neither possible nor desirable. A very close working relationship with the Treasury is, therefore, absolutely essential, and I think the two departments may justly claim to have achieved this.

When I read press reports of division between the Treasury's insistence on financial stability and the DEA's pressure for faster growth, I am tempted to repeat what Mark Twain said when he was told of reports of his death: 'They are highly exaggerated'. Of course if there never were a dilemma between these two objectives of policy half the work of applied economics would become pointless and two-thirds of practising economists would lose their *raison d'être*. But the dilemma arises from certain facts in our economic circumstances; and when it comes to the fore, it is present in the breast of everyone concerned with these problems. In its partnership with the Treasury and other departments the Department of Economic Affairs has had something new to contribute. This feature, which I think is widely accepted, is that it has no 'sectional interest' to advocate. It is for this reason that it is ideally placed to ensure that the overall interests of the long-term development of the economy are allowed full weight in interdepartmental discussions leading to economic policy-making.

THE PLAN

It may seem paradoxical that I have talked so much about the philosophy underlying the machinery for economic planning with only a passing reference to the National Plan. Nevertheless, this logical priority is right. The preparation of the National Plan gives coherence to our work—in interdepartmental discussions, in work directly with industry, in improving the regional structure of the economy—by relating all the aspects together. But the responsibilities of the Department are not co-extensive with the material contained in the Plan. We cannot confine ourselves to the period of five years ahead; we have also to look at policies in the intervening years; and, at the same time, we must also look further into the future than five years. It is true that the need to produce a document of this kind 'concentrates the mind wonderfully'. It is, for example, interesting to recall that the closest we came to having a long-term plan in the immediate post-war period was when we had to produce a 'long-term programme' for the Organization for European Economic Co-operation in Paris. Nevertheless, we must not allow the preparation of a document for publication to become the be-all and end-all to the detriment of the evolution of short-term policies designed to attain the objectives chosen for the development of the economy. In the end, the Plan will only be as good as the policies which subserve its objectives.

THE STRUCTURE OF THE DEPARTMENT OF ECONOMIC AFFAIRS

I have dealt at some length with the general question of planning machinery; now I turn to a description of the staff and organization of the Department of Economic Affairs, and to a more precise definition of its work, showing how in fact the Department participates in the actual operations of government.

The Department has no executive responsibilities in the ordinary sense, and, as a result, is very small in total numbers: 544 on 1 October. This compares with 1,580 in the Treasury, itself a very small department, and 9,500 in the Board of Trade. More significant even than total numbers is the very high concentration of administrators, economists, industrialists and statisticians in the Department. Together they make up more than a fifth of the total establishment, as compared with an eighth in the Treasury and less than a twentieth in the Board of Trade. This staff structure gives to the Department its distinctive character, that of a small, highly integrated group working intimately with other departments and more or less wholly engaged in policy-making.

The Department is divided into five parts: two deal with Economic Co-ordination; the others respectively with Economic Planning, and with Industrial and Regional Policy. Broadly speaking the Economic Co-ordination Divisions lead for the Department in its operations in the 'Whitehall machine'; the Economic Planning Division organizes the preparation of the Plan; the Industrial Division is engaged on work to improve industrial efficiency in the context of the action set out in the Plan; and the Regional Division is concerned with policies designed to ensure that all parts of the country contribute to and share in rapid economic growth.

ECONOMIC CO-ORDINATION

The Economic Co-ordination Divisions are supervised by two Deputy Under-Secretaries of State, one covering the co-ordination of policies affecting the domestic economy, and one concerned with the development of external economic policy. On the domestic front, for example, the Division is engaged in work on the economic effects of various aspects of fiscal policy, the expansion of agriculture, and the demands on the resources of particular industries, for example those on the crucially important construction industries. It works very closely with the Treasury in the planning of public expenditure within the context of the National Plan. Again this Economic Co-ordination Division generally represents the Department in inter-departmental discussions relating to fields where DEA is not itself the department responsible for bringing a subject before Ministers, but where it has a very important part to play in ensuring that the overall interests of the economy are taken into account in the development of policy. Examples which spring to mind are policies for manpower, transport and housing. Of course none of these areas of policy is the preserve of any one Division of the Department, as you will, I am sure, readily appreciate; economists, industrialists and regional planners all have something to contribute.

One area of policy which deserves a special mention here is the Government's policy for productivity, prices and incomes, where the Economic Co-ordination Division has played the major part in advising the First Secretary of State. Here I believe the creation of a new Department with no sectional interest to represent, but concerned with the welfare of the economy as a whole, and which is not itself a major employing authority, has provided a remarkable opportunity for a fresh start in this most important field. The Department has been able to build up extremely close relations with both sides of industry which are complementary with those built up by the Industrial Division in its work to improve industrial productivity. I do not propose to discuss the development of prices and incomes policy or of policy in relation to productivity as such; I draw your attention to them only as outstanding examples of functions which the Department of Economic Affairs is specially fitted to perform by virtue of its position in co-ordinating and reconciling the economic interests of government, management, and unions.

PLANNING

The work of co-ordination on the external front is generally less in the public eye, and is perhaps not so obviously related to the preparation of the Plan. But UK strategy in external economic relations is of primary importance to the development of the economy, both in the longer term where UK interests in Europe, in the Commonwealth, and elsewhere have to be balanced; as do the country's interests as an exporter of manufactured goods and as an importer of food and raw materials. This function includes of course our interests arising from our membership in EFTA as well as our relations with the EEC.

The work of the Economic Planning Division needs little further introduction. The Division, which includes most of the Department's twenty-four professional economists, manages the preparation of the National Plan, and provides a conceptual framework for the development of the economy within which detailed policies can be worked out. The key to the Division's work is the future allocation of resources as between for example public and private consumption, investment and exports to provide a basis for the planned growth of real incomes, a higher standard of social services, an improved industrial structure and above all a healthy balance of payments. Much of this work is done in the closest consultation with the Treasury. It depends for its success on the reconciliation of the short- and long-term interests of the economy. Both day-to-day management and the longer-term developments of the economy are a continuous dialogue—or, perhaps better, a joint operation—between the Department of Economic Affairs and the Treasury.

RELATIONS WITH INDUSTRY

The appointment of a Chief Industrial Adviser, and of seven senior industrialists who are serving under him on secondment to the Department, represents an entirely new departure, at least in peacetime, in the Government's approach to its relations with industry. Their function is to ensure by direct contact that action is taken to make British industry more efficient and more productive. This, together with the increased competitiveness which may be

I

expected to result from the prices and incomes policy, is the essential prerequisite for the more effective deployment of resources which the National Plan requires for the achievement of the growth objective.

The ways to increase industrial efficiency vary a great deal from industry to industry. There are, of course, common factors—the need for more investment, more efficient use of manpower, better management, and the abandonment of restrictive practices. The degree and form in which these problems present themselves differ widely. In some industries the outstanding problem is one of insufficient capacity to meet demand when the economy expands. There is, I think, widespread agreement now that one of the most serious disabilities from which our economy has suffered has been the fact that certain types of investment, for example in the chemical and machine-tool industries, declined so sharply in the 'stop' phase of the 'stop-go' cycle that subsequent expansion led, owing to the absence of adequate capacity, to a sharp increase in imports. In other industries it is uneconomic production arising from insufficient standardization which is the main cause of inadequate competitiveness.

In order to assist the solution of these widely varying problems the Government is fostering, under the auspices of the National Economic Development Council, the creation of Economic Development Committees for individual industries. By the end of this year there will be about twenty of these committees—covering about two-thirds of the private sector of industry—compared with nine at the beginning of the year. The role of these committees—which comprise representatives of management, unions, government and independent members—is to examine in detail the opportunities for growth and efficiency in their industries and to promote action to grasp them. The Industrial Policy Division of the DEA seeks in the EDCs the co-operation of industry in the implementation of the Government's industrial policies; and carries back from the EDCs ideas and recommendations for government action which the Division follows up within the government machine. The Industrial Advisers who represent the DEA on the EDCs have been selected for their special experience and are therefore well equipped to take an active and positive part in establishing good relations with industry which are essential to the operation of the Government's industrial policies.

This can be illustrated by the joint work on the Industrial Sections of the National Plan. In the first place, the Industrial Division and the EDCs played an important role in the Industrial Inquiry, both in the preparation of the questionnaire to industry, and later in the dialogues with each industry on its future prospects. Secondly, the Industrial Division will be working jointly with the EDCs on follow-up action arising from the Plan to secure greater industrial efficiency, and will play its part in securing acceptance, both by individual industries and by the Government, of policies to promote standard-ization, rationalization, better management, more productive investment, and so on.

REGIONAL POLICY

The Department's work in the field of regional economic planning has been summarized by the First Secretary as being:

> ... first, to provide for a full and balanced development of the country's economic and social resources; and secondly, to ensure that the regional implications of growth are clearly understood and taken into account in the planning of land, of development—in particular of industrial development—and of services.[1]

As we have seen, a more balanced economic development through-out the country can contribute to faster growth in two principal ways. Of these the first is the advantage to our economic strength which could be secured by making use of the reserves of manpower in some regions and the modernization of industry in the old industrial areas of the nineteenth century. Secondly, there are also important ad-vantages to be gained from a more even distribution of economic prosperity, which would counteract the inflationary effects of regional concentrations of excess demand, and thus facilitate the manage-ment of the national economy. It is a principal task of the Regional Policy Division, in co-operation with the Planning Division and the rest of the Department, to work out a specific programme of action to reduce regional imbalances.

First, the benefits to be gained by measures directed towards these objectives must be balanced against their cost, which is of two kinds: direct costs, such as financial incentives to industry and public investment in regional development, particularly in communica-tions and housing; and indirect costs, such as may result from restriction of growth in the prosperous areas. Secondly, the nature of the measures required to stimulate economic activity needs careful

[1] *Hansard*, House of Commons, 10 December 1964, c. 1829.

examination. For both these purposes detailed economic analysis (for example of the effects on the industrial structure of the limitations of labour mobility) is needed. Some of these are being undertaken by the Department; but universities and other organizations are also being encouraged and offered financial assistance to initiate research projects.

As well as being concerned with regional policy as an aspect of economic management the Regional Policy Division has the task of co-ordinating the detailed work of regional planning. This involves co-operation with many other government departments, both in Whitehall and through the regional organization. This organization has been enlarged and strengthened by the appointment of Regional Economic Planning Councils and Boards.

CONCLUSION

I have tried to set out the place of the Department of Economic Affairs as a central part of the country's machinery for economic management, and to show the kind of work it is doing. At the end of a lecture of this kind, the question is bound to arise whether the Department's work has been successful. A further question is whether the Department has made good use of the very wide variety of skill and experience, of administrators, industrialists and academic economists, which has gone to make it up.

Of course, a year's work is not much on which to come to a firm judgement. Moreover, much will depend on the view one takes of the progress of the economy itself. Some progress has undoubtedly been made towards the achievement of an effective policy for prices and incomes, and the Department may perhaps claim a share of the credit. The work of the Economic Development Committees in helping different industries to develop ways of improving their efficiency, competitiveness and export performance is still at a formative stage. But, the Department has made a start on new action in fresh fields to correct structural weaknesses in the economy, to improve competitiveness and to increase productivity; and it is to action in these fields that we must look to provide the only solid basis for adequate growth with a viable balance of payments.

As far as this experiment in organization as such is concerned I would, at this stage, offer only a few remarks. In our system of government, perhaps more than in any other, organization is fashioned less by the dictates of its own logic, than by the desiderata of policy and by the personalities of those who make it, i.e. by Ministers. It follows from this, that in the end the 'machine' will always adjust itself to what Ministers want. Does this mean that no objective judgement can be passed? I think not. With due regard for the prudence which should always guide a public servant, particularly in this borderland between the political and the administrative, I would say that the experience of the last twelve months has greatly strengthened the case for a small central co-ordinating economic department, one which has no major executive functions but which also has no sectional departmental interest to defend. In this respect, the DEA is unique in Whitehall, and if it did not exist it is my view that it would have to be invented in some form—for the function it performs will remain central to government for as far ahead as one can see.

The Department of Economic Affairs may be a curious-looking animal among Whitehall departments, but I can honestly say that the experiment of putting together for this co-ordinating purpose of a number of disparate elements—administrators, economists, industrialists—has worked much better than I had dared hope a year ago; and to judge from what many of my senior colleagues in other departments have said it has worked much better than they had feared! It may not be until the end of the Plan period, in 1970, when we see how the economy itself has fared, that we shall be able to pass a definite judgement on the Department; at any rate I believe that any future machinery for economic management will be profoundly affected by the experience of this year. It is safe to predict that it will never again be what it was before October 1964.

THE ECONOMIST IN THE MARKET-PLACE

An article in a series, 'Doers and thinkers', published in The Times Literary Supplement, *3 November 1972.*

That economics is a science need nowadays not be debated, whatever splenetic businessmen or politicians may say from time to time. But what kind of a science is it? What is its practical counterpart? Who are its practitioners? Is it like aerodynamics, nuclear physics, metallurgy, anatomy (together with all the other disciplines relating to aspects of the human body that are encompassed in the study of medicine)? What are the economic equivalents of the designer of an aircraft or of a nuclear reactor; or of a pilot, a production engineer or a surgeon? Does one need to study economics to be a successful businessman or an effective statesman?

These are very puzzling questions. Mere inspection of what has been accomplished and by whom in business or statesmanship is not very enlightening. We can identify the Listers and the Bantings and the Virchows, the Whittles and the Lovells and the Edisons; and we can fairly readily trace the connecting links between their achievement and the corpus of systematic, theoretical knowledge behind each one. We can make due allowance for the appearance from time to time of the sport, the self-taught genius. But what is the relation between the body of economics developed, say, in the 160 years from Adam Smith to Maynard Keynes and the successful operations of Mr. X who has built up a vast financial conglomerate (and a tidy personal fortune) in two decades, or Lord Y who has managed to satisfy millions of High Street consumers over the past hundred years or his more modern counterpart with his many lucky shareholders?

The questions can be multiplied and varied. By the second quarter of the nineteenth century, classical political economy was already fully established. But should one think of Robert Peel, a great administrator and reformer, as the practical emanation of the economics of his day, when one recalls not only the abolition of the Corn Laws, but the reform of direct taxation and the Bank Charter Act of 1844? Was Churchill at the Exchequer a disaster because he did not know economics?

Conversely, have economists made good businessmen, administrators or politicians? The philosopher Thales (let us include him as the equivalent, at the time, of an economist) was said to have wanted to demonstrate, and to have succeeded in doing so, the practical value of philosophy by cornering all the olive presses in anticipation of an abundant olive harvest which his knowledge enabled him to forecast. Ricardo made a considerable fortune on the Stock Exchange; and Keynes is thought to have greatly enhanced not only his own fortune, but also the funds of King's College, Cambridge, by successful speculation. In politics and administration examples are hard to come by. In the United States, Mr. Schultz is the first professional economist to head the Treasury. In our own, the present Permanent Secretary, by common consent a quite outstanding man, is the first ever to have been trained as an economist; the Bank of England has had a deputy Governor who was one. M. Giscard d'Estaing is an *Inspecteur des Finances*; and both Edward Heath and Harold Wilson read PPE (though there are those who do not look upon that as necessarily denoting a training in economics).

Anyway, these examples are few, and these are early days to enable one to arrive at an empirical judgement whether economics has helped practical achievement.

Perhaps a glance at the extent to which economists are held in esteem by the business community, in Whitehall or Westminster, or how far a training in economics proves to be an asset to an aspiring entrant into the worlds of business, administration and politics would be enlightening. As of this moment, I would judge that, except for certain specialized tasks, a degree in economics is not a privileged passport, at any rate in this country. Indeed, in business it is sometimes still a handicap, and in the Civil Service there is still to be found—despite Fulton—the prejudice here and there that the undefinable administrative flair which the highest offices are thought to demand is more likely to flourish against a background of Homer than of Keynes. These, however, are simply symptoms of the inevitable slowness of change, since each generation tries to far as possible to reproduce its own characteristics in the succeeding one. In the United States and Germany, to a considerable extent in Italy, and to a lesser degree in France, the situation is different—curiously, perhaps, when one considers that economics began as, and for a century and a half remained, a predominantly British discipline.

I do not think that these very knotty questions can be answered by looking at the statistical evidence, for this is difficult to assemble and even more difficult to appraise. We must rather try to see whether we can assess the inherent probability that economics could be a help in business or statecraft. To this end, it is necessary to re-call what economics sets out to do and how that relates to the purposes of business and to those of politics; to consider what qualities appear to be required for success in either of these spheres; and then to relate the study of economics to these requirements.

Classical economics began as an essentially practical discipline, having as much 'a tendency to use' as the natural sciences, which experienced their explosion at about the same time. But, like them, it had first to explain its own chosen universe, that of man in the creation, distribution and consumption of wealth. The analogy can be made wide or narrow according to taste, but it is certainly not complete. In most of the natural sciences, initial observation is of external phenomena; action, based on an understanding of these, follows. In economics, as in the social sciences generally, observation is of man himself in action, in a collective environment.

When the economist explains to the average man what it is that that man is doing, he is faced with Monsieur Jourdain learning that prose is what he has been speaking all the time. This revelation may be received with reverence for its author, but more often than not the economist is at once at a disadvantage, since the 'economizing' individual will—not unnaturally—claim to know better what he is up to than the observer. When, in the post-classical period, economics turned more and more towards 'micro-economic' analysis—the study of individual prices and of the supply and demand conditions of particular goods, and so on—it became at once closer to the pre-occupations of the individual businessman, yet at the same time too rarefied to be of much practical use to him. He may marvel at the elegance of the carefully formulated 'opportunity-cost principle' as one of the basic criteria that guide his daily actions, but he may also explain that it 'takes no ghost come from the grave to tell us that'!

Hence, the economics that businessmen tend to respect is not the economics of the textbook: it is to be found (though here America and Germany are ahead of a country in which 'where did you go to school and what games did you play?' are still quite often the critical questions) rather in the multifarious outgrowths of pure economics that contain a liberal mixture of accounting principles, cost accounting techniques, financial and managerial organization and control methods—in short, in the syllabus of the business school rather than of PPE or the Economics Tripos.

But even if training in these subjects is highly regarded, this is by no means decisive. They are at best 'para-economic' subjects; they pertain more to vocational training; they can as easily be added to legal and accounting training as to one in economics; and they can to some extent be learned on the job. More and more business school graduates may be hired by big industry, but the fact still remains that one is likely to find far fewer economists than accountants, engineers, lawyers, and indeed classicists, historians, or mathematicians—or, for that matter, those without any 'tertiary' training at all—among successful businessmen. I can think off-hand of at least four Fellows of the Royal Society among eminent British industrialists, and of very, very few economists among bankers!

Is this state of affairs to be regretted? Essentially not. If one believes, as I do, that economics is both an important and a fascinating subject for scientific study, one would naturally wish to see it studied more, and particularly by those whose own activities lie in the economic field. On the other hand, it would be foolish to pretend that those who study it will inevitably be better fitted for success in a business career as a result of having done so. Their understanding of how the economy as a whole works should, of course, be enhanced; and to the extent to which they are able to relate what happens on their own particular cabbage-patch to the changes on the whole farm, they may work all the better for it. But it must be recognized that in economic matters the general interest and the individual interest do not as a rule coincide, except perhaps in that long run in which, according to Keynes, we are all dead; and an understanding of what the economy may need is not at all the same thing as knowing what one's business needs.

When it comes to public policy conclusions to be derived from economic analysis, even knowledgeable businessmen (or trade unionists), to say nothing of those who have no knowledge of the subject, can be found to propound the most puerile notions. Many standard textbook 'fallacies', such as the 'lump-of-work' or of the wage fund, still raise their heads from time to time; and the idea that a country (at least a democratic one) can be run like a business can be enthusiastically espoused only by those who have little or no learning in economics.

Thus the position is complex as far as the relation of economics to public policy is concerned. The orientation of the subject, from Smith and Ricardo to Keynes is clear: it is both to analyse the working of the economy as a whole and to deduce from this analysis proper guidance for statecraft. For a long time, once Smith and, later, Ricardo had done their work, this was indeed accepted, at least in practice. There can be no doubt about the great influence which the canons of classical political economy exerted over generations of statesmen. The removal of mediaeval and mercantilist restrictions, though they took a long time to be finally achieved, were not to be halted once the benefits of the increasing division of labour and the widening of markets had been clearly enunciated. The reform of the monetary system after the Napoleonic wars owes a great deal to Ricardo, that of the Poor Laws to Nassau Senior. Smith's canons of taxation continued to be accepted as basic for a century or more after they were developed. The mechanism regulating international payments over many decades was in its essence the work of classical economists beginning with David Hume's *Essays*.

However, the influence of economics in what actually happened in government was indirect. The corpus of classical theory had become an accepted part of the mental equipment of those classes of society from whom political leaders and administrators were drawn; the agenda of the State was limited; the principles of the dismal science that had to be acquired to deal with it were few and relatively simple, based as they were on only a few—explicit or implicit—fundamental beliefs (derived for a long time from an attachment to the virtues of the 'natural order', even though its more recondite aspects were discarded); and so no special training was required. A reading of a few books (or at least bits of them) that were part of the standard equipment of any educated man was quite enough. As for the governed, they did not need to know—or accept—the principles by which these matters of taxation, labour legislation, finance were arranged; and if they were curious there were always Mrs. Martineau's *Illustrations of Political Economy* in nine volumes to teach them, in the form of homely tales, the principles of political economy, 'less studied than perhaps any other science whatever', or perhaps Bastiat's *Economic Harmonies*.

This state of affairs did not, however, last. The process by which it was undermined is co-terminous with the whole development—material and intellectual—of our society in the past hundred years. The democratic process itself (which progressed in a reciprocal relationship with economic development) led to pressures by different interests and thus to a much more complicated task of establishing an acceptable agenda of the State—and its implementation—than was ever dreamt of in the simplicity of the harmony of the natural order.

This increasing complexity of the relationship between government and the economy—that is, the external framework within which individuals act—was finally demonstrated after the First World War and, above all, by the Great Depression. A new body of theory was needed to explain the persistence of unemployed resources, the paradox of poverty amid plenty; and new policy prescriptions had to be drawn up to cure this disease. The great change in thinking which brought this about, though contributed to by many thinkers, will always be associated with the name of Keynes, the Newton who brought light where the economy's laws 'were hid in night'.

This is not the place to describe these changes, their effects on the general intellectual climate—now affecting many more people than in Smith's day—or the detailed impact it had on many cherished criteria of sensible government action, from taxation to monetary policy. What is important is that the simple pattern, both of understanding and of policy guidance, was shattered, that economics itself (despite the emergence of a post-Keynesian orthodoxy) became less sure of itself than it had been for a century, and that the rulers—in any event very different people with very different constituencies to be responsible to than those of a hundred years earlier—found themselves faced with a technically highly sophisticated body of analysis and an intricate and controversial body of policy prescriptions for the tasks they were called upon to perform.

Their first reaction was not to attempt to re-establish that integral relationship that had existed before, but rather to hire the technicians; hence the very great growth of the number of economic advisers and specialists in all spheres of government, together with the substantial contributions from public funds for research in economic and allied subjects outside the government establishment. However, the vast bulk of this talent continues to be kept outside the general ranks of administration. More administrators can, of course, be found—though at this time still not much in the highest posts— who have received a (or some) training in economics; but this is not surprising since the study of economics in the universities has spread and has come, either by itself or as part of a more varied curriculum, to represent a respectable form of general academic training. But there is still something of a gulf fixed between the administrator and the economist per se, let alone between him and the politician. His role is looked upon not very differently from that of the military—to be 'on tap but not on top'.

Whether this state of affairs, much studied, though to little effect, by the Fulton Committee, is desirable, or whether it can long continue, are moot questions. The fact that economics has not reached— and it is not in its nature ever likely to reach—the precision of some of the natural sciences in their applied form, and the fact that economic policy decisions must in some degree and in some manner be sanctioned by the mass of people whom these decisions affect, may lead one to the conclusion that a gulf must always remain.

ECONOMICS, GOVERNMENT AND BUSINESS

The Stamp Memorial Lecture, delivered before the University of London on 11 November 1976.

Josiah Stamp spanned all three areas of human activity with which my lecture is concerned and he made remarkable contributions in each. Being first an economist, that is a thinker, he left behind many penetrating reflections on the relationship of economics to the other aspects of human existence, some of them cited a few years ago on a similar occasion by his son. However, he has not left us his own systematic examination of the interplay between the creation and distribution of material goods and services, the role of economic policy, within the wider framework of politics, and the theorizing on both by economists. I cannot pretend to be able to supply that deficiency—certainly not within the compass of this lecture. But having myself had the exceptional good fortune of working in all these three fields, and having always been fascinated by their relationships, I wanted, on this occasion, to make at least a preliminary attempt. Perhaps I could put it differently by recalling what I once heard Josiah Stamp say at the start of a lecture: 'If we must have minds like ragbags, let us at least from time to time sort out the rags'.

Let me say, initially, that like Stamp, I believe that there are reasonably clear dividing lines between the three subjects. While a generalized theory of choice as the essence of human action may conceivably have some philosophical use, and while the principle of choice between the alternative uses of limited resources is certainly a useful tool of economic analysis at certain levels, it can at times come perilously close to tautology and it may elide the very answers in which one is most interested. A more relevant, if more primitive, distinction between the 'material' and other objectives of human conduct is more helpful in tackling this theme.

My title could have been arranged differently. Business certainly preceded Economics, and so did government. I leave it to anthropologists to decide whether government came before business or after. I use these words, of course, in the widest possible sense. Perhaps, even if one is not a Marxist, one can regard the emergence of organized authority as coming after, but probably not much after, anything that can even begin to be regarded as business. However, the order I have chosen happens to match Stamp's experience as well as my own, so it may as well stand.

I begin, then, with Economics. The first point I want to make is that up to about one hundred years ago, Economics was not concerned, or not primarily concerned, with business as such. This may sound odd when one recalls the preoccupations of the mercantilists with trade practices, domestic as well as foreign, the homely examples from trade and agriculture used by Petty to establish his theory of value, and the multitude of references to specific trade matters and business conduct (not only the celebrated case of the making of the pin) in the *Wealth of Nations*. To my mind all these served as illustrations and analogies only. The forerunners of the classics, Smith, Ricardo and their immediate successors, their French and German imitators and opponents—Say, List and Marx—were concerned with the wealth of the nation. They were students of an aspect of society and, in examining the social process as it related to material goods and services, they were anxious to determine what framework of economic policy would be most conducive to maximizing welfare in its material sense. In short, they were concerned with government, and the analysis of the economy and the few, simple and at that time largely implicit propositions about the actions of what later came to be called economic man, were directed to ascertaining clear, practical guidance for the better ordering of human affairs.

This normative character of classical Political Economy though quite plain was not its unique characteristic. It was inextricably interwoven with a description of how the economic system was supposed to work; and that description was based on certain assumptions concerning human conduct culled from moral philosophy. In Adam Smith's work the family relationship between the *Wealth of Nations* and the earlier *Theory of Moral Sentiments* is unmistakable. Furthermore, the prescription, that is the norms laid down for the conduct of government economic policy, is based on certain desiderata for the organization of society which are taken from the then current body of social philosophy, the principal of which is that of individual liberty. In short, therefore, the classical system can be viewed as a closed body of doctrine in which a distinction between description and analysis on the one hand, and prescription or policy guidance on the other is neither necessary nor possible. Subject to the qualification of certain other springs of conduct, man is moved by the desire to improve his material condition; he is the best judge of his own interests (again subject to certain qualifications); individual liberty (with due regard to the liberty of others) is both an absolute good in itself and the best guarantee that man can pursue his own interests; division of labour and extension of 'the circle of exchange' are demonstrably conducive to greater wealth creation; the social contract, or any more sophisticated but essentially similar modern version of the principles of justice, and the objectives of the individual are best furthered by a minimum of interference with the working-out of market forces (d'Argenson's 'to govern well is to govern little').

One more feature must be mentioned. In the narrower economic field, the classics were primarily interested in what today would be called macro-economics, that is in the relations to each other (and in some cases, as in Ricardo and Mill, the changes in that relation over time) of the great aggregates of the system, output, accumulation, consumption; profits, wages, rent; the significance of changes in the supply of money and credit; and so forth. The concern with the prices of individual goods and services, despite the great part which the theory of value plays in the classics, was quite secondary.

I recall in this somewhat crude summary, these characteristics of classical economics for two reasons. First, the central position of macro-economics was something which tended to disappear after the middle of the last century—roughly halfway through the two centuries that separate us from the *Wealth of Nations*—to be rediscovered during the Great Depression. Since then it has held sway, in one form or another, in that part of the discipline that is concerned with public policy. The significance of this factor I shall refer to later. In the second place, the intertwining of normative and analytical elements has left a legacy of ambiguity which has bedevilled thought in this field ever since.

This ambiguity stems from the difficulty of distinguishing between three purposes which the postulates of economics can serve. They can, in the first place, be no more than theoretical postulates, on the ultimate validity, relevance or adequacy of which there can be differences of view. But they are stated and recognized as abstractions used exclusively for the purpose of working out a body of theory, that is to draw conclusions, a process which amounts to little more than extracting and making explicit the implications already contained in the original postulates. The second way in which this type of theorizing can be conceived is by assuming that the postulates are the most relevant abstractions from reality and that a body of theory based on them is the most meaningful description of reality. Third, the postulates and the theory may be admitted to be a far cry from reality, but to represent an ideal state. It is then the duty of policy to ensure that the actual system would tend towards the ideal.

Whereas in the case of the first 'neutral' type of theory, the essence of much of modern Economics, it can be argued that the gulf between analysis and prescription is wide, is there for all to see, and is bridged only after the most rigorous examination of how the 'model' and reality are related, in the case of the other two types of theorizing this is plainly not so. The jump from theory to prescription, which is in any case more tempting in economic and other social affairs than in the natural sciences, is very readily made. Lord Robbins in his latest book, *Political Economy Past and Present*, appears to have opted for the third of these ways of looking at economic problems and economic policy and, while this is to be welcomed in the interests of intellectual hygiene, it transfers much of the debate on to the terrain of social and moral philosophy where, indeed, it all began.

I do not propose to follow it very far in this direction. To me, it is very treacherous terrain indeed. I do not mean by that to say that many if not all the value postulates underlying Economics are not to be held dear by civilized man, at any rate in societies like ours. The 'ultimates': individual liberty, the individual pursuit of happiness, the principle of fairness, in the highly abstract sense in which it appears, for example, in Professor John Rawls's *Theory of Justice*, all these require no argument; but even in regard to these there is, and has historically been, considerable room for wide divergencies in practical interpretation. This is also true of the institutional arrangements which give effect to them, and in the process, give them substance, even if one excludes the much greater part of the world's population which has been brought up on quite different principles.

The difficulties start at a less 'ultimate' stage of the argument, the socio-economic organization best designed to secure the 'ultimate' values. In traditional economic terms these are private enterprise, private property in the means of production, and the free play of market forces. I leave out of account the exceptions recognized from the beginning, the provision of public goods, such as defence, characterized by what Professor Rawls has called indivisibility and publicness, natural monopolies (public utilities) and education, in

respect of which the principle that every individual is the best judge
of his own interests has always been qualified. I am more concerned
here with the belief, I am tempted to say myth, that at some time
between Adam Smith's day and ours, the economic system got very
close to achieving the Smithian ideal, and that since then there has
been a sort of a fall from grace. A *trahison des clercs* partly, but not
only, the result of the spread of socialist ideas, was quickly followed
by a deterioration in practical economic arrangements, so that now
we find ourselves in a new and far from welcome 'mixed economy'.
Nothing in the history of the chief industrial countries of the world
in the last two hundred years remotely justifies such a view of
economic development. But a misreading of history would be the
least of one's worries. What is much more troublesome is that a body
of precepts relating in part to economic mechanisms which should be
advocated and debated on its own merits, derives a certain spurious
weight from this penumbra of association with a 'golden age'.

There is perhaps a curious analogy here with Marx. He was also
a classical economist, after all. His 'Golden Age' lies in the future
and the inevitability of the historical dialectic is the guarantee of its
realization. There is a further point in that the most modern forms
of utilitarianism in their abstract formulations make the precise
organization of production and ownership in the means of production virtually irrelevant. An echo is to be found in Marx's view of the
ultimate Communist Society in which the 'administration of things'
has taken the place of the 'rule over individuals', in which 'from
each according to his abilities and to each according to his needs' is
the guiding principle: a kind of invisible hand must clearly be in
operation if that society is to work.

The increasing preoccupation which began halfway through our
period with micro-economic problems, essentially price formation,
to which I have already referred, has aided the emergence and persistence of the belief in a golden age in which there is free play of
market forces, and free competition prevails. This is not surprising
since the marginalist schools that first appeared one hundred years
ago had strong links with a form of utilitarian philosophy. But even
when shorn of these aspects and of the hedonist principle, even when
it became a 'neutral' analysis of equilibrium states, including de-
partures from and returns to equilibrium, it is not surprising that the
identification of the equilibrium of the abstract model with a desirable state of affairs and the orientation of policy towards achieving
it should have continued, despite the disclaimers in a much earlier

essay by Lionel Robbins that 'there is no penumbra of approbation round the theory of equilibrium'.

All this should have led, and in the case of some branches of Economics did lead, to a presumption that there should be only a minimum interference by government, that an essentially non-interventionist, free-market inspired economic policy was the right one. The claims of reality were, however, too strong. Throughout this period up to the Great Depression, the economic history of the advanced industrialized countries, not only the old ones, Britain and France, but, and more particularly, the newer ones, Germany, the United States and Japan, is marked by a constant struggle. It was occasioned not so much by the tendencies towards intervention against an entrenched free market policy as by a see-saw between the two, and, less successfully, by the advocates of non-intervention to capture some ground from the more powerful forces of interventionism. This was true not only in the traditional field of foreign trade, but also in the regulation of the power of large corporate enterprise, in the claims of organized labour, in the ordering of the capital and banking markets, and the mechanism of the international monetary system.

I consider it important to be clear about all this if we are to examine dispassionately and with some hope of arriving at useful conclusions the relations between Economics and government on the one hand and business on the other as these present themselves today. For I fear that while there is much to be argued about on details of economic policy, including such very large details as the proper role and shape of monetary policy, it is even more important to have a proper framework within which these specific questions are to be debated. I am led to this view by the fact that debates on the proper place and limits of government action, which I had thought long since consigned to the academies and to the non-economic parts of the social disciplines, have recently been strongly revived.

Having dealt so far with the non-interventionist legacy of classical economics, let me, before I look at the matter further, cast a glance at the opposite end of the spectrum. I speak of the theories, rarely accepted as legitimate branches of economics but which nevertheless also stem from classical political economy, which are consciously interventionist and even collectivist. While these are generally free from the difficult philosophical birthmarks of the natural order, they are no less dependent on the implied acceptance of propositions which do not of themselves have anything to do with the most efficient ordering of economic activity. As I have already said, in Marx the dialectical process of the class struggle fulfils this function, and it is this, rather than the elaborate argumentation of the rising organic composition of capital, that is responsible for the policy conclusions. But in all forms of collectivist thinking there is the belief that collective ownership and management (not necessarily the same thing) of the means of production would somehow by itself guarantee an efficient and equitable society. There are, of course, differences between this view and the extreme non-interventionist views. The more sophisticated 'liberal' does at least try to derive his conclusions regarding equity from non-economic propositions (principles of justice); while, on the other side, extreme collectivists tend to equate an efficient and just economic system with a good society. Nevertheless, there is enough similarity for my purpose in these two extreme points of view to make it useful to examine the present state of the theory of economic policy against that combined background.

What then is, at least from outward appearances, that situation? The first thing to be said is that the simultaneous appearance of the economic disturbances of the Great Depression and the war and its aftermath (some would say a fundamental revolution which started with the First World War) and the new emphasis on economic aggregates, largely, though not exclusively, associated with the name of Keynes—I leave it to sociologists of knowledge to determine any causal relationship—has meant an unprecedented growth in the use of economics and economists in government. Josiah Stamp would find it unbelievable that in this country alone there are the best part of three hundred economists directly employed in this capacity in central government. The corresponding relative figure in the USA is no doubt smaller, but there government uses outside economists and institutes much more freely than is done here.

In the second place, the techniques applied have become highly standardized and sophisticated. Especially at the centre, the process of statistical measurement and assessment of the present and immediate past, the forecasting of the medium-term future and the devising of judgements—most importantly the budget judgement—on which policy is then based, has become a virtually routine process with a regular timetable to which ministers and administrators are equally in thrall. For a long time the term 'demand management' which was used to describe this process, brought out clearly what it was about. It was designed to show what the development over the next ensuing period was going to be of total resources and the claims upon them together with the probable division of both resources and demand into their main elements, assuming existing policies were continued. The task of economic management would then be, by suitable fiscal policy of which the budget or, as necessary, a series of budgets are the main instrument, to 'take out of' or 'put into' the economy enough demand so as to achieve a suitable balance. This description, though highly simplified, is a reasonable likeness of a system practised continuously and consistently, though with changing emphasis and with refinements of techniques, for twenty years after the war in this country and with suitable adjustments in the United States and a number of other countries.

The successes of the alliance between the post-Keynesian macroeconomics and the requirements of the administrative machine were so striking and seemed so firmly established that they engendered a high degree of complacency and led to a firm connection between the new economic establishment, the old administrative machine, and even the politicians who seemed only too ready to subject themselves to the yoke of the regular interdepartmental machinery with its Committees, timetables and 'exercises'. As long ago as 1950, the then Stamp Lecturer the late Lord (at that time Sir Edward) Bridges, though allowing that a Stamp Lecturer in 1977 or 1980 might have something different to say, felt that 'the Treasury of 1950 was not ill-equipped to deal with its many and varied tasks'.

Not surprisingly, perhaps, this development coincided with the institution of a much more refined system of control of expenditure—the management of the public sector of the National Economy, which was the title of the 1964 Stamp Lecture by the late Sir Richard Clarke. The system there described had a very clear relationship with the economic management process generally, and it is no mere concidence that one of its authors had also been closely involved with the evolution of the new economic management during its first few years. On this front, too, hopes were running high and Sir Richard Clarke in his final passages was even able to envisage that the new procedures might form the beginning of long-term budgeting thus leading to a 'system for the long-term balancing of the development of the economy, operating side-by-side with the existing system . . . for the short-term balancing of the economy'. Alas, the high hopes entertained for both these pieces of machinery for managing our affairs are still far from realization.

The system, in fact, came under increasing criticism in the mid-sixties, because what appeared to have been earlier successes in maintaining a high level of activity and employment with a fair measure of financial stability (in the sense of prices as well as budgets) were being eroded. This was particularly the result of international developments which were impairing the working of the international monetary system, making it increasingly difficult to achieve equilibrium in international payments.

Exclusive reliance on macro-economic management, therefore, came under increasing suspicion and more and more people came to feel that we were suffering from what I at the time called, 'macro-economicosis'. As a result, a search began almost everywhere, but particularly here and in the United States, for additional instruments of economic policy, ranging all the way from attempts by persuasion to influence wage and price formation to the elaboration in 1965 in this country of a full-blown economic plan. I do not propose to examine the pros and cons of incomes and prices policy, of indicative or of any other kind of economic planning or of any individual piece of specific intervention. Nor am I concerned with the arguments over monetarism as distinct from fiscal policy, though I shall refer to them later. What does concern me are the broader aspects of this trend—and the resistance which it has not surprisingly evoked—and its significance for the question of the relation of economics as the fount of economic policy.

The reasons for questioning this new and, to some, excessive development of economic management are not far to seek. Fiscal and monetary policy are necessarily interventionist. There are extreme non-interventionists who would oppose even the monopoly of a national currency or who would reduce the need for government revenue to a minimum of law and order, excluding even education. But these are eccentricities which we can ignore. There are highly charged and contentious debates possible, and they frequently take place, over the size of the national budget, over the proportion of the national product that should be allowed to go through the public purse, both for economic reasons and because of different views as to the desirability of certain fund-using government activities. Similarly, we have been made very familiar in recent years with the views of those who would restrict the powers of the monetary authorities over the money supply by having a fixed rate of annual growth, possibly administered by an independent Currency Commission, and also, though not necessarily common to all monetarists, the view that intervention to maintain a system of fixed exchange parities is improper. But the principle of fiscal and monetary management as such has not been challenged.

But once one moves from that sphere into all the other paraphernalia of economic management that have been advocated and tried more recently, the problem takes on an altogether different aspect. What is now being attempted over a wide range of economic activities is to produce a result which is different from that which might be expected were the new piece of policy in question not applied. For reasons which I do not think I need elaborate it seems to me to be wrong in this connection to speak of results different from those which would flow from the unimpeded working of market forces. The word 'free' is often not explicitly put in front of 'market forces' although it is often tacitly assumed. As my earlier argument has shown, I suspect that somehow a state of affairs is assumed to exist which does not, and that the desirable result which might—but only might—follow were it to exist is regarded as having been proved.

What is indisputable is that the objectives of incomes policy, of price policy, of regional development policy, of investment policy (all the way from tax write-offs to direction of institutional investment flows) and of direct industrial intervention, are to produce wage settlements, prices, location of investment and its total, and even development of individual businesses, which are different from what they would otherwise be.

Planning writ large is in a somewhat different category, at least in the mixed economies. Whether it be the 1965 British Plan for which the short-lived Department of Economic Affairs was responsible, or the New Industrial Strategy which is being pursued through the tripartite machinery of a very large number of so-called sectoral working parties under the National Economic Development Council, these are not necessarily in themselves interventionist but are to be seen rather as means for ensuring a greater spread of knowledge of the actual circumstances in different industries. They should, therefore, conceivably be welcome to the more intransigent freemarketeers as leading to a greater degree of market transparency. It is, however, to be feared that the continued importance of the macro-economic factors in economic management may be lost sight of in the excitement of the novelty of this machinery. In a country in which the balance of payments constraint remains of overriding importance and in which the volume of public expenditure and the public sector borrowing requirement are of vital concern (whether one accepts the relationship between them claimed to exist by new

Cambridge school, or not), it would be sheer folly to believe that any amount of specific or selective planning can take the place of sound general policies. It was for this reason that I welcomed the Treasury's presenting to the National Economic Development Council its two 'scenarios' of the medium-term future, though I do not like this new jargon. And for the same reason I regretted the cheap jibes directed at them by writers who ought to have known better.

But the main problem is a different one. How should these new additional instruments of economic policy be judged? One reaction to this new trend has been an out-and-out rejection by the new school of free-market advocates. While there is much to be said by way of doubt and warning about some of these developments—and I shall revert to them when I come to discuss the relation of government and economics to business—I doubt whether fundamentalist rejection of economic management is either justified or helpful. I have already said enough about my own reading of the political and social philosophy of the classical tradition to explain why I hold the first of these views. The idea that less government, in the sense of less economic management, can just be taken as automatically promoting the maximization of production and material welfare without any reference to the specific propositions to which it relates is certainly not proven, and will not be accepted by those who have the ultimate decision, namely the voters. Less economic management without qualification seems to me a highly unrealistic slogan in a world of OPEC and CIPEC, of regional economic communities, of 'snakes', of a multiplicity of taxation and foreign exchange regulations that affect the conduct of business at home and abroad, to say nothing of trade union bargaining power, and of the multi-national corporation which, though often unjustly maligned, has nevertheless market means at its disposal that do not readily fit into a modern version of the 'economic harmonies' of Bastiat or even of Say's 'law of markets'.

Above all, with the reappearance of mass unemployment those who simply reject new forms of economic management out of hand on the ground of ultimate principle, with perhaps some portentous reference to the loss of personal liberty, are not helping to better human society. I do not find it helpful to be told in relation to large-scale unemployment in highly industrialized countries such as Britain or the United States that every greengrocer knows that the price of his wares has to be cut until the supply is cleared; nor that a floating exchange rate, provided it is not sullied by the intervention of the Central Bank, will automatically take care of the balance of payments. I have not yet found a convincing correlation between the existence of a high degree of free market, the relative absence of nationalized business or of specific planning on the one hand and a stable, prosperous and growing economy on the other. I may well be told that this is only so because the true condition of free markets and enterprise exist nowhere and that like Bentham's natural order they do not arise spontaneously but have to be created. But this is little comfort in the world of today. But perhaps the greatest disservice is that these views will either be dismissed as entirely irrelevant or provoke such resistance as to strengthen the extreme opposite view which advocates intervention, direction and the supercession of markets à outrance.

There is some evidence that this may be happening in our country and since I believe that the anti-market school is equally to be shunned, this is a development I regret—and not only because polarization of views is itself not a desirable state of affairs in a hitherto relatively stable and civilized society. For let us be clear that there is as little justification for the extreme collectivist view as there is for that of the extreme non-interventionist.

In the first place, it tends to throw the baby out with the bath-water. That the price mechanism is an invaluable piece of machinery for both the allocative and the distributive needs of society there is too much evidence, including evidence from the totally collectivized economies, to be gainsaid. Apart from this, the price mechanism can, and often should, be used as a touchstone of the economy of certain non-price arrangements, whether distributive or allocative. It used to be one of the main arguments in favour of the British system of agricultural protection (that long-standing piece of intervention never quite understood by the free-marketeers), that, being largely a deficiency payments system combined with relatively free imports from the world markets, it made possible a reference to competitive market prices thus revealing more clearly the cost of support, while the Common Agricultural Policy, being essentially a rigged market, did not do this. This particular machinery is now on the way out, but there are other forms of protection or subsidy where the same argument could apply. Furthermore, I would again say that I am not aware of any established correlation between the degree of intervention, or of non-price distribution on any significant scale, or of nationalization of business and either the creation of wealth or economic stability, and growth or the welfare of the people. The nationalized banks of Italy and France have not made the monetary system of these countries the envy of the world; nor has the existence of an Industrial Reconstruction Institute, created under Mussolini, freed its unhappy country from the consequences of an antiquated social and administrative infrastructure.

Indeed, a recent study of inequality in the distribution of national product shows that it is totally devoid of any relationship with the sort of economic institutions, collectivist or individualist that have for some reason which I have not yet fully fathomed become so prominent a theme of much of British contemporary political controversy. France, with a long tradition of economic planning, with a substantial nationalized sector, including banking, comes top of the 'inequality league' with 47.1 per cent of the incomes that go to individuals being appropriated by the 20 per cent of the population having the highest incomes while only 4.2 per cent go to the 20 per cent with the lowest. Spain and the USA come next with 45 per cent and 4.2 per cent and 42.1 per cent and 4.9 per cent respectively. Germany and the UK are about in the middle in that order, and the Netherlands with 36.3 per cent and 9.1 per cent respectively has the lowest 'inequality coefficient'. I can construct all kinds of economic, political and social theories, above all in historical terms, to explain these differences, but none that would have much relevance to the battle between the free-marketeers and the planners.

The basic trouble with much of collectivist thought is that, like its opposite, it too frequently becomes attached to means and forgets the ends which they are meant to serve. Even the mish-mash of our mixed economy today—so offensive to the tidy-minded out-and-outer—is not free from this danger, particularly in the organization of economic policy. As I have already indicated, I find the whole machinery of policy-making often perilously close to making its participants forget what it is for. In the fascination of the sheer mechanical smoothness with which it operates, a danger which applies equally to negotiations, domestic and international, the sport takes over and the objective is forgotten.

All these perils become particularly evident when one examines the relations between business and active government intervention. To this subject I now turn. First, however, a word or two about business and economics. I do not mean by this the relatively new field of business economics. This development of the last twenty years or so has created great job opportunities for the growing output of Economics faculties. Much of the work of economic research departments of large industrial companies and banks is of a very high order indeed and forms a most valuable addition to the volume of work coming from academic quarters, research institutes and governmental or inter-governmental agencies. I refer more to the relevance of the general corpus of economic theory to the preoccupations of the modern businessman and the extent to which economic propositions are taken into account in arriving at business decisions. It is not easy to generalize and individual experiences differ. My own observations, however, lead me to doubt whether the relationship has, at least over the general range of business decisions, grown any closer than it has been right through the history of economics. It is, I believe, true that some of the more elementary propositions in economics when pointed out to the businessman will come as a revelation of something he has been practising all the time. Whether he will readily recognize some of the more recondite theorems in linear programming as being valid representations of the reality with which he is familiar is a little more doubtful though, since many people in important executive positions are now graduates in business administration, the number may be growing. What does, however, remain doubtful in my view, is whether economic propositions are, in fact, applied to resolving business problems. One reason for this doubt is that the prejudice in favour of recruiting graduates in non-economic subjects still seems to persist, at least in this country. Both in business and in government administration economists are either kept in a sort of research ghetto or, where they are allowed out, will need to prove that they have become administrators or businessmen before they will be able to advance to the top. I hesitate to forecast how this relationship will develop. If the United States is anything to go by—and, in a way, Germany and France, curiously enough, rather more than Britain—there should be scope for a further spread of the use of highly refined economic theory in the business decisions of the larger enterprises and for highly specialized purposes; and this should bring with it greater opportunities for economists.

At a much more general level, particularly where the philosophical aspects of traditional economics are concerned, it is by no means clear to me that the businessman would subscribe unhesitatingly to the tenets of the more fundamentalist free market school. I say this not merely because of Adam Smith's well-known suspicions of the motives and actions of those who live from profits and his emphasis on their propensity to get together for purposes inimical to the public interest. (He would have been amused by the story, perhaps apocryphal, of the American banker who being accused in the early days of anti-trust legislation of being involved in creating a trust replied, 'Trust, trust, nothing of the sort, just a few gentlemen sitting around in a co-operative frame of mind.') No, the real reason is that business, like politics, is the art of the possible; and fundamentalist attitudes are not compatible with skill and success in that art.

It is a platitude to say that many business decisions are taken instinctively. In case of doubt, I recommend a reading of the evidence given to the Macmillan Committee by the then Governor of the Bank of England, the redoubtable Montagu Norman. The probing by the economists on that Committee, including Keynes, of the reasons for various decisions produced answers that were so colossally uninformative as to leave in many readers' minds the suspicion that they were uninformed.

To examine the relation of government and business means, in the first place, to exclude the two limiting cases, a virtually non-interventionist economy and a wholly collectivized one. The former of these, however unrealistic such a hypothesis may be, means that there is effectively no relationship and business can carry on without worrying about government. In the latter, business, as we know it, has disappeared, although, of course, the decisions which businessmen have to take—how to organize production, distribution and exchange in the absence of markets, the price mechanism and the private profit motive—has not.

The problem of how business and government relate to each other arises in a significant way in a mixed economy such as ours in which the frontiers of intervention and the application of different macro- and micro-economic policy measures for certain objectives of the national economy are constantly shifting in scope and in degree. The first and obvious thing that can be said is that everything government does affects business. Even if economic policy were to be confined to the broadest macro-economic fiscal and monetary measures, the position of particular branches of business, industry, commerce, finance and, indeed, of individual businesses would be affected. For example, demand management by fiscal policy is bound to affect industries or businesses that are on the margin of profitability. This is, in fact, the whole purpose of demand management. And only if one could suppose that the respective doses of what is periodically 'put into' or 'taken out of' the economy are relatively small, can one expect the adjustment to be smooth.

But the supposition of relatively small changes is hardly a realistic one in present conditions. It is precisely because the amplitude of oscillations that might be produced by fiscal policy alone is so large, not only in Britain with its balance of payments constraints, but also elsewhere, that other policy means have been resorted to.

Monetary policy, as traditionally practised, can hardly have any different effect as far as business is concerned. The impact on business of changes in the quantity of credit and of interest rates is likely to be even more direct and immediate. Whether a truly 'monetarist' monetary policy, that is one which kept the growth of the money supply constant, would be less troublesome for business planning is more difficult to determine. But even if one were to assume that this is so, it does not get one very far, unless one assumes that monetarism in this sense would be accompanied, as its advocates would wish it to be, by the widest possible freedom of operation of the price system.

The problem becomes acute when we move from these well-established instruments of macro-economic policy to the newer ones and to measures of specific or selective intervention. Few businessmen are likely in principle to be opposed to such measures and business has shown a remarkable ability to adjust itself to them. Some are, of course, less acceptable than others and not only on the basis of who benefits (or should in theory benefit) and who does not. Certain forms of investment incentives or the Selective Employment Tax are examples in point.

But, by and large, the more generalized new instruments can be introduced without destroying a sort of *modus vivendi* between government and business. During the last fifteen years, in this, as in a number of other countries, many experiments of this kind have taken place, some with and some without business opposition. Business has shown readiness to co-operate in wages and prices policies, a fact which is as remarkable in the former as in the latter case. It has played its part in working out and operating measures to encourage investment in general as well as in areas of high unemployment. Where, however, the relation becomes more difficult is in those activities of government which affect directly particular industries and individual firms. These have grown considerably in this country in the last fifteen years or so and can be classified under the broad term of industrial policy. This is an area in which basic principles are almost by definition of little use, for what is attempted here is quite deliberately selective. From time to time attempts have been made to lay down certain broad criteria which have to be met before positive intervention by government can be justified. Leaving aside such relatively obvious and not particularly novel ones as defence or advanced technology, these criteria have included preservation of employment, particularly in high-unemployment areas, the further-ing of exporting or of import-saving industries and more generally the maintenance of production—and productive capacity—against a future up-turn when, by past experience, domestic production might prove to be inadequate and imports would be 'sucked in'.

There are a number of very difficult problems that arise once the government ventures into this intermediate zone, lying between the nationalization of industry through the public corporations, which behave more or less like private ones, and the area occupied by private enterprise unfettered except by the broad constraints of public policy, including economic policy generally. The criteria for selection are clearly highly contentious once one moves from the general statement to the actual picking out of the firm or firms. Who is to make the selection? And by what instruments? Once the choice has been made the specific measures by which it is to be implemented is another very difficult and contentious question. Since in many, if not all, cases the expenditure of public funds is involved, the precise way in which accountability is to be safeguarded is yet another one. So is the monitoring of the actual progress of the policy in regard to the management performance of the firms affected. The reconcilia-tion of sometimes highly antagonistic principles and objectives, for example, the preservation of employment versus profitability or the avoidance of monopoly, is often very difficult. And the machinery by which such reconciliation is to be sought is not always available or, if so not always suited to the purpose.

No wonder, then that the history of the last ten years should be full of examples of failures, sometimes gross and often very harmful failures, of these policies. They are well illustrated by the almost kaleidoscopic changes in the institutional arrangements made to deal with these matters. The creation in 1964 of the Department of Economic Affairs with some macro-economic functions but essen-tially as a sort of micro-economic pendant to the macro-economic, demand-managing Treasury, was the high-water mark of this wave of concern with industrial policy. The fact that it disappeared fairly rapidly and that its functions are now divided between the Treasury and the Department of Industry is only a change of form. But it is more the revised and enlarged functions of the Department of Industry and the creation of Departments of Energy and of Prices and Consumer Protection that now represent the Whitehall expression of the move towards more selective interventionist policies, the constellation of Committees and working parties around the National Economic Development Council forming a bridge with the actual world of business, including its trade union element.

While all this governmental machinery has, I suggest, in essence not changed a great deal since 1964, the changes of form and of personnel at all levels have been considerable and have created some confusion in the business community as to where to go for what. This in itself is not serious. Despite a certain inexorable continuity in the concern of government with these matters, the changes, first at the political level, then in terms of the more detailed organizations other than in Whitehall, have undoubtedly created a sense of lack of continuity of policy. The programme on which the Administration of 1964 came in was not exactly its programme when it went out in 1970; and the programme which the following Administration pursued from 1972 onwards was certainly not the programme on which it came in in 1970. The businessman may be forgiven for being bewildered and for not knowing, for example, whether and if so for how long, lame ducks are to be helped, rather than to have their demise accelerated, or on what grounds this decision would be taken. This uncertainty arises most obviously where there are changes of government or of the balance of opinion within the same government. But even when there are no great movements of opinion, the subject by its very nature contains an inherent uncertainty; and all decisions, however carefully made, contain an element, sometimes a very strong element, of arbitrariness.

Can this be removed, or at least minimized? The arrangements made between Westminster and Whitehall on the one hand and between the departmental machines and business on the other are of some consequence; but there is as yet no clear indication whether the various Corporations, Commissions and Boards that have in recent years been set up, or the Parliamentary Committees and sub-committees that have recently shown much more activity, can provide a safeguard. On the other side, the dangers are clear. In some, perhaps in many cases, in which permits, licences, orders, funds and so on are at stake, the power of an official, a Minister, or a statutory board can literally amount to the power to decide, commercially speaking, who shall live and who shall die. The injection of this new powerful factor into a situation in which, as it is in Britain, so much of our business conduct is still subject to self-discipline, a sort of mixture of the honour system tempered by the old-boy network and strengthened by self-regulatory panels or boards, it must be clear that uncertainty and opacity (the opposites of the conditions supposed to exist in a classical market economy) are at a premium.

Some eight years ago I asked in a different context whether they ordered these things better on the other side of the Atlantic. In the eyes of some, even to ask the question is equivalent to behaving with a lack of patriotism. But it must nevertheless be asked. The answer is not to be found by comparing in decibels the complaints of British and American businessmen respectively about the misdeeds of their Governments. The difference, if any, is probably slight. It does, however, seem to me to be the case that despite the much more complex American Constitution and political system and the further complications of a federal structure, American business operates within a more clearly defined set of rules than does British business. Whether this is in some large sense desirable or not, I leave on one side. It is the case that many Americans are known to be as concerned about the growing assumption of power by statutory agencies as many on this side of the Atlantic are about the unexpected and very powerful role which British officialdom now plays in business. It is also true that the clearer and tighter the framework of statutory regulation, the greater the role of the lawyer in business decisions. America, it is sometimes said, is a lawyer's paradise—a situation which is not necessarily desirable unless one is particularly concerned to improve the status and income of that profession.

But there is something to be said on the other side and I am not sure that answers to certain difficult questions, for example those which balance monopoly, against other considerations are best reached by Ministers advised by officials rather than by a statutory body, though I know that this view runs counter to a strong British tradition. However, if the number and complexity of the individual cases coming before senior officials and Ministers is going to go on growing at the rate they have in recent years, a much greater delegation of decision to statutory bodies may be inevitable. And if, for example, the rules governing the take-over of public companies are to have increasingly the form of law and effectively the force of law, and if the manner in which they are administered is to approximate more and more to procedure in a court of law, then the question whether the citizen and the businessman would not be better off with a Securities Exchange Commission can no longer be lightly dismissed. I suspect that the tendency to delegate many decisions away from Ministers to various boards will, in fact, increase, and that this will put an increasing strain on the British propensity to leave many aspects of regulations vague and to be settled case by case. A much closer statutory definition of the powers and duties of boards and similar agencies and the institution of procedures much more akin to legal ones will then become inevitable.

Let me now try to sum up and see if any conclusions can be stated— whether, in Stamp's words the rags have now been sorted into some kind of order. I hope that you will allow me, for the sake of clarity, to put these conclusions in the form of personal views on the points at issue. Tempting though it may be in this dual bicentennial year to urge a return to unadulterated Adam Smith, I would not do so. I think that neither intellectually nor in practical terms is the new fashion of relating current policy prescriptions to pure free-market doctrine helpful. I hope I have made it abundantly clear that I consider the clichés of collectivism as equally inappropriate. Indeed, since the latter have more chance in our society to influence action than the former, they are more dangerous. Both derive from what is no doubt a deep-seated human urge, namely, to have simple formulae that can be taken as axiomatic and that avoid the painful choice between practicable alternatives—practicable in terms of the social, political and, indeed, economic realities. In the extreme cases of price/free market fervour (and in much of extreme monetarism) there is also evident the desire for automatic decision (ostensibly out of distrust of the capacity and disinterestedness of the deciders) which I regard as ultimately inimical to the evolution of a rational and civilized way of dealing with these matters.

So, I would advocate that one should cease to invoke ultimate principles at least in the daily interchange of practical economic-political debate. There is no inherent reason, for example, why some nationalized industries should not be run efficiently and profitably. Perhaps they should be allowed access to the—one would hope continuing free—capital market; and opposition to this possibility, whether from collectivist dogmatists or from misguided bureaucratic planners, should not be allowed to cloud the dispassionate examination of what might be the single most effective incentive to good management. On the other hand, adherence to the full programme of the old 'clause four' seems to have about as much relevance to the problems of the very people who are ultimately supposed to be helped as the discovery of micro-organisms on Mars.

The solution of the problems of incentives, efficiency, individual freedom and equality, economic growth and avoidance of inflation as well as maintenance of a high level of employment is not in my view likely to be furthered either by reference to somewhat antiquated social philosophical speculation or by the repetition of slogans. A high level of individual taxation does not necessarily destroy incentives as quickly as some people claim. On the other hand, there is little evidence that it promotes equality, in whatever sense that troublesome word is used; indeed by redirecting the channels through which incentives operate, it may produce—perhaps has already produced—a society much less approaching the ideals of the equalizer, or, indeed, of liberals.

So much then for the relevance of some of the fundamental tenets behind classical political economy and its collectivist mirror image. Is there any hope that a new political economy could be developed which would have a substratum of theory concerning the behaviour of modern economic man as well as a new theory of liberty and justice? Is there any hope that a new political economy could, in combination with the new insights which modern economics, in its narrower, analytical sense, has made available, serve as well as a similar combination did with classical political economy a long time ago? I am not very hopeful, but the search for such a new political economy may help to guard against the ideological excesses against which I have warned, and against the danger of an economic technology—of 'economic engineering'—to which modern economic techniques may predispose ministers and administrators alike. I have, I think, said enough about business in its relation to economics and government to make a summing-up unnecessary. I would only repeat that in this, as in so many other spheres, we are fortunate in having the United States as a gigantic laboratory from whose experiences we can learn with some reduction in the pain involved. For in that country readiness to experiment in matters of social, including economic, organization is strong and is happily combined with an ability to absorb the inevitable errors which is much greater than ours, or, indeed, that of many other highly industrialized countries.

I spoke of the dual bicentennial year. But 1776 saw not only the appearance of the *Wealth of Nations* and the birth of the American Empire, but also the publication of the first volume of that unequalled description of the decline and fall of an earlier empire, Gibbon's great work. It is, I think, worthwhile to recall this, since re-reading Gibbon should encourage us to think of the problems I have discussed against a broader background of what makes and unmakes a society.

In the end, our success in these matters will be measured by our ability to live up to the prescription of a great English mathematician who, transplanted from Cambridge, England to Cambridge, Massachusetts, became a great American philosopher. Alfred North Whitehead thought the art of free society consisted in the maintenance of the symbolic code with fearlessness of revision. This is what he said: 'Those societies which cannot combine reverence to their symbols with freedom of revision, must ultimately decay either from anarchy, or from the slow atrophy of a life stifled by useless shadows.' What a warning, and what a challenge!

INDEX

Affluent Society, The (J. K. Galbraith), 43
After the Common Market (Douglas Jay), 203–6
American Economic Co-operation Act, 158
America's Stake in International Investment (Cleona Lewis), 92
Australia, 169, 172, 178–82 *passim*, 186, 189, 205
Austria, 32, 171, 192

Bagehot, Walter, 71, 80, 85
Bank for International Settlements (BIS), 107, 117
Bank of England, 73, 105, 107, 111, 117, 207, 221
Governor of, 111, 221, 283
Bentham, Jeremy, 56, 280
Bretton Woods, 95, 97, 120–1, 128, 136–7, 207, 208, 209, 217, 221, 229
Britain's Economic Prospects (R. E. Caves and Associates), 21, 138–42, 146
Brookings Institution, 21, 138, 139
Burns, Dr. Arthur, 116–17, 217

Canada, 160, 166, 169, 172, 178, 179, 181, 186, 189, 205, 246
Canada's Balance of International Indebtedness (Jacob Viner), 92, 93
Cannan, Edwin, 48, 49
Capital (Karl Marx), 58–65
Caves, Professor Richard E., 138–9
CEEC (Committee of European Economic Co-operation), 156–7
Civil Servants, 23–4, 26, 238–48
Civil Service, 26, 29, 238–48, 263
Clarke, Sir Richard W. B., 250 and fn., 252, 276
Colton, Charles, 91–2
Common Agricultural Policy (CAP), 168–70, 175, 181–2, 183, 197–9, 203–4, 226, 228, 280
Common Market, 81, 171–85, 203–6; *see also* European Economic Community
Commonwealth, The, 135, 161, 169, 170

Commonwealth Sugar Agreement, 183
Communist Manifesto, The (Karl Marx), 61–2
Cripps, Sir Stafford, 133, 250

Denmark, 43, 171, 192, 231
Departments:
Agriculture, 253
Aviation, 239
Defence, 24, 239
Economic Affairs, 249–61, 278, 284
Energy, 286
Housing and Local Government, 253
Industry, 285–6
Labour, 253
Power, 24, 253
Prices, 286
Public Building and Works, 253
Social Service, 24, 239
Technology, 24, 253
Trade, 24, 252, 253, 255
Transport, 24, 253
Treasury, 239–40, 245, 250–7 *passim*, 263, 285

EFTA (European Free Trade Association), 171, 205, 257
Essay on Medieval Economic Teaching (G. O'Brien), 30
Euro-bond, 73, 98, 99–105
Euro-currency, 73, 74, 75, 80, 91, 98, 101, 105–11, 113–15, 117, 122–3, 221
Euro-dollar, 73, 75
European Coal and Steel Community, 76, 162, 212, 223
European Economic Community, 70, 76, 81, 84–9, 162, 168–70, 171–85, 193–4, 197–8, 205, 212–27, 228–233; *see also* Common Market
European Monetary Support Fund, 231–2
European Monetary Union, 88–9, 161, 213, 228–33
European Payments Union, 159–60, 161

Fragment on Government (Jeremy Bentham), 56

France, 98, 113, 146, 213, 263, 274, 282

Friedman, Professor, 40–1

Galbraith, Professor John Kenneth, 42–3

GATT, 36, 175, 177, 180, 185, 194, 205, 209

General Theory of Employment, Interest and Money (J. M. Keynes), 30, 45, 64

Germany, 98, 101–2, 104, 113, 146, 148–50, 182, 192, 194, 198, 205, 210, 213, 246, 263, 264, 274, 281, 282

Great Depression, 32, 33, 47, 188, 271, 274, 275

Gross National Product, 35, 36, 43, 51

Group of Ten, 95, 107, 213

Guth, Wilfried, 90, 116

Holland, 104, 246, 281

Hume, David, 56, 92, 266

Interest Equalization Tax, 79, 100, 145

International Monetary Fund, 36, 88, 95–6, 116, 122, 126, 136–7, 208, 210, 213, 215–16, 231

International Sugar Agreement, 183, 201

International Trade Organization, 36, 95, 209

Irish Banking and Currency Report, 1938 (Per Jacobsson), 91, 93–4

Italy, 98, 182, 213, 231, 263

Jacobsson, Per, 90, 93–4, 96, 121–2

Japan, 44, 98, 104, 146, 148–50, 180, 210, 225, 274

Jay, Douglas, 201–6

Joint Stock Banks, 74, 77–8

Keynes, John Maynard, 17, 27, 28, 44–5, 46, 57, 58–9, 81, 88, 91, 97, 136–7, 208, 251, 267, 275, 276, 285
and Clearing Union, 95–6
London influence, 94
short-money flows, 105–6, 112
as businessman, 262–5
as symbol of change, 30, 31, 33–6, 54–5, 64
reactions to, 39–42

London, City of, 73–88, 94, 99–100, 111, 140–1, 208, 226

Machlug, Professor, 106, 107

Marjolin, Robert (Secretary-General, OEEC), 157

Marshall Plan, 36, 121, 163, 165, 167, 209

Marx, Karl, 32, 46, 58–65, 188, 270, 273, 275

Meade, Professor, 197–8

Migration of British Capital (Jenks), 92

Ministries, *see* Departments

National Economic Development Council, 252, 258, 278, 279, 286

National Economic Development Office, 252

National Plan, 252, 254–5, 256, 257, 258, 261

NATO, 160–1, 162, 185

New Industrial State, The (J. K. Galbraith), 43

New York, 75, 99, 208

New Zealand, 169, 181, 182–3, 192, 205

O'Brien, George, 30

O'Brien, Sir Leslie, 114–15

OEEC, 155–67, 209, 255

Phillips Curve, 38–9

Physiocrats, French, 51, 53, 188

Political Economy Past and Present (Lord Robbins), 272

Principles of Political Economy and Taxation (David Ricardo), 50

Rawls, Professor John, 272–3

Ricardo, David, 31, 32, 33, 50, 60, 91, 92–3, 188, 263, 265–6, 270, 271

Robbins, Lionel, 56, 274

Robinson, Professor Joan, 63

Roosa, Robert, 93, 104

Schumann Plan, 135, 162

SDRs, *see* Special Drawing Rights

Smith, Adam, 17, 29, 31, 33, 46–57, 60, 199, 244, 262, 265–7, 270, 273, 282–3, 288

Smithsonian agreement, 210, 215, 230

Special Drawing Rights, 27, 88, 105, 116, 117, 126, 128

Stamp, Josiah, 92, 121, 269–70, 275, 288

Switzerland, 99, 104, 107, 171, 246

Theory of Justice (John Rawls), 272

Theory of Moral Sentiments, The (Adam Smith), 47, 48, 53, 271

Tract on Monetary Reform (J. M. Keynes), 81

Treatise on Money (J. M. Keynes), 81, 106

Treaty of Rome, 162, 169, 171–85, 204–5, 224

United States:
Bureau of the Budget, 239

Department of Commerce, 22
Federal Government, 94, 247
Federal Reserve Board, 22, 88
State Department, 155
Treasury, 25, 117, 263

Wealth of Nations, The (Adam Smith), 30, 46–57, 270, 271, 289
Werner Report, 86–7, 213, 230
Working Party Three, 95, 213
World Bank, 36, 89, 95, 118, 123